Practical Raspberry Pi

Brendan Horan

apress®

Practical Raspberry Pi

ISBN 978-1-4302-4971-9

ISBN 978-1-4302-4972-6 (eBook)

President and Publisher: Paul Manning
Lead Editor: Michelle Lowman
Technical Reviewers: David Hows and Peter Membrey
Editorial Board: Steve Anglin, Mark Beckner, Ewan Buckingham, Gary Cornell, Louise Corrigan, Morgan Ertel, Jonathan Gennick, Jonathan Hassell, Robert Hutchinson, Michelle Lowman, James Markham, Matthew Moodie, Jeff Olson, Jeffrey Pepper, Douglas Pundick, Ben Renow-Clarke, Dominic Shakeshaft, Gwenan Spearing, Matt Wade, Tom Welsh
Coordinating Editor: Christine Ricketts
Copy Editor: Christine Dahlin
Compositor: SPi Global
Indexer: SPi Global
Artist: SPi Global
Cover Designer: Anna Ishchenko

Distributed to the book trade worldwide by Springer Science+Business Media New York, 233 Spring Street, 6th Floor, New York, NY 10013. Phone 1-800-SPRINGER, fax (201) 348-4505, e-mail orders-ny@springer-sbm.com, or visit www.springeronline.com. Apress Media, LLC is a California LLC and the sole member (owner) is Springer Science + Business Media Finance Inc (SSBM Finance Inc). SSBM Finance Inc is a Delaware corporation.

For information on translations, please e-mail rights@apress.com, or visit www.apress.com.

Apress and friends of ED books may be purchased in bulk for academic, corporate, or promotional use. eBook versions and licenses are also available for most titles. For more information, reference our Special Bulk Sales–eBook Licensing web page at www.apress.com/bulk-sales.

Any source code or other supplementary materials referenced by the author in this text is available to readers at www.apress.com. For detailed information about how to locate your book's source code, go to www.apress.com/source-code/.

To my wonderful wife, 穎琪 Vikki. I could not have done all this without your support and understanding and, most of all, your love. Thank you for your help and countless trips to the electronics market. None of this book would be possible without your help.

Contents at a Glance

Contents

About the Author

Brendan Horan is a hardware fanatic, with a full high rack of all types of machine architectures in his home. He has more than 10 years of experience working with large UNIX systems and tuning the underlying hardware for optimal performance and stability. Brendan's love for all forms of hardware has helped him throughout his IT career, from fixing laptops to tuning servers and their hardware in order to suit the needs of high-availability designs and ultra low-latency applications. Brendan takes pride in the Open Source Movement and is happy to say that every computer in his house is powered by open source technology. He resides in Hong Kong with his wife, Vikki, who continues daily to teach him more Cantonese.

About the Technical Reviewers

Peter Membrey is a Chartered IT Professional with nearly 15 years of experience using Linux and open source solutions to solve problems in the real world. An RHCE since the age of 17, he has also had the honor of working for Red Hat and writing several books covering open source solutions. He holds a masters degree in IT (Information Security) from the University of Liverpool and is currently a PhD candidate at the Hong Kong Polytechnic University where his research interests include cloud computing, big data science, and security. He lives in Hong Kong with his wonderful wife Sarah and son Kaydyn. His Cantonese continues to regress.

David Hows is an Honors graduate from the University of Woolongong in NSW Australia. He got his start in computing trying to drive more performance out of his family PC without spending a fortune. This led to a career in IT where David has worked as a systems administrator, performance engineer, software developer, solutions architect, and database engineer. David has tried in vain for many years to play soccer well, and his coffee mug reads "Grumble Bum."

Acknowledgments

I'd like to thank Peter and David for all their hard work as technical reviewers. It's not easy working with me but I have enjoyed working with you! Lastly just for Dave, read the data sheet, mate!

I'd also like to thank the Apress team: Michelle, Matt, and Christine, who helped me throughout the process of writing. We've had our ups and downs but I would gladly work with you all again. All of you have given me the feedback and help I needed.

Lastly, I thank the open source projects that made this possible for me: LibreOffice, Dia, GIMP, gEDA, and a whole host of smaller applications.

Introduction

Practical Raspberry Pi sounds more like a math book than something you voluntarily pick up to read for fun. Luckily for you, there will not be much math content and it will be fun. So what is *Practical Raspberry Pi* all about? It's about simple day-to-day projects–ones that are fun, functional, and for everyone to do–for your Raspberry Pi.

I would hope that you would have some idea of Linux; any distribution is okay and I will cover a few different operating systems in this book anyway. If you feel a little uncomfortable with Linux or the Raspberry Pi is your first Linux machine, I urge you to read over Peter Membrey's *Learn Raspberry Pi with Linux.* I also hope you can tell the hot end of a soldering iron from the cold end, even though you don't need to be a soldering expert for the projects in this book. By now you should have at least one operating system installed on your Pi; if you don't, not to worry because it will be one of your first tasks in this book.

So what makes the Pi something you hunger for? Everyone loves cheap hardware and I love all hardware, no matter how old or obscure. The Pi is a very capable little machine; also for hardware projects, it's not bad! You could get more on the hardware side out of an Arduino but the Pi offers something more than just hardware. It's not just one slice of the computing world: it's the whole pi. From hardware-level projects to software-level projects you have it all in front of you with the Pi. So you have a world of opportunities. For example, you could carry around the Pi with you or set it up inside your house as an IP-enabled power switch.

I have always liked to pull electronic things apart to see what's inside them and how they work. Collecting assorted chips and other electronic junk seemed second nature to me; I had always pined for a computer of any sort as a child and when I finally did get one I just wanted to pull the case off it!

Well, the Pi comes with no case so that's not much of an issue. Even without a case to remove it's a very exciting piece of hardware. Finally we have a cheap solution that can bridge the hardware and software gap that will take advantage of Linux. Given the Pi's price, I hope you feel more willing to experiment with the software and hardware. Given this, I want to talk about how to approach the hardware and not feel worried about it. Don't feel upset or annoyed when things don't work out. Hardware has a tendency not to work for the smallest reasons. You might have had a bad solder joint or soldered something in backward. You may think it sounds so silly, but it's often the smallest things that trip you up.

Here's some personal experience to illustrate this point. Living in Hong Kong gives me access to cheap electronics and I've always wanted a Hakko soldering iron but back in Australia they are very expensive as they need to be imported from Japan. So recently I became the proud owner of a nice Hakko station and on that particular day I brought it home, unboxed it, and smiled at its majesty. I plugged it into the wall and broke out a test printed circuit board (PCB) I had lying around and waited for the unit to heat up.

After some time I noticed it was not heating up. I tried everything to make it work: changing fuses and double checking everything, or so I thought. It was only when my wife walks in and asks why it was turned off that I glance down at the small power switch on the unit to notice it was off.

Sometimes it's so simple you miss it!

Take a step back and relax: your Pi will be fine. Most of the time things don't work for me the first time; in fact I cannot recall when they ever do. This used to get on my nerves a lot and I would end up sitting there forcing myself to sort it out. I now know this is the wrong approach with electronics: you will make mistakes and you will let the magic smoke out!

WHAT IS THIS MAGIC SMOKE?

The magic smoke is an inside joke in the electronics field. Supposedly there is a magic smoke that lives in all electronics components and that makes them work. So if you were to let the magic smoke out of the component, it would no longer work. In short, you blew it up. Some larger integrated circuit devices do in fact let out a small puff of blue smoke if you blow them up. Thus, the magic smoke story was born.

Just take a step back and go over the basics and you will find your problem. Now that you feel more relaxed, let's talk about the tools you will need to work with for the projects in this book. You will already have a Raspberry Pi in your hands and for a lot of the below projects you will need the Model B.

Basic Tools

You should already have an SD card by now. Unfortunately you cannot net boot the Pi! I would suggest you get a few different SD cards: one 32-GB card for the main work and some 16-GB or 8-GB cards for the smaller project work. Separation will make it less confusing when you swap between operating systems.

I would also assume you have a power supply of some sort but if you don't have one, go and grab any wall plug that has a micro USB plug on it. There are a lot of phones that have this. Don't try and power it from your desktop or laptop if you have the Model B as it requires up to 700 mA and your USB bus maxes out at 100 mA unless the USB device negotiates for more power (which the Pi does not).

You will also need these basic tools:

- A set of small cutters and pliers.

- A half-decent multimeter (no need to go over the top on the multimeter). Personally you should aim for a meter that can measure voltage, current, and resistance down to at least two decimal places; I like meters that come with a stand but that's a personal preference.

- A soldering iron. You should be able to get away with a basic iron. A small hand iron with a normal tip will be fine. I never had the luxury of a good iron until recently. The tools are not 100% of the end result; your skill will play a large part. Take good care of the soldering tip and use it correctly and you will be fine. Clean your tip with some steel wool made for soldering irons rather than a wet cloth and the tip will last longer.

- Some solder. Do keep in mind that lead-free solder is harder to work with and melts at a higher temperature but is better for the environment.

- A desoldering wick.

- A screwdriver.

In Figure 1 you can see the basic tools you will need.

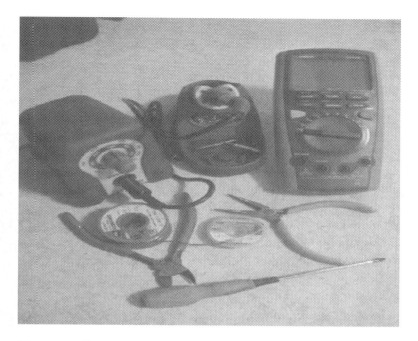

Figure 1. *Collection of necessary tools*

For each project you may need different components or cables. I will address the needs of each project in its own chapter. If you can I would recommend buying better-quality tools. They will work well and last longer but remember that the skill of the operator does not come from the price tag of the tools.

▓ **Tip**   I like to have a bright light when I am doing my soldering work. I picked up a nice flexible neck light from IKEA that fits the bill perfectly but this is purely optional.

Some small prototyping boards may be of use as well or you can use PCBs that are made by hand or premade: it's up to you and I won't dictate what is right or wrong. I prefer to use prototype boards. As you can see in Figure 2 I like to use breadboards that have a handy USB power source attached.

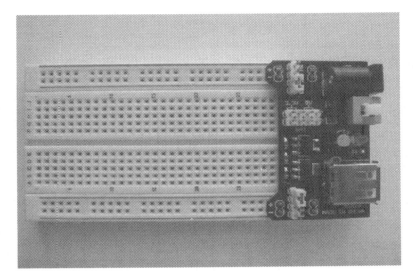

Figure 2. *A small breadboard with a USB power adapter*

DANGERS OF MAINS VOLTAGE

Because this book contains a project that involves being close to mains AC power I will pay due diligence and talk about the dangers of mains voltage, even though we never touch AC mains power in this book! Let's start off with a small story about myself and how I found this out the hard way.

When I started fixing blown capacitors in my friends' PCs many, many years ago, I did not grasp the danger of mains power or what capacitors did apparently. One fine evening one friend asked me to extend the wires on his power supply unit, or PSU (an easy job for me). So I unplug the machine, yank out the PSU, and open the case of the PSU within minutes of turning it off. Then with an uninsulated screwdriver I accidentally discharged a large capacitor into my right hand, which caused much discomfort and a shaking arm for quite some time. Not a fun experience!

I now take twice as much precaution than is needed when I am around high voltage or any voltage for that matter.

You won't be working with AC and you will not be exposed to it at any time in the projects in this book, but I want you to understand it can be lethal. I was just very lucky. Don't open anything mains-powered and don't work on exposed mains circuits. Of course, if you are an AC electrician by trade you know better than me and I take my hat off to you.

Measure Twice, Cut Once

Here is a quick rundown of the functions I will mostly use on the digital multimeter, or DMM. I would not expect you to be using an analog multimeter, although it would work just fine. The most basic of the functions I will be describing will be available on any multimeter. What will be different are the resolution and sensitivity that the meter can measure. On a more expensive meter you may find that the sensitivity goes down to four or five decimal places and that the resolution will go down a lot lower. As long as you can get at least two decimals on your meter you will be fine. Most common meters will do just that.

These days some multimeters are autoranging, which makes the value range easier to select. They can select the correct range for the measured voltage. If you are measuring 10.5 V on your probes the autorange function will display this as 10.00 V, for example, rather than 00.10 V if you had selected the wrong range. If your meter is not autoranging, that's fine: just select the correct range for what you are measuring. This value is the maximum value that the meter can read in the selected range. If you were to measure 15 V DC then you would select the 20 V DC range. If your meter is autoranging it will take care of this for you. For the needs of the projects you will get by with just an inexpensive meter. At a minimum it should be able to measure voltage, current, and resistance.

When you set up your multimeter for the first time it should come with at least two probes. The black probe will stay connected to the plug labeled "COM." The end of this probe will usually be connected to the negative terminal on what you are trying to measure. The other probe, the red one, can be connected to the socket with an ohm and volt symbol that may look like "VΩ" but the writing or logo may be slightly different on each meter. One of the most-used functions on your multimeter will be the DC voltage measurements. The DC range will be indicated by a V with a solid and dotted line next to it. To measure DC voltage, place the probes on the negative and positive parts of the component/circuit you wish to measure.

To measure current, you need to move the red probe to the socket labeled most commonly with a capital "A". This will measure amps. Some multimeters also have an "mA" socket that is designed to read milliamps. Select the DC voltage range and now you can measure amps rather than volts. It's important that you move the probes from the "VΩ" to the "A" or "mA" socket, otherwise you will still be measuring volts. The last thing we are going to measure is resistance and of course that is measured in ohms. Move your red probe back to the "VΩ" socket and move your multimeter's dial to the "Ω" symbol and select an ohms range. This range works similar to the voltage range as before. A lot of the other functions on the multimeter you won't need to worry about.

Basic Schematics and Electronics

Let's talk about some basic electronic concepts that you will need to know to complete the projects in this book. Where possible, I will display photographs of my work and circuit schematics.

Schematics

I used gEDA to do my electronics schematics: it's open source and feature-rich. In addition to that, gEDA supports the industry-standard electronics design automation (EDA) format, meaning that you could use the created files on any system that supports EDA. So let's kick off and talk about some electronics fundamentals. Because I use gEDA, and gEDA abides by the EDA standards I would like to talk about the conventions used in my schematics. I assume you are familiar with reading electronics schematics at a basic level; if you're not, don't worry because they are not that scary. I will start off by showing what crossed unconnected wires look like versus connected wires.

Figure 3 (the left-hand side) is what wires look like that are not joined in any way. Figure 4 (the right-hand side) has wires that are joined. You can see this by the little dot in the center of the diagram.

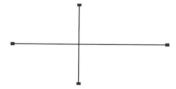

Figure 3. *gEDA image of an unjoined connection*

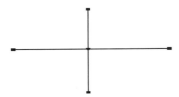

Figure 4. *gEDA image of a joined connection*

Throughout the following chapters, we will need to connect to the headers. Headers are the small metal pins you see on the Raspberry Pi board. You will use them for connections later on. Figure 5 shows the type of diagram I use to represent the headers. Don't worry too much about how it looks. You just need to know what it represents.

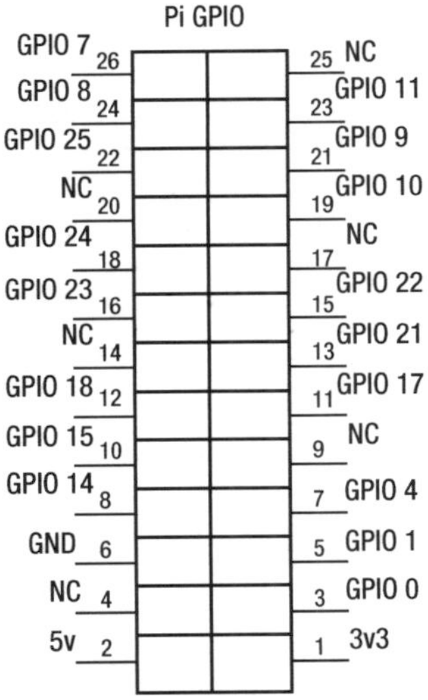

Pi GPIO

GPIO 7 26		25 NC
GPIO 8 24		23 GPIO 11
GPIO 25 22		21 GPIO 9
NC 20		19 GPIO 10
GPIO 24 18		17 NC
GPIO 23 16		15 GPIO 22
NC 14		13 GPIO 21
GPIO 18 12		11 GPIO 17
GPIO 15 10		9 NC
GPIO 14 8		7 GPIO 4
GND 6		5 GPIO 1
NC 4		3 GPIO 0
5v 2		1 3v3

Figure 5. *gEDA representation of pin headers*

Power sources don't need much representation in our schematics as the Pi is powered externally. However, some of the GPIO projects need external power as well.

So here is what they will look like. Figure 6 shows the 3.3-V power rail and in Figure 7 you can see the ground (gnd) rail.

+3.3V

Figure 6. *gEDA 3.3-V source diagram*

gnd

Figure 7. *gEDA ground diagram*

> ▓ **Note** In the electronics world you refer to a ground or voltage source as a rail. When you see the term "ground rail," for example, that would mean the ground terminal on the physical circuit.

You may wish to find different methods for powering your Pi. I will guide you through testing your power supply because this may cause unknown issues with your projects if your operating voltage is too low.

Electronics Concepts

Let's start with a refresher about Ohm's Law. After all, any basic electronic function we need would be close to impossible without this little equation.

Ohm's Law

Ohm's Law states that the current between two points is directly proportional to the potential difference between the two points of contact (see Figure 8).

$$I = \frac{V}{R}$$

Figure 8. *Ohm's Law*

In Figure 8, I equals the current, V equals the voltage, and R equals the resistance. I is measured in amps, V is measured in volts, and R is measured in ohms.

So if we know the voltage (V), for example, is 5 V and we have a resistance (R) of 50 ohms, our current (I) must be equal to 0.1 amp. Ohm's Law can be written in any of the following ways:

- I = V/R
- R = V/I
- V = I×R

Thanks, Mr. Ohm! We all owe you a beer or two.

Now I will discuss resistors, as they are one of the first things you are likely to use. Resistors are aptly named because they resist current.

Resistors

Resistance is measured in ohms (Ω) and it's the measurement of the amount of resistance the current flow will be impeded by. You can think of a resistor as similar to something that pinches a tube to let less water through. Figure 9 shows what a resistor looks like in the schematics.

Figure 9. *gEDA image of a 1k resistor*

So what's your friendly resistor going to do for you? Well, say you wanted to connect an LED to a 5-V source: an LED's normal voltage is less than 5 V. Now it's fairly obvious that if you connected a 2.2-V LED to the 5-V source you would smoke the LED (not the desired effect). This is where our friendly resistor comes into play.

Your LED has an operating voltage of 2.2 V, which is also known as the forward voltage drop, and a current rating of 18 mA. You need a resistor that can bring down the voltage to the correct level. We can use Ohm's Law to work this out. First, take away the forward voltage drop (2.2 V) from the source voltage (5 V). This gives us 2.8 V, so V is equal to 2.8. You already know I, in this case, 18 mA. So it's quite easy to work out R. You just need to divide V by I, in our case, 2.8 divided by 0.018, which gives us 155. So we need to use something close to a 155-ohm resistor, most likely a 150-ohm resistor.

To work out a resistor's value, look at the bands printed on it. Table 1 will help you work out resistor values from these bands, where digit 1 is the band closest to the wire of the resistor out of the bands in the tight group; the tolerance band is not in this group and will be at the opposite end of the resistor.

Table 1. *Resistor value calculations*

Color	Digit 1	Digit 2	Digit 3	Multiplier	Tolerance
Black	0	0	0	x1	
Brown	1	1	1	x10	
Red	2	2	2	x100	
Orange	3	3	3	x1000	
Yellow	4	4	4	x10000	
Green	5	5	5	x100000	
Blue	6	6	6	x1000000	
Violet	7	7	7	x10000000	
Gold	None	None	None	x0.1	5%
Silver	None	None	None	x0.01	10%

▒ **Note**   The third digit is only used for five-band resistors. If the tolerance band is missing, this indicates a value of 20%.

Take a look at your resistors and try to work out their value from Table 1. You will soon see that they all follow a simple pattern.

Next up, we visit my close friends, the capacitors.

Capacitors

A capacitor stores a certain charge. This charge is known as capacitance and is normally measured in farads. Because we are working with relatively low voltages, our capacitors will be measured mostly in microfarads (μF) or nanofarads (nF); see the "SI Units and Measurements" section later in this chapter for more on micro and nano. A capacitor's job is to store a charge for us. It is used mostly to stabilize a voltage flow. You may want to think of a capacitor as a barrel of water that you can always draw a constant flow from while the barrel keeps getting filled up. Figure 10 shows what a capacitor looks like in the schematics.

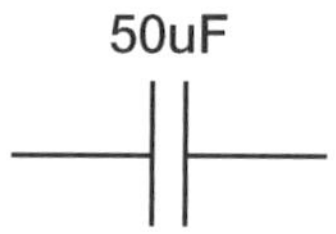

Figure 10. *gEDA representation of a 50-uF capacitor*

So what's so good about a capacitor? It just stores a charge, right? It seems useless, apart from electrocuting yourself. So why do we see them everywhere? Simply put, they are highly useful! One of its most common functions is to regulate voltage flow. If you have a Model B Pi, take a look near the micro USB power port. See that round thing labeled C6 on the PCB? That's a capacitor, not a handle to pull the USB plug out! As the good people at the Raspberry Pi Foundation know, they can't guarantee the Pi will receive a stable 5 V from any power source. So that's what the little C6 capacitor's job is. It will be charged from the USB input and discharge a constant and stable 5 V into the Pi's circuit; if you were to rip out the capacitor your Pi would function but you may shorten its life. No one benefits from an unstable life; therefore, use a capacitor to smooth out your Pi's power source.

Diodes

A diode's basic function is to allow current to flow in one direction but not in the other. Diodes are a wonderful way to prevent damage to delicate circuits if you accidentally reverse the input polarity (for example, you plugged something in backward). If you were to reverse the input polarity without a diode you will most certainly let the magic smoke out of your device. Diodes are like one-way doors; you can only push them from one side. I like to think of them as the revolving doors of the electronics world.

The two main things you need to keep in mind are the diode's maximum current handing and maximum reverse voltage. If you exceed the maximum reverse voltage on a diode it will blow up, as things do in electronics.

All this protection won't come for free: diodes have an unfortunate effect called forward voltage drop. This is the tax you pay in voltage by using the diode's protection. Figure 11 shows what a diode looks like in the schematics. The direction of the arrow indicates the direction of allowed current flow in the circuit.

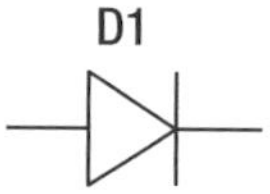

D1

Figure 11. *gEDA representation of a diode*

You will most likely encounter a diode in a power segment of a circuit although it also may be found elsewhere. Let's think about a portable radio for a moment. A massive boombox will need a lot of batteries. What would happen to the delicate circuitry inside that fancy radio if you put the batteries in backward? Nothing, you say. Well, of course, nothing will happen because you have your best friend, Mr. Diode, blocking all that reverse voltage.

Series and Parallel Circuits

You also may encounter the terms "series circuit" or "parallel circuit." When components are installed in a series they are connected to each other, one after the other. When components are connected in parallel they are connected side by side. Figure 12 shows a serial placement and Figure 13 shows a parallel placement.

Figure 12. *Resistors in serial placement*

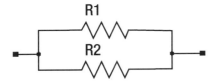

Figure 13. *Resistors in parallel placement*

Each component will react differently when it is placed in serial or parallel. Let's take the above example with resistors. In Figure 12, when the resistors are connected in a series, working out the total resistance is simple. We add the resistors' values together.

```
R1 + R2 = total resistance
```

To work out the total resistance in a parallel circuit has a few more steps. If R1 has a value of 50K and R2 also has a value of 50K you first need to multiply R1 and R2; you then add R1 and R2. Finally, divide the product by the sum to get the total resistance. For example, if your resistors were each 50K the formula to work out the total resistance would be

```
50 x 50 / (50 + 50) = 25
```

Now that you have some fundamental electronics knowledge, let's do something with it. You will start off by testing your Pi's power source in the next section.

Pi Power and Clean Input

We have capacitors, so who cares about the power source? Well, your Pi will, especially when you fry it and you need to wait for a new one to be delivered.

Your Pi, while being ultra-cheap, is a highly sophisticated electronic device with a very complex system on chip (SoC) on board. So having a reliable power source is very important. If your voltage is too low, your Pi may boot and run but crash, or you may crash your Pi when using the GPIO because this puts higher demands on the power source. A simple capacitor can smooth this out and do its best to supply a stable voltage source. Like in my water barrel example, if your barrel runs low you are not going to get a constant flow of water. Instead, you're going to get spurts and air bubbles. This is why it's important to have a decent power source.

So how can you test a power supply with no load? Well, you can't really. The good people at the foundation have given us a very useful way to test the power source when the Pi is running. You are going to need your Pi running with some basic load booted into an OS. You will also need your multimeter. Set the multimeter to the 20 V DC range or your lowest range above 5 V DC.

If you take a look at your Pi board you will notice some small round through-hole contact points. Look for two called TP1 and TP2. TP1 is located under the Raspberry Pi logo and TP2 is located between the GPIO and the RCA video jack. In Figure 14 you can see the TP holes.

Figure 14. *The TP measurement holes*

TP1 is where you will place the positive probe from the multimeter. TP2 is where you will place the negative probe from the multimeter. Be careful not to touch anything else with your probes as you may damage your Pi. Now look at the multimeter's screen. You should see a voltage in between 4.75 and 5.25 V DC. The Pi has a voltage tolerance of 0.75 V DC or 15% tolerance. Anything outside this range is bad and you will need to investigate your power source or cable or maybe both. If your voltage reads very close to the 15% tolerance I would suggest that you take a look at your power supply or cables. Being very close to the 15% is just as bad as being over it; when you put the Pi under load you will go over the 15% tolerance very quickly.

So why am I getting negative voltage readings? Has my Pi gone crazy? No, it's not crazy and you haven't damaged anything: you have your probes backward. This is still a valid reading of the voltage if you ignore the negative sign. I would recommend that you swap the probes and check it again. It's a good idea to get into a good habit from the start. In Figure 15 you can see how to measure the TP1 and TP2 voltage points.

Figure 15. *Checking the running voltage on your Raspberry Pi*

The Dangers of ESD

When you handle your Pi you may not think of it as being similar to a desktop or laptop PC. With the Pi, however, you need to worry about electrostatic discharge, or a charge building up inside your body. This stored charge can be of quite a high voltage. A good example is when you walk around carpet and you touch something metal: the charge wants to escape from you into the metal object.

Given the potentially high voltages you may carry if you were to touch your Pi you may discharge the electrostatic charge into the Pi and render it inoperable. You should always ground yourself before touching anything electronic: you can do this by touching a metal object first. If you're worried about electrostatic discharge you can use an ESD mat or an ESD wrist strap to ensure that you never get a buildup. You may want to get a case for your Pi to keep you from accidentally discharging into the Pi. There are some nice cases that have support for a ribbon cable to the GPIO ports, which will protect your Pi from ESD and any other accidents.

SI Units and Measurements

Unlike units of measure in Hong Kong, which can range from catty to pound, electronics normally stick with a standard. This standard is SI units and uses SI prefixes. All other measurements used throughout the book will also be in SI units.

So when you get to the temperature-sensing projects, my examples will be in degrees Celsius. For the electronics side of things you will most likely encounter the following terms: "n" for nano, "μ" for micro, and "m" for milli. To put that in more practical terms, 20 mA is 20 milliamps and 1 μF is one microfarad. This is all pretty logical and easy to follow.

You may encounter some odd written terms that are not part of the SI standard or any other real standard. This is where the decimal point in a value is replaced with the unit of measure. I'm not sure where this came from but it's also easy to work with once someone tells you what's going on. Take, for example, the 3.3-V voltage rail on the Pi. You could write that as 3.3 V but often you will see it written as 3v3, meaning 3.3 V (the decimal is replaced by the unit of measure).

What to Expect

Now that we have the formalities out of the way, what can you expect from each chapter of this book?

- Up first, I will guide you through the hardware of the Raspberry Pi. I will start off with the ins and outs of every plug and socket. I will talk about the benefits of the architecture and the potential pitfalls. There will be diagrams for all the outputs and for some of the more common configuration settings needed to boot the Raspberry Pi.

- Next I will go through the installation of what may be your first Linux operating system on the ARM architecture. Fedora will be the choice of operating system for this book but you can use any operating system that has an ARM port. I will also explain where Fedora falls short and what optimizations can be done. I will also talk about your SD card (after all, it's no standard hard disk).

- Your first hardware project will be in Chapter 3, where I will go over the fine points of the GPIO pins and how to use them and how to protect them from danger. Your first project will use Fedora and a temperature sensor to read the temperature of your room or something else like a full high rack you may have inside your home.

- For anyone who remembers the craze of setting up small LCDs in their PCs running off parallel ports, the name HD44780 will ring bells. Nearly everyone I know has a few of them. In Chapter 4 I will show you how to use one via the GPIO and simple Linux LCD software.

- For those of you out there that are security conscious, Chapter 5 will give you a nice guide on how to set up a passive infrared motion sensor and a security pressure mat. I will also show you some simple scripts to make use of the security devices in a more automated way.

- The Raspberry Pi is no place to fire up the GNU Compiler Collection (GCC). In Chapter 6 I will walk you through the setup of a cross compiling environment, and I'll provide some tips and tricks for making the GCC work better for you. It's important to remember that the Raspberry Pi is a lot slower than your desktop and lacks any real hard disk. So to save time and hardware it's best to cross compile from a faster machine. You'll need these skills for Chapter 7.

- It has an HDMI port: quickly, make it do something in HD! The Raspberry Pi is small in size so it could be well suited for that odd media PC you've always wanted. Also the Broadcom VideoCore GPU is designed for HD playback. In Chapter 7 I will guide you through the installation and configuration of the popular open source XBMC.

- In Chapter 8 you will build a piece of hardware that is missing from the Raspberry Pi: a real-time clock. You may not know what a real-time clock is but I am sure most of you will have seen the silver shaped coin battery on your motherboards. Chapter 8 will give your Raspberry Pi the ability to keep time by itself!

- Everyone loves console access over a serial port or maybe that's just me. Whatever your preference is, you may find it useful to make the Raspberry Pi into a remote console server for accessing the console of your router or other devices. I will also discuss how to access the Raspberry Pi headless via the console port. If that all sounds like fun, Chapter 9 will be of interest.

- In Chapter 10 I discuss how you can safely control a mains appliance with your Raspberry Pi. In this project you will not be exposed to any dangerous mains voltage. I will also give you basic code examples for how to control this device. You may want to use this to automatically turn on an air conditioner, for example.

- Chapter 11 will discuss other operating systems. I will cover Android; after all it's an ARM, so how could you not at least run Android once? I will also cover RISC OS: a bit of a revival in an older operating system never hurt anyone. Finally, I will talk about my personal favorite operating system: Gentoo Linux. I will demonstrate a full hard-float installation of Linux and your standard applications.

In the projects in this book, I use all sorts of different chips from temperature and humidity sensors to TTL converters. I will explain their use in the appropriate chapters so don't feel worried if you feel something is missing. It will come together when you build the projects. It is a good idea that you go down to your local electronics store and buy packs of resistors of common values, some capacitors, and some small lengths of wire known as "hook-up" wire. This should get you off to a good start. For me, I just take the bus to the electronics district here in Hong Kong or a train to the Shenzhen electronics markets but not everyone is that lucky. (If you ever do make it to Hong Kong, I recommend you visit Sham Shui Po, Apliu Street, and the Golden Computer Arcade.)

By the end of this book you will be able to configure any operating system and tune it for good performance for your Pi. It's important to understand how the hardware and software go together on the Pi and that is also one of the foundation's key goals. Not only will you be able to select any operating system for your Pi, but you will also be able to read the temperature, control appliances, and much, much more. The next time someone asks you what you can do with such low-specification hardware, show them the Pi. For around $25 you get a serious amount of computing power, and you just need these projects to unleash the power of the Pi.

CHAPTER 1

■ ■ ■

Hardware Overview

Now that you have all the tools, components, and electronics knowledge from the introduction, you should be able to carry out the projects in this book. Let's talk about the hardware in detail on the Raspberry Pi. A whole chapter dedicated to some cheap hardware? You may ask why do I need this much information on such cheap hardware? Well, to get the most out of the software you're going to need to know the details of the hardware.

In addition, a lot of projects will make use of the low-level hardware inputs and outputs on the Raspberry Pi, so knowing how best to use the hardware at hand is very important. The Raspberry Pi Foundation also wants to reignite people's interest in the hardware and writing code for that hardware; I guess they miss their BBC Micros. In case you have not noticed I am a bit of a hardware fan and I've got a soft spot for hardware of all sorts. I feel that today's computers are far less interesting with just the x86 lines and a few remaining miscellaneous architectures left. So seeing the Pi and the ARM become more widespread makes me a little happy. After all, I do have a full high rack of different architecture machines in my home, ranging from the PA-RISC and Itanium 2 to the IBM Power, and, given Hong Kong's impossibly small apartments, that's a pretty big commitment. Adding one more makes me happy though I don't think I'll rack-mount my Pi (although a small rack cluster of Pi sounds quite tasty)!

Looking back at the ARM's humble development it is interesting to know that back in 1986 Acorn Computers created an interface for an early ARM processor that could be connected to the BBC Micro via its tube interface. This was critical in the ARM's development many years ago. In terms of the tube bus on the BBC Micro, the outset of GPIO (General Purpose Input Output) pins would be more useful nowadays. So if back in the day Acorn can interface a completely different CPU architecture, you should be able to do some interesting projects with the GPIO and the other interfaces on the Pi.

The Pi has a large range of inputs and outputs that we can make use of in the following chapters. In the following pages I will cover the inputs and outputs and how to use them. I will also give you an overview of what's special about the ARM11 architecture and how certain parts of this architecture can affect the operating system we select. The video output will be quite important to those of you who wish to connect the Pi to a video display of some type. The Pi has also included a lot of low-level inputs and outputs: some of them we can use and some of them we cannot use at the moment. That's unfortunate, but I am sure the foundation has its reasons for this. Unfortunately, not all documentation on all parts of the Pi is released for a public audience.

I am an open source supporter so I hope one day the documents are released to the public, giving all of us the chance to fix issues in this hardware and make improvements with Linux on the Pi. In particular, the Broadcom VideoCore IV that is part of the Broadcom BCM2835 has its documents stored far away from public view. The unfortunate effect of this means the community at the moment will need to make do with a binary blob driver for Linux.

■ **Note**   A binary blob driver refers to the way you receive the driver or module. In most Windows machines you receive an installer for your hardware and, once installed, your hardware can be used by the system. This is a binary blob: it just means a precompiled driver or module for your given hardware. In the world of Linux this matters because you cannot integrate this driver into the kernel source and most of the time you never see the source code. This makes it impossible for the community to support the hardware if the vendor were to stop making a binary blob driver available.

Given the price of the hardware I am sure we can all make do and work with what we have.

Pi In, Pi Out

Let's start off with the most common ports on the Pi. Figure 1-1 is a reference image of a Raspberry Pi.

Figure 1-1. *Raspberry Pi Model B*

Let's look at the Pi from the top side, starting off with the USB port and moving clockwise around the board since I am sure all of you know what a USB port looks like by now.

USB Port

The USB functions are provided by the SMSC LAN9512 on both the Model A and Model B. The LAN9512 is an interesting package and a very good way to save PCB space; I can see why the foundation has selected this chip. The USB ports on the Pi are USB 2.0 and provide everything you normally would need from a USB port with one small drawback. The maximum recommended current draw is 100 milliampere or mA for short, compared to the possible 500 mA of a normal USB port in device-negotiated mode. So if you need to draw more than 100 mA you should look at a powered USB hub or power the device externally. Devices like a USB flash drive should be fine; a 2.5-inch external self-powered hard drive will not be fine on the other hand. So give some thought to what you're going to plug into your Pi's USB ports.

While it's unlikely you will damage the Pi your device may not work or it may act very oddly. There is another potential issue with the USB ports and also the LAN port. Why the LAN port, you ask?

LAN Port

The little SMSC LAN9512 used for the USB ports has LAN in the part name for a reason. If you were to take a look at the high block-level design of the LAN9512 you will notice that it has one upstream USB port and three downstream ports. A downstream USB port is what you, the end user, can use to connect into and the upstream ports are what the USB hub uses to talk to the rest of the computer system. Hang on, you said three USB ports? Yes, and you get only two. The other USB downstream port is internally connected to the Ethernet physical layer interface chip (or PHY) in order to provide you with network functions. That's an amazing amount of functionality from such a small package. Like I said, it comes at a price: we now have two USB ports and a LAN port sharing the one single upstream port. Obviously you may encounter bandwidth issues when using the USB ports for storage and when accessing the network functions. It's the price we must pay to save cost and space on the Pi.

The Ethernet PHY that I spoke about previously is feature-rich for such a small package: it even supports Wake-on-LAN functions and TCP/UDP checksum offloading. Checksum offloading will be very appreciated, given that we have limited CPU cycles. The offload functions allow the Ethernet PHY to calculate the TCP/UDP checksum rather than leaving this task for the main CPU.

CSI Header

Moving on, we have a little black connector behind the LAN port. This black header is a 15-pin flat flex cable header for the MIPI Alliance's CSI-2 interface. CSI stands for Camera Serial Interface and the 2 stands for version 2.

What's so good about the CSI then? The CSI interface standard defines a unidirectional serial interface standard for a CSI-compliant camera device. The good thing about the CSI standard when compared to a cheap USB web camera is that the standard defines what they call the command control interface (CCI) master and slave and the CSI transmitter and receiver. The architecture of the CCI master and slave is what makes this interface a good idea for the Pi.

The CCI master, according to the CSI standard, can be an application or some low-level hardware controller; in the case of the Raspberry Pi it's inside the low-level hardware as part of the Broadcom GPU. The GPU can talk via the CSI interface to act as a CCI master for a cheap camera unit. The camera can then communicate directly to the GPU via the CSI interface: the camera will be the slave device to the GPU. This is a really great way to set up a camera as the GPU will take care of decoding the raw video from the camera. Given that the Raspberry Pi has limited CPU cycles this is a very clever use of the GPU (by limited CPU cycles, I mean that you're working with a slower processor; for example, your Pentium 3 would be considered slower than your Core i7 processor or you could say the Pentium 3 is CPU cycle–limited when compared to the Core i7).

Now that you know that I like about the CSI interface I am going to talk about where it falls very short on the Pi. CSI defines the hardware-level interface–nothing more, nothing less–and if you just take the hardware at face value it's quite simple. Unfortunately, as everyone knows, you need a little something called software to make use of the hardware.

CSI defines nothing about how you write the software or even where it runs. You could embed code in firmware or have it running fully in software.

▓ **Note** Firmware is the name for code that is stored inside the chip itself or inside a small flash chip attached to the device. An example is a common MP3 player, which uses firmware to store its small operating system.

It also will not define how you communicate over the CSI bus. While it may be easy to find a camera that will physically fit and is compliant with CSI-2, the chances of it working with the Pi are nonexistent. After all, the GPU is a proprietary device and the CSI interface is part of it. The foundation is looking at making a small CSI camera available to the community later on. For the time being we can do nothing useful with this interface.

HDMI Port

The HDMI interface is a little boring compared to the last three. No matter how boring this interface is, it will be pretty important to you for any of your media-related projects. This interface is a pretty standard HDMI 1.3a–compliant port. Do keep in mind that you will not be able to get a VGA signal from this port: only HDMI and DVI-D signals are supported.

▒ **Note**   The foundation thinks that VGA is outdated; that's fine, as they also give us a composite output to make up for the lack of VGA or another analog output. If you're going to use the HDMI port with a DVI converter, you will need to use the 3.5-mm audio socket for audio out. If you wish to have sound on your HDMI interface you will need to edit the `config.txt` file in your boot partition to have this setting: `hdmi_drive=2`. Don't worry about how to edit this file just yet; I will talk about this later in Chapter 2 when you install Linux. HDMI is a digital connection; it's not analog. Buying a $300 HDMI cable will not help your Raspberry Pi. Just use your common sense and pick a cable that looks okay. You can save the extra money from an expensive HDMI cable and buy another Pi.

Power to the Pi!

The power port is pretty useful; it's a micro USB-type B port. It cannot be used for anything other than powering your Pi. You will have come across this type of USB connector on a lot of different devices but most likely you would have found one on your mobile phone. Watch out that you don't bump off that C6 capacitor! There is not much more to say about this input.

DSI Header

Keeping on the top side of the Pi for the moment you will see another black connector facing the rear of the Pi. Its 15-pin flat flex cable connection looks exactly like the CSI-2 interface I already discussed. This is a DSI port. More acronyms, so what's a DSI port?

DSI stands for Display Serial Interface, which sounds oddly close to CSI. Well, that would be because it's a standard defined by MIPI once again. Unlike CSI, DSI is widely used in cheap LCD displays like the ones you would find in older phones or in the first-generation Nintendo DS. Just like the CSI, the DSI is directly connected to the GPU. Unlike the CSI, the DSI defines the protocol between the display and the host processor (in our case, the GPU). The DSI can also be used in addition with an inter-integrated circuit bus (I²C bus) to give you touch-interface capability. While this is not part of the DSI specification or the I²C specification, often I²C or serial peripheral interface (SPI) buses are found on the displays you may encounter.

Given that we have a hardware interface defined by the DSI and a protocol to communicate via the DSI that is defined by the DSI specification, you would expect any old DSI display should work on this interface. Unfortunately, you would be wrong. In the same way that the GPU limits our ability to access the CSI bus, the exact same thing happens with the DSI bus. There are simply no drivers for any operating system to interface with the DSI. Nor do we have access to any documentation on the GPU to be able to write one. The foundation is talking about the possibility of providing a binary blob driver for Linux in order to be able to access this bus. It would be nice if they do, as DSI displays can be found cheaply and they are a lot more useful than a character-driven LCD display. Well, at least they are cheaply found where I live. A quick bus ride down to the electronics district and I would have more choice of DSI displays than character LCD displays.

SD Card Slot

Flip over your Pi and you will see the SD card slot at the rear end of the Pi. If you're using a full-length SD card, watch out because they poke out the back of the Pi pretty far. The SD card slot is labeled as an SD/MMC/SDIO card slot. Exactly what does that all mean, because it sounds pretty useful on paper? Well, it's not.

What Is SD?

SD as you most likely know by now stands for "Secure Digital" and it is a standard held by the SD Association. As you would expect, there are also standards for all the SD cards; the main one you need to pay attention to is the "speed class" rating. The speed class rating starts at 2 and works its way up to 10 (unfortunately, it does not go up to 11). All speeds of cards should work fine, although I recommend you stick with speed 6 as that type of card will provide the best mix of speed and compatibility.

Speed class 10 may work but be sure to check the Raspberry Pi hardware compatibility list as there are lots of reports of the speed class 10 cards not working correctly. You can find an updated list of what SD cards have been tested at the following site:

```
http://elinux.org/RPi_VerifiedPeripherals#SD_cards
```

You will also want to stay away from any cards with a "UHS speed class" as they are not compatible at all with the Raspberry Pi. UHS cards use a different timing source for access. The SD card slot on the Raspberry Pi is unable to provide the correct timing for you to be able to use UHS SD cards. Even Micro SD cards with adapters can be known to cause issues as well. Do yourself a favor and pick up a quality speed class 6 nonmicro SD card.

You may also see a reference to SDHC and SDXC: they are SD High Capacity and SD eXtended Capacity and both will work on the Pi without any issues. SDXC will be at 32 GB and greater in size. SDXC cards come preformatted with the exFAT filesystem. If you format the card in your Raspberry Pi, it may no longer work in other SDXC devices like digital movie cameras and digital picture cameras.

What Is MMC?

The next set of letters to learn is MMC. MMC is another standard and stands for Multi Media Card. Nowadays the SD standard supersedes the MMC standard. I would not expect that you would find many pure MMC cards for sale new today. Your SD card may well be MMC-compatible, and the Raspberry Pi will read and write to your old MMC cards as well. MMC cards will be slower and potentially of smaller capacity: while they will work fine on the Raspberry Pi, I would recommend you buy a newer SD card.

What Is SDIO?

Lastly, we have SDIO. You may have guessed that the IO part of the name stands for input/output. SDIO cards have some form of input and output; the most common are WiFi and Bluetooth. This means that when you insert an SDIO card into a device it will be seen as a WiFi device or a Bluetooth device if the host device and operating system support that. You will come across two types of SDIO cards: pure IO cards and mixed-storage IO cards. Given that the Raspberry Pi must boot from the first partition on the SD card, this makes the pure IO SD cards useless because your Pi won't be able to boot anything. The mixed-storage cards will work as long as the operating system has drivers for the IO part of the card. SDIO cards are not all that popular and will cost a lot more than adding a USB WiFi or Bluetooth dongle to your Raspberry Pi.

I would suggest you avoid the SDIO cards completely: not only will they cost more but there is a good chance that Linux won't support it.

GPIO Headers

GPIO is the next set of headers you will find on the Raspberry Pi. The 26-pin header is known as the GPIO connector (P1); while strictly not all pins are GPIO in the pure sense of the meaning the collective set of pins is called GPIO by the community.

When referring to a pin on the GPIO connectors, use the convention of "P1-XX" where XX is the pin number of the GPIO pins. This is done to avoid confusion with Broadcom's naming convention for the GPIO pins on the system on chip (SoC). When you look at the Pi you will see a label near the bottom of the PCB called "P1": this indicates pin 1 of the GPIO, or P1-01. Opposite to that is P1-02. The pin at the opposite end of P1-01 is P1-25 and the pin at the opposite end of P1-02 is P1-26. Some pins are labeled as "NC" or DNC": that means "no connect" or "do not connect" and you should not be connecting anything to these pins. They will either be physically or logically not connected to anything or reserved for future use.

■ **Warning**   Before we talk about the functions of each of the GPIO pins, I wish to offer you a small but highly important warning. **The GPIO pins on the Raspberry Pi are not tolerant of 3.3 V and above:** the GPIO are purely 3.3 V only.

With that out of the way, let's take a look into the pins and what each pin can do. I've made a nice table that lays out all the GPIO pin functions and their alternate functions if available. Refer to Table 1-1 to see what each pin can do.

Some notes on these pins. P1-01 has a maximum current draw of 50 mA. Like I have said, it's best to power your heavy projects externally rather than via the Pi. P1-02 is a 5 V input: you can use this to power the Pi rather than the micro USB port. I highly suggest you use some type of protection circuit when you power the Pi via the GPIO power pins.

Table 1-1. The Available Pin Headers on GPIO

Pin Number	Primary Function	AlternateFunction	Alternate 1 Function	Pin Number	Pin Name	Function	Alternate Function
P1-01	3.3 V			P1-02	5 V		
P1-03	GPIO 0	I²C SDA		P1-04	NC		
P1-05	GPIO 1	I²C SCL	GPCLK0	P1-06	GND		
P1-07	GPIO 4			P1-08	GPIO 14	UART0_TXD	ALT5=UART1_TDX
P1-09	NC			P1-10	GPIO 15	UART0_RDX	ALRT5=UART1_RXD
P1-11	GPIO 17		ALT3=UART0_RTS ALT5=UART1_RTS	P1-12	GPIO 18		ALT4=SPI1_CE0_N ALT5=PWM0
P1-13	GPIO 21	PCM_DIN	ALT5=GPCLK1	P1-14	NC		
P1-15	GPIO 22		ALT3=SD1_CLK ALT4 = ARM_TRST	P1-16	GPIO 23		ALT3=SD1_CMD ALT4=ARM_RTCK
P1-17	NC			P1-18	GPIO 24		ALT3=SD1_DATA0 ALT4=ARM_TD0
P1-19	GPIO 10	SPI0_MOSI		P1-20	NC		
P1-21	GPIO 9	SPI0_MISO		P1-22	GPIO 25		ALT4=ARm_TCK
P1-23	GPIO 11	SPI0_SCLK		P1-24	GPIO 8	SPI0_CE0_N	

Remember that the GPIO pins are behind the power protection circuits on the Pi: given this, it would be very easy to let the magic smoke out of the Pi. A power protection circuit would stop any unsafe voltage from entering into the Raspberry Pi. It would also prevent any reverse polarity issues that may come up if you attempt to plug in the power the wrong way.

So what is this about primary function, alternate function, and alternate 1 function? The primary function is what the pin will be when the Pi boots by default with the sole exception of GPIO 14(P1-08) and GPIO 15(P1-10). These two pins are automatically switched to the alternate function of providing the universal asynchronous receive/transmitter function (UART). Also note that this UART runs at 115,200 bits per second by default. This is done so that you can watch the Pi boot over a serial console that is completely headless. Without this happening automatically, you would need to wait until the operating system boots to activate the serial console. That would be pretty inconvenient if you had a low-level boot issue.

The alternate and alternate 1 functions can be set at the operating-system level. P1-03 and P1-05 can also be used for the I²C bus: they have had an additional 1.8K pull-up resistor added. The addition of the pull-up resistor for the I²C bus is a nice touch because now we can set the bus high or low without adding any external pull-up resistors. By setting the bus high, we can place the voltage level to 3.3 V; to set the bus low, we could set the voltage of the pin back to 0.

Each GPIO pin can supply a set maximum amount of current; if you go over this you may damage the GPIO pin or, worse yet, destroy the 3.3 V supply on the Pi itself and that would be a very bad thing. Exactly what is the current limit then? Well, that's easy: it's a maximum of 16 mA. I want to talk a bit more about this limit as it can be a little confusing at first. Each pin can sustain a maximum of a 16-mA draw but you can't have every pin drawing that much current or you will fry your 3.3 V supply. The 16 mA is a total for one or all the combined GPIO pins so take care to design your projects so that you don't go over this limit.

Analog Video Output

Up next is the Pi's only analog video output. It's in the form of a composite RCA output. There is not a lot to say about this as there is not a whole lot to it. The foundation has tried its best to make this composite interface usable on a wide range of devices and it seems to have done a good job. You cannot use the composite and the HDMI interfaces at the same time: you must pick an output and use it. If you have both outputs plugged in, the HDMI interface will be the active output, rather than the composite.

For fun you can also set the composite output to be black and white via the `sdtv_disable_colourburst=1` setting in the `config.txt` file. The `config.txt` file has all the values you will need for basic operation; by default it will be set to `sdtv_mode=0` and `sdtv_aspect=1`. If you need to edit this file, take a look at Chapter 2 when you install Linux. I've created Table 1-2 to help you set the modes if you need to.

Table 1-2. *Video Modes Supported by the Composite Video Out*

Setting in config.txt	Description of Setting
sdtv_mode=0standard	NTSC
sdtv_mode=1	NTSC-J
sdtv_mode=2	standard PAL
sdtv_mode=3	PAL-M
sdtv_aspect=1	aspect ratio of 4:3
sdtv_aspect=2	aspect ratio of 14:9

JTAG Ports

Between the composite video out and the 3.5-mm audio out, you will find two rows of pin headers labeled P2 and P3.

- P2 is the JTAG, or Joint Test Action Group, interface for the Broadcom SoC. There is not much you can do with this JTAG port at the moment.

- Likewise, the P3 header is the JTAG port for the SMSC LAN9512 chip. It is also of not much use right now.

The JTAG interfaces are used to initially program the SoC chip and the SMSC chip on the board. The manufacturer can also use the JTAG to test the hardware at the time of its manufacture. If the Raspberry Pi did give us access to the JTAG interface you could re-flash the Broadcom chipset with your own firmware to run your own software.

Audio Output

Wow, another somewhat boring output. It's the 3.5-mm stereo audio socket. Just like with the HDMI and composite outputs, you can only output audio to one output at a time, such as HDMI or the 3.5 mm. You can use HDMI video with the audio disabled: this will enable you to use the 3.5-mm audio with the HDMI output.

By default if you use HDMI, the audio will go via HDMI; if you want HDMI video and 3.5-mm audio, set this in your `config.txt` file using `hdmi-drive=1`. Sound-quality wise, the HDMI output will provide you with a better output but if you don't have that then you can make do with the 3.5-mm stereo output.

LEDs

Lastly, on the edge of the Raspberry Pi you will find five LEDs. While not inputs, they do have an output: their ability to emit light. This output tells us a few key status points about the Pi's operation state and the link state for the Ethernet on the Model B only. In Table 1-3 we can see the modes for the LEDs.

Table 1-3. *LED States on the Raspberry Pi*

LED and Led Color	Description
D5 Green	System okay/SD card access
D6 Red	Power okay, 3.3 V
D7 Green	Full duplex; half duplex if the LED is off
D8 Green	Link activity for the LAN

That's it for the inputs and outputs on the Raspberry Pi. There are a few miscellaneous chips on the back but none of these are important to discuss.

Pi Brains

What's this in Figure 1-2? It's the ARM11 core block diagram that makes up part of the SoC. This is only one part of the Broadcom BCM2835 SoC and it is officially called the ARM1176JZF-S core. Don't feel too bad if Figure 1-2 looks like just a bunch of shapes thrown onto the page or if anything in this next section seems way too technical. As you go though each chapter and learn more about the Raspberry Pi and its hardware, this section will start to make more sense. Give it a read over now but don't worry if you just don't get it. Please do come back to this section when you're involved with the projects; you will be surprised at how much more it makes sense.

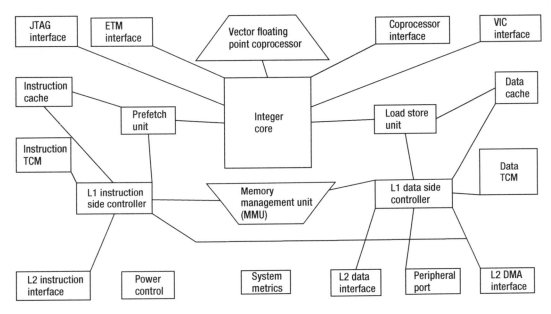

Figure 1-2. *The block diagram of the ARM1176JZF-S core*

The ARM11 core is built around the ARMv6 architecture: it brings advancements in the processor's pipeline, caching, and multimedia aspects of the core.

Let's talk about the ARM11 core in some detail now. It is built around an integer core that has three main instruction sets.

- The ARM instruction set is the main instruction set, and it is where most of your code will execute.

- The 16-bit thumb instruction set is a subset of the most common instructions from the main ARM instruction set. The thumb instruction set will be of most use to embedded devices but won't be of much use to the projects in this book.

- The last set is the Java byte code instruction set that supports hardware and software execution of variable-length Java byte codes.

In addition to the three main instruction sets, the ARM has two subsets of instructions called media and digital signal processing (DSP) instructions, which help speed up multimedia functions, especially the Single Instruction Mutable Data (SIMD) instruction. The SIMD speeds up MPEG-4 and digital audio by a factor of two. This makes all the difference in the world if you were listening to your MP3 collection. To play an average MP3 file you would need twice as much CPU power without SIMD instructions to play the exact same song. More power used on the CPU would mean more battery power used on your portable MP3 player. No one would like an MP3 player with only 15 minutes of runtime.

Processor Pipeline

The ARM11 core has increased the length of its pipeline depth from three stages to eight stages. Each stage has a set function and to a certain level having more stages allows you to process more data in the same clock cycle. This is where some of the efficiency of each clock cycle comes in. So, is the pipeline like a water slide?

Well, no, but they do share one common theme though: each segment connects to the next. In the case of the pipeline in the ARM, one stage's output is the next stage's input. Let's look at the ARM11's Algorithmic Logic Unit (ALU) stage in Figure 1-3. The ALU stage is responsible for all algorithmic functions, such as addition or multiplication.

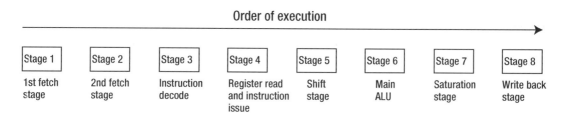

Figure 1-3. *Flow chart of instruction execution*

The stages are executed in order from one to eight in one single clock cycle; so one clock cycle can provide one ALU operation. Now think about if the pipeline was four stages long and not eight: it would then take two full clock cycles to complete the same instruction. This makes the process half as efficient. However, the ARM11 is a superscalar architecture so it can do more than one operation per clock cycle, as can most modern processors. Superscalar means that functions inside the CPU core can operate in a parallel fashion. You can think of a superscalar architecture like a grocery store with multiple checkout lines. You have many operators serving many customers. The opposite to this is scalar: scalar would be a small green grocer with only one checkout that can serve only one person at a time.

Eight stages up from six must be better, right? To a certain degree it is: you now can get more done per clock cycle.

So why can't the ARM add 30 stages then? Very simple: the more stages you add, the higher the clock frequency you need to drive the stage. This has the very unfortunate side effect of increased heat and power usage. Given that the ARM11 is targeted to low power and low heat-embedded devices more stages would be very bad.

The ARMv6 is special in another way too; it is the first ARM core to contain a vector floating point coprocessor. This coprocessor meets the IEEE standards for floating point arithmetic by giving the ARM11 a low-cost, high-performance, single-precision and double-precision computation ability in hardware. A lot of the performance improvements will come from this coprocessor that is potentially more than 10 times faster for certain operations.

▓ **Note**   A coprocessor is very much like a copilot. Its job is to assist the main process with functions that can be better handled by the coprocessor, leaving the main processes free to handle the bigger tasks.

To best illustrate how this will give increased performance I created some diagrams. First, in Table 1-4 we have two ranges from 1 to 5: the first range will be called "A" and the second range will be called "B".

Table 1-4. *A Table of Integers*

A	B
1	1
2	2
3	3
4	4

Let's take, for example, a nonvector processor and add each number from ranges A and B: it would need to loop through this table five times. In a vector processor all the values from ranges A and B are loaded in one loop as shown in Figure 1-4.

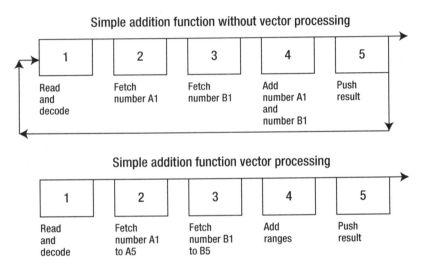

Figure 1-4. *Flow charge showing the difference between vector and nonvector function execution*

So, given Table 1-4 and Figure 1-4, we can see that it would take the nonvector processor five loops of steps 1 to 5 to add all the numbers from each range. The vector-enabled processor can do the same work in one single loop of steps 1 to 5.

In the Raspberry Pi world, this can be called a hard float or a soft float. A hard float is making use of the coprocessor; a soft float is doing the same operation in software. Wherever possible you should be looking at trying to get a hard float enabled to help speed up the applications and give your Raspberry Pi's CPU more free cycles.

Caches

As you can see from Figure 1-2 the ARM11 provides separate data and instruction caches (a cache is an area of very fast memory that can be directly accessed by the main CPU). On the Raspberry Pi these are sometimes known as "D-cache" and "I-cache." In the case of the ARM1176JZF-S each cache is 16 KB in size and each cache can be locked independently so they are four-way associative. The I-cache and D-cache make up what is commonly called the L1 cache.

Hmm, 16 KB seems pretty small. Well, it's not so bad for an L1 cache when you compare it with the Intel Core i7. The Intel L1 cache is only 32 KB in size so for the Raspberry Pi to have 16KB by 16 KB, it's not doing too badly for itself. Next up you would see figures on the level 2 cache, or L2 cache. If you were to use the same Intel Core i7 example, the current generation of the i7 ships with anywhere from 8 MB to 16 MB for the L2 cache.

So what about the L2 cache on the Raspberry Pi? It's there in a fashion: Broadcom has assigned the L2 cache to be used by the GPU; in terms of clock cycles the L2 cache is closer to the GPU than the ARM11 core. In addition, by dedicating the L2 cache to the GPU you can get more performance from the GPU. The CPU will map requests around the L2 cache; after all, our main system memory is sitting on top of the SoC so don't be concerned about the Raspberry Pi mapping around the L2 cache. It's not going to give you any big noticeable performance issues.

No L2 cache has to be bad: will the sky fall? It's hard to compare CPU architectures and how more or less cache will affect that CPU without understanding that you are comparing apples and oranges. A different CPU architecture will benefit from more cache whereas in some CPUs the addition of more cache will not give you a lot of notable benefit. The ARM cores are not starved for data unlike some of the powerful x86 chips. So I urge you to not worry about the L2 cache; if the ARM1176JZF-S suffered that badly from the lack of an L2 cache ARM would have added one.

The ARM1176JZF-S has a good way of controlling the caches too. It makes use of a dedicated coprocessor to handle all cache functions. This means that the main integer core can focus more on the task at hand, which is processing your request and not controlling the cache. This coprocessor also takes care of the main system memory access. It will control what is in the cache and how the main system memory has been accessed and how each cache has been accessed as well. Each data path between the caches and main system memory is 64 bits wide, giving the ARM11 a bit more throughput. This allows more data to flow though each path concurrently.

Memory Chips

On the topic of main system memory, if you take a close look at your Pi board you will notice an absence of a separate DDR2 memory chip. So where is all of that 256 MB of DDR2 stored?

Surprisingly it's a single chip on top of the SoC chip. The main chip in the center of your Pi is in fact two chips stacked together like a sandwich but using an array of little conductive metal balls and sockets called a ball grid array rather than mustard to connect the layers. On the bottom and connected via the ball grid array to the mainboard is the SoC and stacked on top of that once again via the ball grid array is the 256-MB DDR2 memory chip. This is called "package on package" and not "sandwich," though I like sandwich better: it sounds tasty and package on package sounds boring.

Power States

Lastly I want to talk about the power states of the ARM1176JZF-S. This may be of great interest if you're going to leave your Raspberry Pi on for long periods of time, say, for example, in Chapter 9 when you will set up the serial server as a headless remote terminal. You may need the remote terminal only once a month, so why let the core and peripherals run at full speed and voltage?

The Raspberry Pi has four distinct power modes.

- The first mode should be pretty obvious: it's called the run mode and it means that the CPU and all functionality of the ARM11 core are available and powered up. This is the default mode of operation of the core. If you are using your Raspberry Pi for everyday use I would recommend you stick with this mode because you will need all the power you need.

- The second sate is the standby mode. In this mode the main core clocks are shut down although the power circuits on the core are still active. By this, I mean that the parts of the CPU that process your instructions are no longer running. They are in the same state as if you were to remove the power from the Raspberry Pi. This makes the core draw less current as it's not actively running anything, so it's just like a zombie. In this mode the core can be quickly woken up by a process generating a special call to the CPU called an interrupt. This interrupt will stop any current processing and do what the calling process has asked for. This mode is known as Wait for Interrupt, or WFI.

- The third mode should be all too familiar to everyone. This is the shutdown mode. In this mode there is no power. The best example of this power mode is that you have pulled the power cable.

- The last power mode is the dormant mode. In this mode the core is powered down and all caches are left powered on. This mode is only partiality supported in the ARM1176JZF-S core at the moment and I do not suggest you use it.

Performance per Watt

So what's with the block diagram before? Well, now that you know all the detail and effort that has gone into the ARM11 processor you can look back at the block diagram and appreciate that while the Raspberry Pi is a very cheap system this CPU is no toy. For the performance and feature set per watt the ARM11 is nothing short of amazing. Performance per watt is king in major data centers now.

So the next time you hear someone complain "oh, it's only 700 MHz!" you can retort with "Why, the ARM11's 700 MHz will handle a whole lot more than you think it can." Now that you understand the architecture you can make better use of it. You can use the additional instructions or you can rely on the ARM11 to act in a certain way. Go forth and optimize your code and your hardware around this amazingly cheap SoC device.

There is always a negative to every positive. One unusable function at the moment on the ARM1176JZF-S is the dedicated DSP core: currently there is no publicly documented API to access this core inside the ARM11 CPU, and this is unfortunate because our media projects could have made good use of this core.

Pi Eyes

I have talked about the AMR11 side of the Broadcom BCM2835. Now let's talk about the Broadcom VideoCore IV side of the SoC. This part of the Broadcom BCM2835 is protected by non-disclosure agreements, making it hard for the open source community to optimize its code and better utilize the VideoCore. This all comes back to the fact that the driver is supplied as a binary blob. For example, if the VideoCore code were open source it would be allowed into the Linux kernel, or end users could patch and fix bugs that they come across. Given that the VideoCore's main audience is the highly competitive mobile phone market it's no surprise that there is an NDA on the design and on the APIs for this part of the Broadcom BCM2835. What we do know is that the VideoCore can in fact run by itself and execute limited amounts of ARM code at the moment. Normally the VideoCore chip is paired with an ARM processor and is just used to accelerate media playback and capture, as is the case with our Pi. The VideoCore supports 1080p playback and should be able to handle all of our playback requirements quite nicely. You can set how much memory is assigned as video memory (also known as VRAM) by using different executable and linkable file formats. These files will have the extension of elf boot files.

The foundation provides three elf files to boot the Raspberry Pi: they control the system/VRAM split. They are arm128_start.elf, arm192_start.elf, and arm224_start.elf. The number in each of the file names determines how much system memory you have, and whatever is left is allocated to the VRAM. So in the case of arm128_start.elf you have 128 MB of system memory and 128 MB of VRAM. This file needs to be copied to /boot and must be called start.elf, otherwise the GPU will not read it when the system starts and your whole system will fail to boot.

Hang on, you said the GPU reads that? This seems a little confusing: why is the GPU reading a boot file? Remember when I talked about how the VideoCore GPU can run code? Well, the Raspberry Pi uses the GPU to initialize the SD card slot and read the config.txt and start.elf files from the SD card. It then hands off the boot process to the CPU.

What Happens at Power On?

This may seem a little out of place compared to the rest of the topics but given the Raspberry Pi's unique hardware and odd boot sequence it seems very fitting. You may have noticed that there was no BIOS screen when you first powered on the Raspberry Pi. That's because the Raspberry Pi has a very strange way of running the power-on self-tests (POSTs). I am going to give you a quick overview of exactly how the Pi performs POSTs.

The following occurs in order once power is applied to the Raspberry Pi. The example will use Linux as the operating system but the concept applies to all operating systems booted on the Raspberry Pi. Step 1 assumes that you have just plugged in the power.

1. The ARM core is not running, SDRAM access is disabled, and the GPU is on.

2. The GPU starts executing the first-stage boot loader that is stored inside the SoC package. This first-stage boot loader is programed into the SoC and cannot be edited or changed.

3. The first-stage boot loader reads the second-stage boot loader into the L2 cache that's mapped to the GPU: this is also known as the bootcode.bin.

4. The bootcode.bin enables access to the SDRAM. The bootcode.bin then loads the third-stage bootloader, known as loader.bin. This is loaded from the SD card into the SDRAM.

5. The loader.bin then reads the start.elf file from the SD card.

6. The start.elf file then reads the config.txt, cmdline.txt, and the Linux kernel.img files from the first partition on the SD card.

7. The boot process is handed over to the Linux kernel.

The files mentioned in this boot process can be obtained from the foundation's GitHub site. The files can be obtained for no cost and are licensed under the Broadcom Corporation license; please take a moment to read this license.

Also keep in mind that the Raspberry Pi can boot from only an SD card. The Linux kernel and the boot files that I listed must be present on the SD card and not on an external drive.

Pi on Your Face

If all this sounds too good to be true, then some of it is. I am personally a big supporter of open source software and hardware. Everything used to write this book was performed with open source applications and open source operating systems. I also would love to see hardware be more open but given how competitive some markets are I cannot see this ever changing.

This is unfortunate and will somewhat limit us now and in the future if documents and APIs are never available to the public. For example, to boot the Raspberry Pi we use a premade binary file that is placed on the SD card. End users have no way to re-create this or change anything about it if they encounter a bug with it. If these files were to all of a sudden stop working, the hardware we have would be rendered totally useless.

The Raspberry Pi also needs the binary blob file in order to drive the functions of the GPU; this has the unfortunate effect of locking us out of the CSI and DSI buses. As end users, we cannot currently make use of them: the foundation is hoping to provide us with a way to get access to the buses at a later stage. For the moment, don't consider the CSI and DSI interfaces a selling point.

You will also notice the clear lack of any onboard battery or anywhere to set the date and time like you do on your normal PC. The foundation expects that the Raspberry Pi will use NTP for the Model B and that the time will be set manually on the Model A on each boot of the device. This is a little inconvenient but it makes perfect sense when you think about the PCB space and component cost that would make up the real-time clock (RTC). This would have pushed the cost and the size of the Raspberry Pi well above what it is now.

Summary

This brings us to the end of talking about all the aspects of the Raspberry Pi's hardware. We started our journey with looking at every input and output and there are a lot of them: you won't run out of ideas and projects anytime soon.

I then talked about the heart and brains of the Raspberry Pi and how amazing it is that you get such a sheer amount of processing power for such a small and cheap device. I then guided you though the features and configuration options for the VideoCore GPU, which prompted me to then talk about the boot order since it's directly tied to the GPU of all things.

Lastly I spoke about any currently unusable connectors and interfaces and missing hardware. This section may come off sounding a little harsh but it's not intended to be: for the price you are paying, the Raspberry Pi is an amazing piece of hardware. I waited for more than three weeks for mine and each day I would check my inbox to see if it had shipped out. You would think that living in Hong Kong I would get it a little quicker but that was not the case.

You've most likely noticed that there is a lot of detail in this chapter and that's just my love for hardware shining though. Don't get too caught up in all the details of how everything works. I really want you to enjoy the hardware; if you find that reading more about the hardware is something you enjoy be sure to check out the ARMv6 reference manual and the Broadcom BCM2835 web documents (unfortunately, the latter are a bit lacking in useful information).

Enough of the details! Let's do something with the Raspberry Pi. So we'll kick off with something useful and get Fedora installed.

CHAPTER 2

■ ■ ■

Installing Fedora

You now know all about the hardware on the Raspberry Pi and have all the parts you need to get it up and running. You may have even already got a version of Linux installed. Most likely you have installed the Debian port known as Raspbian. Raspbian is fine and has all the latest fixes and it's also the easiest to install. I prefer to use Fedora because I deal with Red Hat Enterprise Linux (RHEL) each day at work and it makes it a little easier for me. I am not that familiar with Debian so I feel I can offer you more with Fedora. However, I am not going to force you to use any particular Linux distribution. You are quite free to choose any distribution; use whatever you are comfortable with. All the tools and code in this book will use open source build tools or utilities so any distribution of Linux will be fine. After all, I intend to show you more than one operating system on the Raspberry Pi anyway.

In Chapter 11 I will also help you with how to install my first and favorite Linux distribution, Gentoo. Coming from a NetBSD background, I liked the way the portage system worked. My main goal at the time was to learn Linux, and Gentoo is a great teacher. Centos/RHEL also taught me a lot about enterprise Linux and why doing things a certain way is a very good thing.

A lot of the functionality you need will come from the Linux kernel. All the hardware headers are exported by the kernel as built-in functions or as modules. This is one of the reasons that make Linux so good. No matter what distribution you pick, the kernel will be based off the same tree of code. This is also why you will often see Linux distributions described as being GNU/Linux, because they use GNU applications in user land (applications that you run and use yourself) and Linux to give you an open source kernel. This exciting combination of software makes up your distribution.

WHAT'S A DISTRIBUTION?

In the Linux world a distribution is a bundle of end-user software and a kernel. It is a full working system, if you will, ready to be installed and operated. Each part of the distribution could be distributed independently as well. A distribution just packs it all up in one easy-to-use bundle.

In this chapter I will talk about the different ways you can install Fedora to your SD card and how your SD card will be set up. This is not too hard but it's good to know the different ways you can set up your card. SD cards are not hard disks and Fedora expects to be installed on a hard disk so you need to take a little care.

I will also talk about the importation files that live on the /boot partition of your SD card. I will talk you through the files' functions and how you can replace or edit them if you want. These files can have a large effect on the way your Raspberry Pi will work, so it's important to know where to find them and edit them.

Of course I will talk about the first boot of Fedora and what to expect via traditional access with a keyboard and screen and also via headless with just an Ethernet cable. I will also talk about some of the basic settings you may want to configure on Fedora. The big one will be the network time protocol (NTP), unless you like setting the date and time at each reboot of the Raspberry Pi.

Lastly I will talk about what optimization can increase the performance and life of your SD card. With not a moment to spare, get your SD cards ready because next up is the creation of the SD card.

Dissecting the Image

First you're going to need two critical pieces of hardware:

- An SD card, or a few of them, with a minimum size of 2 GB. This size will just get you up and running but will leave you only a few 100 MB of space. I would suggest 4 GB as a good starting size.

- An SD card reader and writer. I use Linux to build all my SD cards. I don't own a Windows or a Mac machine so you may need to change your method to build the SD card if you are using a Windows or Mac machine.

So let's get down and build the SD card. What's exactly on this SD card image we're about to work with? It's a bit of mystery for the first-time user of the Raspberry Pi. What exactly needs to go on the SD card? Well, not much really. The Fedora image you get will have all the necessary files as well as special files in /boot.

Everything that you need to have a fully functional system is included. You may want to change some of the settings or adjust the memory assignment via the files in /boot. No matter how you look at it, the image is a full operating-system image. It's a little different from, say, using an install CD. You won't get to pick the packages you want to install. You get an already configured operating system. All you are doing is placing this image on the SD card.

Fedora has a nice little installer for many different operating systems. For the Linux users out there, myself included, there are two main ways to get the Fedora image on your SD card:

- A GUI installer

- At the command line

Using the GUI Installer

The first and most widely used method is the GUI installer, using an application called faii. You can download it from either of the following places:

- http://raspberrypi.org/archives/tag/fedora

- http://rpi.horan.hk

The installer is a Python script and most distributions will come with Python so there is no need to worry about dependencies on the script. Here's how you use it:

1. Download a copy of the faii-1.0.0.tar.gz tarball to your machine and extract it.

2. Once you have extracted it you should see an executable called fedora-arm-installer. You may need to open this executable first. If you are running Fedora or Ubuntu, make sure you also have the python-qt4 package installed, otherwise the GUI will not launch. Now if you run this you will get a nice little GUI pop up, as seen in Figure 2-1.

Figure 2-1. *The Fedora Raspberry Pi installer on Linux*

3. In the Source section of the tool, click the little blue arrows. This will refresh the source list from the Internet.

4. Select Raspberry Pi Fedora Remix 14 (r1). If you don't want to download a new source image, you can also use the Browse button to select an already downloaded image file to use.

5. In the Destination section, click the button with the blue arrows again to refresh the device list. You may need root privileges to install to your removable media device. In Figure 2-1 my removable media is /dev/sde.

6. Once you're done, click the Install button and wait for the tool to finish writing the image to your SD card. Once it's done, remove your SD card. You are ready to place it into the Raspberry Pi; the tool takes care of everything for you. How nice of it to do so!

Using the Command Line

The second method of installing Fedora to the SD card is my personal favorite. After all I am more than a little bit attached to the command line. I use it every day at work and I use it extensively at home. I prefer a command-line option over a GUI option, especially when you want to make more than one SD card's worth of images. The command-line option makes this a lot faster. Recall when I said the install was in fact just an image of a working system? Well, this image can be written to the SD card by a tool called dd. dd is used to copy a set number of blocks (or bytes) from one device or image to another. In our case we have an image file, which is the Fedora image. Then you have a device, and that's your SD card.

You are going to need to find a mirror of the Fedora install image. You can find a list of mirrors on the http://elinux.org web site. Or you can download the image directly from the following places:

- http://raspi.bullet-irc.net

- http://rpi.horan.hk/chapters/02/chapter02.html

In Figure 2-2 you can see the exact tarball you need.

19

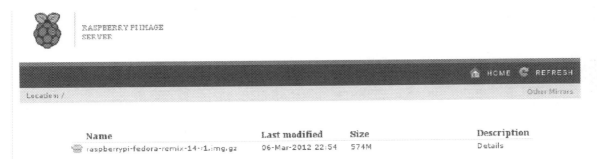

Figure 2-2. Fedora remix download image

Once you have downloaded this image, you need to extract the file. To extract the file use the following command:

```
# gunzip raspberrypi-fedora-remix-14-r1.img.gz
```

You should now end up with an .img file. This file is what you will use with dd to write to the SD card. Next up, insert your SD card and find the device name. The quickest way to find the device is by using the dmesg command. I use the following command to see the last few lines of the dmesg output:

```
# dmesg | tail
```

You are looking for a line that has sdX where X is a letter: in my case it was sde. Now you want the whole device, not a partition. Don't try and write the fedora image to sdX1, for example. Now you need to issue the following dd command as root at your shell and type the following, substituting the X for your device letter:

```
-# dd bs=1M if=raspberrypi-fedora-remix.img of=/dev/sdX
```

Be very careful with the dd command: it's quite easy to destroy your data. dd will not give you any feedback while this process is under way. Just wait for it to return your shell prompt. Once this has finished, you must issue the following command as root to flush any data caches to disk:

```
# sync
```

■ **Warning**   If you don't do this and you remove the SD card the card may be missing parts of the image. The sync command may take some time to complete but it's very important that you let this run. You will corrupt your image if you remove the card while the sync command is running.

Installing the Image on Windows

If you are using Windows to write the image, you need two tools: one to extract and one to write the image.

- To extract, you can use a tool called 7-Zip that can be found at http://7-zip.org/.
- To write the image to the SD card you can use a tool called Win32 Disk Imager that can be found at https://launchpad.net/win32-image-writer/+download.

Of course, it would be nice if you are using Linux on your host machine.

Booting Your Pi

Whatever method you take, you should now have two partitions on your SD card:

- /boot
- /root

For the Fedora image, the /boot is called Raspi_Boot and the /root is called Raspi_Remix_14. See Figure 2-3 for a listing of the partitions.

```
Filesystem      Size  Used Avail Use% Mounted on
/dev/sde1       100M   36M   64M  37% /media/Raspi_Boot
/dev/sde2        30G  2.1G   26G   8% /media/Raspi_Remix 14
```

Figure 2-3. *Partition listing on a Fedora SD card*

Oh No, Goes Crash!

Now that you have a Linux image on your SD card you can insert the image into the Raspberry Pi. Ensure that the power is off to the Raspberry Pi before you do this. Fedora will boot up in different ways, depending on what you have plugged into the Raspberry Pi. If you have a video source and a keyboard and mouse plugged in, you will be booted into the graphical display, whereas if you just have Ethernet plugged in it will acquire an IP address from the local DHCP server and will start SSH. The default username and password are root and fedoraarm.

Unfortunately you may notice that the current 14-r1 release of Fedora hangs the Raspberry Pi's boot. Your boot process will be stuck on either a USB message or it may just hang at the Ethernet detection stage. These sorts of issues are quite hard to debug. The operating system has hung quite early on in the boot process and you used a ready-made image. What could be the matter? The first step I normally take when I have this sort of issue is to ensure that I have the latest firmware for the device. Remove the power from the Raspberry Pi and take the SD card back to your host machine: it's time to update the firmware. Remember when I spoke about the special files that live on /boot? Well, that's where our issue is located. In Figure 2-4 you can see the out-of-date files on the /boot volume of the Fedora image.

Name

- kernel.img
- start.elf
- loader.bin
- cmdline_testmode.txt
- cmdline.txt
- bootcode.bin
- arm224_start.elf
- arm192_start.elf
- arm128_start.elf

Figure 2-4. *Boot files for the Raspberry Pi*

Now, the above files not only boot the Raspberry Pi but also contain some firmware to drive certain parts of the SoC. So if the above files are corrupted or way out of date they will cause you a lot of boot issues or maybe even hang at the Ethernet detection part of the kernel.

So now that you have a good idea what the issue may be, I will show you how to update the boot files and boot loader on the SD card. I feel it is pretty important to have the latest boot loader and boot files. So out of habit I grab the latest files from the Raspberry Pi Foundation's GitHub site. There are a few main files you should keep updated and they need to be updated outside of your normal distribution's update process. You can find the GitHub site at https://github.com/raspberrypi.

It's quite simple to update the files. First, shut down your Raspberry Pi and mount your SD card into your host machine. You should see two mount points. One will be /boot and the other will be your root filesystem on the SD card. Open up the /boot mount point and replace the following files from the latest copy on the GitHub firmware section. You can find the latest firmware at https://github.com/raspberrypi/firmware/tree/master/boot. The files you need to add and update are

- fixup.dat
- kernel.img
- bootcode.bin
- start.elf

Overwrite all files with the versions from the GitHub site. You don't need to remove any files from the /boot partition; they no longer will be used during the boot process. Once you're done, eject your SD card from the host machine and insert it back into the Raspberry Pi.

Your Raspberry Pi will now boot without error. It will then reboot itself the first time in order to resize the filesystem on the SD card. This may take some time if you have a large SD card. Go grab a drink or some food, and by the time you get back it should be done and waiting for your login. The bootup speed is quite quick!

Configure and Look Around

Now that you have a functional Raspberry Pi running Fedora, it's time to take a look around. If you have no keyboard and screen attached, use SSH on the Raspberry Pi with root and fedoraarm as your username and password. If you have a keyboard and mouse attached, you will find yourself in front of a series of prompts to set up the Raspberry Pi. Because I connected over SSH, all the steps below are for the SSH install.

■ **Note** All the projects in this book will require command-line access and I personally prefer the command line although the choice is yours if you want to use a keyboard and monitor.

Whenever I get a new piece of hardware I like to take a look around the hardware. I like to run the following command first:

```
# dmesg | more
```

The dmesg command stands for display message and its main function is to print the output of the message buffer of the kernel. In this case it should be the boot messages from the time that the power was applied to the Raspberry Pi. It's a good idea to check over the dmesg for any errors or hardware that are not correctly set up by the kernel.

You may have noticed this error about not having a real-time clock (RTC) during the boot message stage:

```
drivers/rtc/hctosys.c: unable to open rtc device (rtc0)
```

If you missed it, you can find it easily by using the following command:

```
# dmesg | grep rtc
```

This will search the boot messages for the string rtc. You will then be able to see the error without staring at the output of your boot process. This error occurs because Linux expects most hardware nowadays to have an RTC. Because you have no RTC you need a way to get time set up correctly. I will show you how to set up NTP and set the correct time zone for your Raspberry Pi now.

The first thing you need to do is copy the time zone file for your time zone from /usr/share/zoneinfo/COUNTRY/CITY and overwrite the /etc/localtime file. I did this to set my time zone to Hong Kong, as you can see from the below command:

```
# cp /usr/share/zoneinfo/Asia/Hong_Kong /etc/localtime
```

Now just set your time with the date command. Using the date command you would set the date and time like this:

```
# date MMddHHmmCCyy
```

An example of this would be:

```
# date  0102201309302013
```

This would set the date and time to January 2, 2013, and 9:30 in the morning. Next up take a look at the settings in /etc/ntp.conf; by default this file should have the Fedora NTP servers set up and ready to go so there is no need to edit anything. Start the NTP daemon with this command:

```
# service ntpd start
```

Make sure it's set to start upon boot:

```
# chkconfig ntpd on
```

NTP can take a few minutes to adjust to the local time. After a short while, run the following command to see if you have a working time source.

```
# ntpq -pn
```

In Figure 2-5 you can see a * alongside one of the IP addresses; this is the time source the machine is currently using. The + indicates a candidate time source.

```
[root@hobo ~]# ntpq -pn
     remote           refid      st t when poll reach   delay   offset  jitter
==============================================================================
*202.131.74.126  133.100.9.2      2 u   16   64    1   18.635    5.169   0.146
+169.229.70.201  169.229.128.214  3 u   15   64    1  178.903    4.164   0.247
+203.129.68.14   192.168.51.202   2 u   14   64    1   11.627   -0.080   0.256
```

Figure 2-5. *A working output of the ntpq command*

▓ **Note**   A candidate time source is the next best time source that the system has configured. If the system was to lose the primary time source it would select the next time source marked with a + in the list.

Now that you have fixed the only error in the system's dmesg output, let's take a look around at the hardware a little more. Next up I normally like to run:

```
# lspci
```

You will notice that you will get an error from this command rather than a listing of your PCI devices. That's because the Raspberry Pi has no PCI bus; hence the lspci tool cannot find any information. How can you find out what buses the Raspberry Pi has? That's quite simple with Linux: just do a directory listing on /sys/bus/platform/ devices/; as you can see in Figure 2-6 we have our I²C, SPI, and GPIO buses.

```
[root@hobo ~]# ls -la /sys/bus/platform/devices/
total 0
drwxr-xr-x 2 root root 0 Jan  1 1970 .
drwxr-xr-x 4 root root 0 Jan  1 1970 ..
lrwxrwxrwx 1 root root 0 Jan  1 1970 alarmtimer -> ../../../devices/platform/alarmtimer
lrwxrwxrwx 1 root root 0 Jan  1 1970 bcm2708_dma.0 -> ../../../devices/platform/bcm2708_dma.0
lrwxrwxrwx 1 root root 0 Jan  1 1970 bcm2708_fb -> ../../../devices/platform/bcm2708_fb
lrwxrwxrwx 1 root root 0 Jan  1 1970 bcm2708_gpio -> ../../../devices/platform/bcm2708_gpio
lrwxrwxrwx 1 root root 0 Jan  1 1970 bcm2708_i2c.0 -> ../../../devices/platform/bcm2708_i2c.0
lrwxrwxrwx 1 root root 0 Jan  1 1970 bcm2708_i2c.1 -> ../../../devices/platform/bcm2708_i2c.1
lrwxrwxrwx 1 root root 0 Jan  1 1970 bcm2708_powerman.0 -> ../../../devices/platform/bcm2708_powerman.0
lrwxrwxrwx 1 root root 0 Jan  1 1970 bcm2708_sdhci.0 -> ../../../devices/platform/bcm2708_sdhci.0
lrwxrwxrwx 1 root root 0 Jan  1 1970 bcm2708_spi.0 -> ../../../devices/platform/bcm2708_spi.0
lrwxrwxrwx 1 root root 0 Jan  1 1970 bcm2708_systemtimer -> ../../../devices/platform/bcm2708_systemtimer
lrwxrwxrwx 1 root root 0 Jan  1 1970 bcm2708_usb -> ../../../devices/platform/bcm2708_usb
lrwxrwxrwx 1 root root 0 Jan  1 1970 bcm2708_vcio -> ../../../devices/platform/bcm2708_vcio
lrwxrwxrwx 1 root root 0 Jan  1 1970 bcm2835_AUD0.0 -> ../../../devices/platform/bcm2835_AUD0.0
lrwxrwxrwx 1 root root 0 Jan  1 1970 leds-gpio -> ../../../devices/platform/leds-gpio
lrwxrwxrwx 1 root root 0 Jan  1 1970 serial8250.0 -> ../../../devices/platform/serial8250.0
lrwxrwxrwx 1 root root 0 Jan  1 1970 wl-gpio -> ../../../devices/platform/wl-gpio
```

Figure 2-6. *Available buses on the Raspberry Pi*

Last, I like to look at the USB bus with the following command:

```
# lsusb
```

You may not have this tool as part of your base install. I would suggest that you install it with:

```
# yum install usbutils -y
```

This tool will show you what downstream USB devices you may have connected. In my case in Figure 2-7 you can see I have only one device connected. That is Device 004.

```
[root@hobo ~]# lsusb
Bus 001 Device 004: ID 04d9:1503 Holtek Semiconductor, Inc. Shortboard Lefty
Bus 001 Device 003: ID 0424:ec00 Standard Microsystems Corp.
Bus 001 Device 002: ID 0424:9512 Standard Microsystems Corp.
Bus 001 Device 001: ID 1d6b:0002 Linux Foundation 2.0 root hub
```

Figure 2-7. *USB bus on the Raspberry Pi*

"Hang on, in Chapter 1, you said the Ethernet was on the USB bus, didn't you?" I did and I was right, but it's not visible via lsusb. That's because it's not on the downstream USB bus. It presents itself directly to the internal upstream port. When you think about USB ports you normally think about the port on the back of your PC where you plug something in. This type of connection is known as a downstream USB port because it is connected internally to the USB host controller. On the USB host controller itself, there is an internal connection port called the upstream port. This is how USB devices are interconnected; as an end user you would not plug anything into an upstream USB port.

To see the Ethernet devices, use the grep command to see the kernel's dmesg output:

```
# dmesg | grep  usb-bcm2708_usb-1.1
```

Looking at the output of this command in Figure 2-8 you can see that eth0 has registered itself to the smsc95xx device; this provides the physical layer interface. Then you can see that smsc95xx has registered on the upstream USB bus on usb-bcm2708_usb-1.1.

```
[root@hobo ~]# dmesg | grep usb-bcm2708_usb-1.1
[    3.301866] smsc95xx 1-1.1:1.0: eth0: register 'smsc95xx' at usb-bcm2708_usb-1.1, smsc95xx USB 2.0 Ethernet, b8:27:eb:a9:85:d1
```

Figure 2-8. *The USB Ethernet interface*

Lastly, you may want to have sound on your Raspberry Pi. Sound is provided from the Broadcom SoC as well. Fortunately this module is provided as part of the ALSA kernel modules. You can enable the sound devices by probing the snd_bcm2835 module. In Fedora, if you want this to be loaded on each boot you're going to need to create a file called bcm-snd.modules in the directory /etc/sysconfig/modules/. The contents of that file should be what is listed below:

```
-#!/bin/bash
lsmod | grep -q snd_bcm2835 || /sbin/modprobe snd_bcm2835 >/dev/null 2>&1
```

Now every time your Raspberry Pi boots, it will load the snd_bcm2835 module. You can check that it's working correctly with this command:

```
# aplay -l
```

The output should look similar to Figure 2-9.

```
[root@hobo kernel]# aplay -l
**** List of PLAYBACK Hardware Devices ****
card 0: ALSA [bcm2835 ALSA], device 0: bcm2835 ALSA [bcm2835 ALSA]
  Subdevices: 8/8
  Subdevice #0: subdevice #0
  Subdevice #1: subdevice #1
  Subdevice #2: subdevice #2
  Subdevice #3: subdevice #3
  Subdevice #4: subdevice #4
  Subdevice #5: subdevice #5
  Subdevice #6: subdevice #6
  Subdevice #7: subdevice #7
```

Figure 2-9. *aplay -l listing for the Raspberry Pi*

You can see from the above examples that the Raspberry Pi is a highly integrated unit and you need to make the most of the resources you have on hand.

Now that you know your Raspberry Pi's hardware a little better, let's fix and update any issues with Fedora Remix 14. One of the first tasks you should do is update the kernel, firmware, and applications that are provided by the foundation. Unlike with a normal x86 install of Fedora, the kernel is not supplied from the standard upstream repos but from the foundation's GitHub site. Speaking of GitHub, that's where our next tool will come from, so make sure your Raspberry Pi has an Internet connection.

Updating the Firmware and Operating System

A nice community member has created a script called `rpi-update`. This script will download the latest firmware, kernel, and applications for the Raspberry Pi. You can download this script from the following page on GitHub:

- https://github.com/Hexxeh/rpi-update

Follow the instructions on the web page to download the script. Once you have it downloaded, execute it like this:

```
# rpi-update
```

The first time this tool runs, it will take some time to download all the new updates and apply them. You can see in Figure 2-10 the update process on my Raspberry Pi.

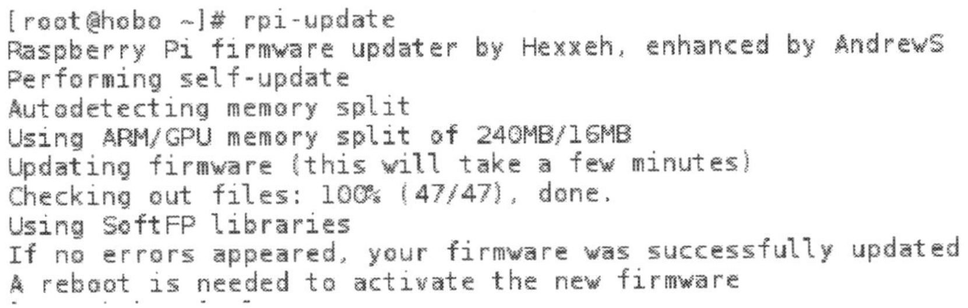

```
[root@hobo ~]# rpi-update
Raspberry Pi firmware updater by Hexxeh, enhanced by AndrewS
Performing self-update
Autodetecting memory split
Using ARM/GPU memory split of 240MB/16MB
Updating firmware (this will take a few minutes)
Checking out files: 100% (47/47), done.
Using SoftFP libraries
If no errors appeared, your firmware was successfully updated
A reboot is needed to activate the new firmware
```

Figure 2-10. *Running the rpi-update script*

I would suggest at this point you reboot your Raspberry Pi for the new kernel and firmware to take effect. After the reboot it would be wise to check that the updates have applied.

It's also a good idea to run the following to get all the latest application-level updates:

```
#yum update
```

Now that everything is updated, you need to ensure that you are using the correct kernel and VideoCore binary driver versions. First, since the `rpi-update` script gets the latest VideoCore tools, we should remove the ones that came with Fedora:

```
# yum erase raspberrypi-vc-utils-20120217-4.armv5tel
```

The new VideoCore tools are located in /opt/vc. Because we are using the foundation's version of the VideoCore tools, you need to update your path and library path.

▓ **Note** In Linux and Unix there is a special system setting called your library path. This setting tells the operating system where it can locate all of your application's library files that support the application. This path is not updated automatically by the system and if you were to install a library outside of the path the system would not read it when attempting to run an application. This would prevent the application from running.

First, I will show you how to update the path for all users.

1. Create a file in /etc/profile.d/ and call it videocore.sh. Add the following into the file and close it:

   pathmunge /opt/vc/bin afterSave

2. Next you need to update the LD_PATH for all users. To do this, create a file in /etc/ld.so.conf.d/ and call it videocore.conf and add /opt/vc/lib into the file.

3. Once you have done this, log out and log back in. You should now be able to run the following command as a test to ensure it's all working (this should give you a reading in degrees Celsius of the VideoCore's temperature):

   # vcgencmd measure_temp

4. It's a good idea to check the kernel version and GPU firmware version. To check the kernel version number, use this command:

   # uname -a

5. To check the GPU firmware version number, use this command:

   # /opt/vc/bin/vcgencmd version

Take a look at Figure 2-11; this is the display before I ran the rpi-update script. In this figure you can see that I am running kernel number 143 and VideoCore version 336078.

```
[root@hobo ~]# uname -a
Linux hobo 3.2.27+ #143 PREEMPT Tue Sep 11 02:02:37 BST 2012 armv6l armv6l armv6l GNU/Linux
[root@hobo ~]#  /opt/vc/bin/vcgencmd version
Sep 11 2012 02:17:45
Copyright (c) 2012 Broadcom
version 336078 (release)
[root@hobo ~]# reboot
```

Figure 2-11. *Display of preupdated firmware and kernel versions*

After the changes you will now see that the version numbers of the kernel and the VideoCore have changed. You can see in Figure 2-12 that I am now using kernel number 160 and VideoCore version 337601.

```
[root@hobo ~]# uname -a
Linux hobo 3.2.27+ #160 PREEMPT Mon Sep 17 23:18:42 BST 2012 armv6l armv6l armv6l GNU/Linux
[root@hobo ~]#  /opt/vc/bin/vcgencmd version
Sep 18 2012 01:44:00
Copyright (c) 2012 Broadcom
version 337601 (release)
```

Figure 2-12. *Versions after the rpi-update script*

The best part of the rpi-update script is that it will keep you up to date daily with the foundation's GitHub repository, unlike your distribution's repository, which may lag a little.

Lastly, for your handy reference I have included a full kernel module listing with this command:

```
# lsmod
```

If you're having issues with any of the hardware projects, check Figure 2-13 to ensure that you have all the correct modules loaded.

```
[root@hobo kernel]# lsmod
Module                  Size   Used by
ipv6                  271235  12
binfmt_misc             6888   1
dm_mod                 70034   0
snd_bcm2835            20157   0
snd_seq                52536   0
snd_seq_device          6300   1 snd_seq
snd_pcm                74834   1 snd_bcm2835
snd_timer              19698   2 snd_seq,snd_pcm
snd                    52489   5 snd_bcm2835,snd_seq,snd_seq_device,snd_pcm,snd_timer
snd_page_alloc          4951   1 snd_pcm
spidev                  5136   0
evdev                   8682   2
i2c_bcm2708             3542   0
spi_bcm2708             4401   0
```

Figure 2-13. *Kernel module listing for the Raspberry Pi*

Now your Fedora installation is current. It's now time to strip out the fat and configure the Raspberry Pi.

Cutting Out the Fat

Why do you need to optimize Fedora, I hear you say, it's already running quite well? Out of the box, Fedora runs quite well; the Raspberry Pi remix has done really well to have such a low memory footprint. Still, even with this excellent out-of-the-box install, there are a few simple tweaks that will make the Fedora remix on the Raspberry Pi work better under a high load. In addition to just saving CPU cycles the other parts of the Raspberry Pi will benefit too.

Optimizing the SD Card

An SD card behaves very differently than a standard hard disk drive. SD cards have a limit on the number of write-and-erase cycles that they can perform, unlike a traditional hard disk drive where there is no concept of a write-and-erase cycle.

WHAT IS THIS WRITE-AND-ERASE CYCLE?

With a normal hard drive, every time you write something to the disk a sector on the disk changes its magnetic state. This is a physical change in the disk platter and causes no wear to the platter itself. Now when you read from that same sector the physical platter has no change in state at all.

An SD card obviously has no physical platters but has small memory chips that contain cells. A cell is where the bits of data are stored, much like a sector on the physical hard disk.

Now, unlike the physical hard disk, when you read or write to a flash cell it will change its state.

This is because the flash cell uses a small amount of stored electrical charge to indicate that the data bits are stored. This is where the write-and-erase cycle comes in: each time you read or write to a flash cell a cycle of the cell is used. It moves from one state to another and there are a limited amount of cycles that each cell can sustain before it will no longer hold any charge.

In the case of a standard SD card it has an endurance rating of around one hundred thousand cycles. A cycle can be a write or an erase. Really, any time the voltage state on the flash cell is changed that's a cycle. Once you have used up all of the one hundred thousand cycles your flash cells will simply stop working. Once your flash cells stop working your SD card will be useless as you can no longer read or write to it.

One hundred thousand cycles may sound like a whole lot at first and for a digital camera, for example, it would be. Now I want you to think about a journaling filesystem like EXT3 that the Fedora remix uses. A journaling filesystem will write small amounts of data (called metadata) to the underlying device quite frequently. On top of the journal writes you also have file and directory update times being written to the disk every time you update a file or directory. You can see the erase cycles getting chewed up now!

By default the mount options for EXT4 on Fedora will use an option called atime, which will update the last accessed time every time a file is touched by the operating system. Think about that in flash cell cycles again: all of a sudden one hundred thousand cycles seems to be quite limited! Let's put an end to that updating of access time for no valid reason.

There are two mount options that can be used to achieve this:

- The first is noatime, which simply won't update the access time. This is good for your flash cells but bad for you, if you want date and time stamps on your files, for example. It may also break some applications that rely on the access time stamp on their files.

- To get a good balance of the two extremes you have the option of using the relatime mount option. The relatime option will update only the access time stamp if it's before the modification time stamp. This will cut down a lot of writes to your flash cells. To turn relatime on, edit your /etc/fstab file and make your root and boot filesystems look like Figure 2-14. Note that in Figure 2-14 the fstab file has no swap set up. We'll look at this issue in the next section.

```
/dev/mmcblk0p1          /              auto    defaults,relatime    1 1
/dev/mmcblk0p1          /boot          auto    defaults,relatime    1 2
```

Figure 2-14. *Root and boot filesystem options*

First, remount each filesystem:

```
# mount -o remount / && mount -o remount /boot
```

Now check to see you have relatime enabled by using this command:

```
# mount
```

This will display all mounted filesystems and their mount options. In Figure 2-15 you can see that the relatime option has been added to the filesystem mount options.

```
[root@hobo ~]# mount
/dev/mmcblk0p1 on / type auto (rw,relatime)
proc on /proc type proc (rw)
sysfs on /sys type sysfs (rw)
devpts on /dev/pts type devpts (rw,gid=5,mode=620)
tmpfs on /dev/shm type tmpfs (rw)
/dev/mmcblk0p1 on /boot type vfat (rw,relatime)
none on /proc/sys/fs/binfmt misc type binfmt misc (rw)
```

Figure 2-15. *Filesystems mounted with relatime*

Thinking About Swapping

Given that the Raspberry Pi has limited amounts of system memory you would assume a swap device or swap file would help out.

WHY YOU DON'T NEED TO CARE ABOUT SWAP

In the Linux and Unix world, machines are configured to have a swap space on disk. A swap space acts like additional system memory; it's just a lot slower. If your machine were to run low on system memory it may choose to swap a process running in memory to disk.

With a normal hard disk you would be correct on this assumption. Once again it comes back to the flash cell cycles. A swap would consume a large amount of cycles on the SD card, which in turn would dramatically reduce the life of your SD card. This is yet another reason why it's important to have your Raspberry Pi set up to best utilize the resources at hand. It's all about understanding the hardware and its limitations.

Optimizing CPU Cycles

Because CPU cycles are precious, a static IP address will be better suited for headless operation. Therefore, I will show you how to first set up the machine to boot with a static IP address. By having a static IP address you won't need to run a DHCP client agent, thus saving a small amount of CPU cycles. This is an optional step, but I feel it's wise to give a headless device a static IP address. The reason behind this is that if your machine is headless you won't be able to see the IP address that the DHCP server has given out to your Raspberry Pi. A static IP solves this issue. If you wish to leave your machine on DHCP you don't need to do anything because the Fedora image is configured to use DHCP by default.

1. Create an `ifcfg-eth0` file under /etc/sysconfig/network-scripts/. It may look something like Figure 2-16. Don't try and use the `ifcfg-usb0` file; remove this file to make the network start cleanly.

```
[root@hobo ~]# cat /etc/sysconfig/network-scripts/ifcfg-eth0
DEVICE="eth0"
BOOTPROTO=none
ONBOOT=yes
NM_CONTROLLED="no"
NETMASK=255.255.255.0
IPADDR=192.168.0.199
```

Figure 2-16. *Example of an ifcfg-eth0 file*

2. Ensure that you have your /etc/resolv.conf set up to have your DNS servers set and /etc/sysconfig/network to have your default gateway set.

3. Set the network to start on boot and to not fall back to DHCP by running this command:

    `# service network start`

4. Ensure it starts up on the next boot:

    `# chkconfig network on`

Another small tweak you can do is change the number of TTYs running. I don't feel you need six active TTYs. Take a look at the file /etc/sysconfig/init. You will see a line that looks like this:

```
ACTIVE_CONSOLES=/dev/tty[1-6]
```

You can change the six to a three, which will spawn only three TTYs on the next reboot. You can see the change to the init file in Figure 2-17. This will only get you a small amount of performance, but it all helps.

```
# What ttys should gettys be started on?
ACTIVE_CONSOLES=/dev/tty[1-3]
```

Figure 2-17. *TTY spawn settings*

I/O Tuning

Lastly I want to talk about the I/O scheduler. An I/O scheduler is responsible for controlling how the block-level access requests are handled. In the case of the Raspberry Pi the block device is your SD card, and an example of access could be the syslog daemon writing log files to the disk. This is where the I/O scheduler comes into play. Say, for example, that you have syslog doing its thing and writing logs and now you want to save that OpenOffice document you're working on, what now? It's not like you can just yell out to the syslog process and ask it nicely to stop writing because you need the disk at the moment. The solution to this is the I/O scheduler. The I/O scheduler will decide who needs access and in what order they can have access. It can create a queue of I/O requests and decide the order in which each needs access to the underlying block device. By default, Linux uses the CFQ, or Completely Fair Queuing, I/O scheduler. This I/O scheduler works very well for most users and most common drives. There is a good reason why it's the default option for the Linux kernel. The CFQ scheduler is designed to be fair to all running processes and aims to avoid starvation of I/O to any one process.

Understanding the CFQ Scheduler

Let's take a look at how the CFQ works. In Figure 2-18 you can see two processes called "Process 1" and "Process 2." Each process has a block of pending I/O. For Process 1 this is "I/O 1 and I/O 2" and for Process 2 this is "I/O 3." In the CFQ the blocks of I/O get grouped together so that the underlying hard disk won't need to seek on disk as much. The syslog, for example, may have two blocks of I/O: they are each appended to the same log file on disk. In the case of a traditional hard disk, this makes sense.

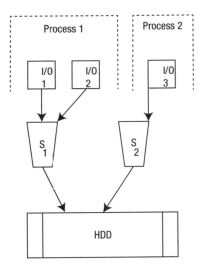

Figure 2-18. *The CFQ scheduler*

This sounds good. So how can you tell what your I/O scheduler is?

Quite simple. You can make use of the sys filesystem to see what the current I/O scheduler is. Just find the /sys/block/mmcblk0/queue/scheduler file and look at its output. Do note that mmcblk0 is what the Linux kernel sees our block device (SD card) as. If you look at Figure 2-19 you can see that the CFQ has brackets around it; that's the current scheduler in use.

```
[root@hobo queue]# echo cfq > scheduler
[root@hobo queue]# cat /sys/block/mmcblk0/queue/scheduler
noop deadline [cfq]
```

Figure 2-19. *The current I/O scheduler in use*

You can see by default that Fedora uses the CFQ. So what's bad about the CFQ? The CFQ makes two main assumptions that are not the best for Raspberry Pi users; after all, we don't have standard hardware or a traditional block device. The two assumptions of the CFQ are as follows:

- Your hard drive needs to move a physical read/write head around the disk platter.

- On a modern system, CPU cycles are plentiful.

It also assumes that CPU cycles are plentiful and that the underlying block device has some form of access latency. Now the Raspberry Pi needs all the CPU cycles it can get. If you can make the I/O scheduler put less load on the CPU and still get performance for the workload in question, it would seem like a good idea. Second, an SD card has very little access latency. A block request on the SD card could have less than one millisecond of access time, whereas a traditional hard disk drive could have up to 7 milliseconds of access time. That's a fairly big difference between the access times. When you have pending operations queued based on a scheduler that is not designed for your I/O subsystem you're going to have a performance issue.

There is a scheduler that better fits the needs of the Raspberry Pi, and that is the noop scheduler. The noop scheduler is the most basic I/O scheduler in the Linux kernel. It works off a simple File In/File Out (FIFO) queue and makes use of request merging to manage the queue. The noop scheduler is very simple; it has very little CPU overhead. That makes it perfect for the Raspberry Pi. Also the noop scheduler expects that the underlying block device has very little access time latency. Once again this suits our SD card perfectly.

Understanding the Noop Scheduler

Let's take a quick look at how the noop scheduler works. Unlike the CFQ scheduler the noop scheduler only has one queue.

Take a look at Figure 2-20. Once again you can see our two processes with the same workload I explained for the CFQ scheduler. Unlike the CFQ, there now is one queue only and all the I/O requests go into this single queue on an FIFO basis. The only exception to this is a function called "merging." This is where the noop scheduler detects that it could group an I/O action together. As you would expect, FIFO to a normal hard disk would cause it to seek all over the platters, but for us there is no seeking because we have no write heads! This is where the advantage of noop comes in for the SD card.

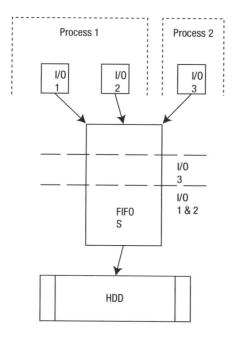

Figure 2-20. *The noop scheduler*

Changing the Scheduler

Now that you know noop is better than the CFQ for your needs, how do you go about changing the scheduler? There are two ways to set the kernel I/O scheduler. The first method I will talk about is a temporary way to change it. After a reboot it will go back to the default CFQ scheduler. In Figure 2-21 you can see all the available I/O schedulers. The one in the brackets is the current scheduler. To change that to the noop scheduler, run this command:

```
[root@hobo ~]# cat /sys/block/mmcblk0/queue/scheduler
noop deadline [cfq]
[root@hobo ~]# echo noop > /sys/block/mmcblk0/queue/scheduler
[root@hobo ~]# cat /sys/block/mmcblk0/queue/scheduler
[noop] deadline cfq
```

Figure 2-21. *Changing the I/O scheduler*

```
# echo noop > /sys/block/mmcblk0/queue/scheduler
```

You can see in Figure 2-21 I have changed the scheduler from the CFQ to noop.

The next way to change the I/O scheduler is more permanent. This is the method I recommend you do, as it will help your Raspberry Pi's I/O performance. Ensure that you have your /boot filesystem mounted. If it is not, you can simply mount it with this command:

```
# mount /boot
```

Once you have your /boot filesystem mounted, open up the file /boot/cmdline.txt and append it to the end of the kernel boot line:

```
elevator=noop
```

You can see in Figure 2-22 an example of my kernel boot line.

```
[root@hobo ~]# cat /boot/cmdline.txt
dwc_otg.lpm_enable=0 console=ttyAMA0,115200 kgdboc=ttyAMA0,115200 console=tty1 root=/dev/mmcblk0p2 rootfstype=ext4 rootw
ait elevator=noop
```

Figure 2-22. *Kernel boot settings*

After all that effort, you can run top to see how little memory your Raspberry Pi is now using. In Figure 2-23 my Raspberry Pi is actively consuming approximately 21 MB of memory.

```
top - 21:28:22 up 52 min,  1 user,  load average: 0.05, 0.06, 0.05
Tasks:  49 total,   1 running,  48 sleeping,   0 stopped,   0 zombie
Cpu(s):  0.3%us,  0.7%sy,  0.0%ni, 99.0%id,  0.0%wa,  0.0%hi,  0.0%si,  0.0%st
Mem:    237880k total,    44688k used,   193192k free,     9200k buffers
Swap:        0k total,        0k used,        0k free,    23428k cached
```

Figure 2-23. *The top command showing memory usage*

Now that the operating system takes up very little memory and system resources, make sure that your applications are also lightweight where possible.

Lighter Applications and Tools

Without major modification to the Fedora install you've seen about all you can do to optimize it. With that in mind you should be looking at using lightweight applications and daemons where possible. I tend to use the network scripts to configure my networks as it is less overhead. If you do need a GUI to configure your wired or WiFi networks I suggest you take a look at the Wireless Interface Connection Daemon (WICD). WICD is a lightweight network configuration tool that achieves a similar outcome as a network manager.

You should also try using a lightweight editor. I personally like vi or Vim. Their features are rich and very easy to use, no matter the connection source. There isn't space in this book to cover vi or Vim, so refer to *Learn Raspberry Pi with Linux* from Apress, which contains a chapter on the subject, or visit the Vim web site at `vim.org`.

Whichever resource you use, try it out; give it a go for a few days or weeks. It will grow on you.

Summary

In this chapter I talked you through the two ways to install the Fedora Raspberry Pi remix distribution. I guided you though the first boot issue you had on the Raspberry Pi and helped you though firmware updates and where to get the firmware. After all, did you really expect your Fedora remix for Raspberry Pi to "just work"? I sure did not. If you are after an easy-to-install, no-hassle distribution I would suggest you take a look at Raspbian. After you finally got a working install I went through the steps to update the kernel and firmware from the foundation's GitHub site. After that we took a walk through the hardware and looked at the buses and tools needed to examine them. Next up, I worked on tweaking the installation for better performance, by removing heavy applications and configuring the system by hand. Not so hard, was it?

I then went on to talk about I/O schedulers and why they are important for the Raspberry Pi. You now know how to change the scheduler on the fly and set it permanently to your desired scheduler. Lastly, I talked quickly about the benefits of using applications that are light on system resources.

In the next chapter you will finally get to make use of the Raspberry Pi as a hardware project. I will guide you through setting up a simple temperature sensor via the GPIO, and I will also help you to access the temperature sensor from the Linux operating system.

CHAPTER 3

■ ■ ■

A Simple Temperature Sensor

Unlike a standard computer, the Raspberry Pi is unlikely to alter the temperature of your room (well, unless you have a cluster of them: then you may have heat issues). It's widely known that high temperatures can affect your computer. Nowadays most new machines have protection circuits to ensure that they do not let the magic smoke out, although this has not always been the way with electronics in computers. Not so long ago, if you seated your heatsink incorrectly you were more than guaranteed to let the magic smoke out, usually with a loud bang or a lot of smoke (see Figure 3-1 for the results).

Figure 3-1. *Someone let the magic smoke out!*

I am sure most people will know someone or have heard of someone who had seated a heatsink incorrectly on socket A of the AMD Athlon. That never ended well, given the heatsink had no thermal shutoff; more often than not it simply exploded. In addition to this, the CPUs of the late 90s often did not have the advanced temperature monitoring that you see today. A lot of the time the temperature was measured with a simple thermistor placed in the bottom of the socket, which made it a little hard to know when the CPUs were getting a little too hot because you were never measuring the actual core temperature. That's why it was important to have an external sensor if you wanted a good idea of the temperature. Nowadays this is less of an issue, so this chapter will look at monitoring the temperature of your room or some other space like inside a rack, for example (or your cluster of Raspberry Pis). The Raspberry Pi as it comes has no way for you to monitor an external temperature source. There is no sensor on board like you often see on common motherboards. The only temperature you can measure is the internal graphics processing unit (GPU) that is part of the SoC. That won't be very helpful to you for reading an external temperature.

This is not too much of a worry for you because the Raspberry Pi comes with very useful GPIO headers. There are quite a few different ways you could read an external temperature from the Raspberry Pi's GPIO pins. You could use a simple thermistor if you wanted or you could use something more advanced, based on the 1-wire protocol. The GPIO pins you have access to could support any of these methods.

This all sounds a bit complicated. Why can't you just use a digital temperature sensor? Aside from that being extremely boring it's also not very versatile. With the Raspberry Pi you can do much more. You now have the option of using many different types of sensors and different connection methods. You now also have the ability to log the data for future reference. Or you may want to perform an action once the sensor hits a certain reading. Or maybe you just want to broadcast to the word what temperature your home rack is at. Given the Raspberry Pi's small size and low power requirements you could be coupled with WiFi to set up a remote temperature station outside. The possibilities are endless.

This project is designed to be simple and cheap; at the same time I hope that it opens your eyes to how easy a hardware project can be with the Raspberry Pi. It's not scary and it's not overly hard to understand. I will start off by talking about the GPIO pins a little more. After that I will discuss the sensors I will be using and how they will be connected. This will include an introduction to the 1-wire protocol and why it's good for this type of project. After that I will show you a basic circuit that requires no soldering in order to take your first temperature reading.

Breadboards and GPIO Pins

Since this is the first time you have used the GPIO pins, I would like to spend a little bit of time discussing the physical side of them. After reading Chapter 1 you will have a good idea what makes up the GPIO pin headers and also what functions you can get from them. I won't go back over all those details in this chapter. There are a few simple guidelines you should follow when working with the Raspberry Pi's GPIO pins.

The first point and the most important one to remember is that the GPIO pins are not tolerant of 5 V. If you try and source 5 V from your GPIO headers and you're lucky, your project just may not work. If you're unlucky, you will let the magic smoke out of something and if you're really unlucky that something will be the Raspberry Pi. If your project has more than 5 V and your Raspberry Pi's GPIO pins get connected to this you will let the magic smoke out of your Raspberry Pi.

There are various methods for protecting your GPIO pins. You can use something fancy like an optocoupler to fully isolate your Raspberry Pi. This may be needed for some projects, like if you were going to interface with high-voltage circuits. You could also do something super basic and use a Zener diode. If you place a 3.3 V Zener diode between the ground and the GPIO pin you intend to use, you will have a small amount of protection. If you attempted to apply more than 3.3 V, the diode would burn out. Once this occurs the circuit is broken and the dangerous voltage would never be received by the GPIO pins.

Personally, unless I am designing a project that absolutely needs protection, then I don't worry. I'd rather take the approach of checking everything I do more than once, making sure I won't supply 5 V to the GPIO pins. This is a good habit to get into, as you will find mistakes and fix them before they become an issue. I don't like to be sloppy as I know the protection will save me: I'd much rather check it and get it right. I also tend to use breadboards for all my prototyping work. This makes things so much easier to work on. Do yourself a favor and get a few of them of various sizes: you won't regret it! In Figure 3-2 you can see some of my breadboards.

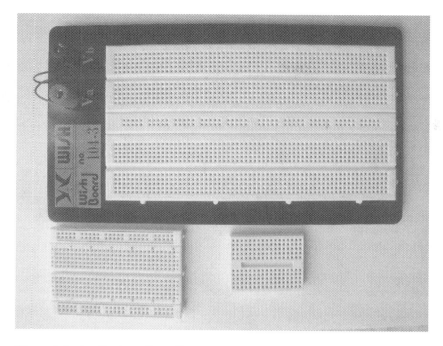

Figure 3-2. *A collection of breadboards*

Also by using breadboards you can simply use a jumper wire from your Raspberry Pi and connect it to the breadboard. By doing this you won't accidentally connect the wrong GPIO pin; it makes it much clearer when you're building the projects. If you take a close look at Figure 3-3 you can see that the holes are in certain patterns.

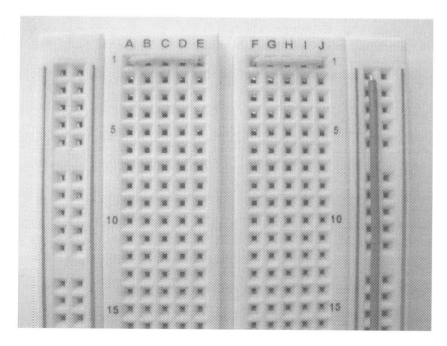

Figure 3-3. *A closeup of a generic breadboard*

On most breadboards you will find the two edge tracks that are connected down the length of the breadboard. These are normally used as your voltage source and your ground tracks. You can then see that the breadboard is divided into two equal halves. No current can flow across the divider strip in the middle of the board. The holes in these sections are connected across the width of the board, but only in their set section. Other breadboards may have different configurations. If you are ever unsure of how the holes are connected you can use the following simple method to check.

1. Place a jumper wire in one of the holes and then place another jumper wire into the next hole.

2. Run a continuity check on your multimeter.

3. Keep moving the second jumper wire around the adjacent holes to work out how the breadboard is connected.

Once you know how the tracks on your breadboard flow, you can work out how best to place your components. There are no hard rules about the placement of components. Just do your best to keep it neat and logical. This will make it easier to debug if you need to. To insert wire or components into the breadboard, gently press their legs into the hole: they won't go in too far and you will have things that stick out. Removing them is just as easy. Pull directly upward and not at an angle to remove the components. If you pull them out at an angle you may bend the legs. If they seem hard to remove, use a little flat-bladed screwdriver to lever each side up gently. I find that some integrated circuits (ICs)s tend to be hard to remove and you often need to gently lever them up.

Sensors

I will be using two different sensors. Each sensor will be connected in different ways to the Raspberry Pi, so that I can show you how flexible the Raspberry Pi really is. Let's start with the sensors.

Introducing the DHT11

Although I do have a strong preference for which sensor is better when connected to the Raspberry Pi, I'll start off by talking about each sensor and why I like a certain type. First up I will talk about the DHT11. The DHT11 is an eight-bit restive-type temperature and humidity sensor in one small package. The eight-bit value refers to the temperature restitution. These will come in many different colors and appearances: it's a very generic part made in China. They are easy to find and very cheap.

Sensitivity-wise, they are not too bad. The temperature range is 0 to 50°C and humidity is 20% relative humidity to 90% relative humidity. Given that Hong Kong is often above 90% relative humidity it's not the best choice for me. The good thing about the DHT11 is that it is in such a small package you can sense both temperature and humidity. It also has a low pin count. You will most often see the DHT11 shipped with four pins although you only need three. You can see the pins in Table 3-1.

Table 3-1. *The pins for the DHT11*

Pin Number	Function
1	Voltage Drain To Drain or Vdd (3–5 V dc)
2	Data (proprietary digital signal)
3	No connect
4	Ground

You may have noticed I mentioned the fact that the data signal is proprietary. When I say proprietary I don't mean it in the sense that all documentation is locked away under a nondisclosure agreement, although some is. What I mean in this case is that it's not using a well-known bus or protocol, say, like, 1-wire or the I2C bus. While this makes it slightly harder to use, it's not impossible. The DHT11 is very sensitive with timing. When you first start communicating with the sensor the following must occur.

1. First, the controlling device must pull the data bus low. When the controlling device pulls this bus low it must take at least 18 ms. Otherwise, the DHT11 will not detect that the controlling device wants to do something.

2. After this 18 ms the controller then pulls the data bus high. The controller must do this for between 20 and 40 μs. During this time the DHT11 will send out a response.

3. As soon as this occurs the DHT11 will then pull the data bus low for 80 μs. If the controller attempts to pull this bus high at this time the start process would be aborted.

4. After the 80 μs is up without interference, the DHT11 will then pull up the data bus.

5. The DHT11 will keep the data bus high for another 80 μs. At the end of this time frame the DHT11 will finally start to transmit actual data.

Take a look at Figure 3-4 and you can see an example of the start signal.

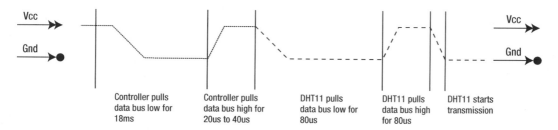

Figure 3-4. *The start signal for the DHT11*

You can see that the DHT11 is quite timing-sensitive. This is where the first issue under Linux comes in. Linux will do its best to abstract the hardware from you, by providing device nodes from the kernel. In normal situations this is a very good thing. For example it makes it simple to access your serial port and use it as a TTY terminal. Where it's not very good is for low-level hardware operations, for example, a timing-sensitive temperature sensor. The only real way to ensure that the DHT11 works correctly under Linux would be to write some C code to handle the low-level timing that is required. This type of sensor is best used on a micro-controller like the Arduino. Because I have an Arduino, this was the first sensor I picked out for this chapter, only to come to the conclusion it's not the best fit for the Raspberry Pi. So if the DHT11 is not a good fit, what is and why?

Introducing the DS18B20

The DS18B20, of course! The what? The DS18B20 is a 9 to 12-bit temperature sensor; unlike the DHT11 it's just a pure temperature sensor and is not capable of sensing humidity, although the sensitivity of the DS18B20 is much better than the DHT11 with a range from -55°C to +125°C. With the sensor being so small you could place it anywhere; it's about the size of your common TO-92 transistor. There is one feature that the DS18B20 has that the DHT11 is missing and that is a temperature alarm. The DS18B20 can alert you over its bus when it hits a user-set temperature. You can set one high-temperature alarm and one low-temperature alarm. For its voltage and current draw, it's perfect for the Raspberry Pi, only needing +3 V and under 1.8 mA. You could power and drive this sensor with one wire from the

Raspberry Pi, but more on that later. It has the same number of legs as a transistor as well. Take a look at Table 3-2 to see what each leg (pin) of the DS18B20 is used for.

Table 3-2. *The pins of the DS18B20*

Pin Number	Function
1	Ground
2	DQ (data input/output)
3	Vdd (optional)

You will notice I've left the Vdd as optional in Table 3-2. How can Vdd be optional? The DS18B20 can support parasite power. This means that with only one wire you can power and transmit data to and from the device. This is part of the 1-wire protocol. I have not listed a protocol or talked about the protocol that the DS18B20 uses. Unlike the DHT11, the DS18B20 uses an industrial standard called the 1-wire bus.

The Amazing 1-Wire Bus

What exactly is a 1-wire bus? Excluding the ground connection of the 1-wire device, both data and power can be transmitted across one wire, hence the name "1-wire." The 1-wire bus was developed by Dallas Semiconductor, now called Maxim Integrated. The 1-wire bus has been around for a very long time. It's been used in public mass transport systems all the way down to simple security tokens. Its main benefit over other similar low-speed buses is that the 1-wire device can be on the end of a very long cable run without too much signal degradation. Like other bus systems the 1-wire bus supports more than one device on the bus, which is referred to as multidrop in 1-wire deployments. Each 1-wire device has a unique 64-bit serial code embedded into the device. This is how the controller device can identify each device on the 1-wire network. The embedded serial code can be broken up into three distinct segments.

- The first segment is called family code; this segment identifies what type of device it is and it's eight bits wide. There is a set device list that all 1-wire devices must comply with.

- The middle segment is called the ID segment and it's 48 bits wide. This 48 bits of data must be unique within the given family of devices. This is what gives you the ability to have many 1-wire devices on the same wire.

- The remaining eight bits of serial code are a cyclic redundancy check, or CRC, checksum and must match the rest of the address.

See Table 3-3 for an example of a serial address.

Table 3-3. *Example of a 1-wire address*

Family Code	ID	CRC
8 bit	48 bits (unique to family)	8 bits
10	0008027e34	ca

In Table 3-3 the full 1-wire serial code would be "100008027e34ca." This is very simple to break down.

- The first part of the address, "10," maps to the "high precision digital thermometer" class; you will need access to the list of devices and their family for this. You can find the device and family table at http://owfs.sourceforge.net/commands.html.

- The next 48 bits ("0008027e34") compose the unique address.

- Finally, the "ca" is the CRC checksum of the address.

The 1-wire network is called a micro LAN. On the micro LAN there can only be one master controller and many slave devices. A key feature about the 1-wire bus is that it's implemented at a software level. You don't need special hardware or a special bus to be able to run the 1-wire devices. In fact the 1-wire bus at a hardware level is very boring and very simple. This makes it perfect for your first project. Take a look at Figure 3-5. You can see an example of a 1-wire bus using parasite power for two temperature sensors.

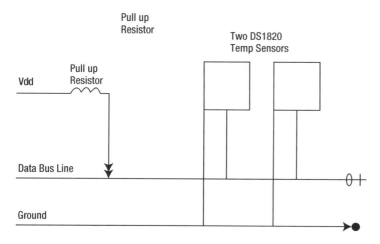

Figure 3-5. *An example of a 1-wire bus*

Parasite power is a magic part of each 1-wire device. Without this you would need a minimum of three wires for each device. A 3-wire bus sounds nowhere near as impressive as a 1-wire bus, now does it?

How can you have Vdd and data signals on the same bus? It's simple really; it's all a matter of timing, but you can't have them at the same time. Whenever the 1-wire device is not communicating with the controller, the data bus is pulled high. When this state occurs, an internal capacitor inside the 1-wire device will receive a charge from the data bus. This internal capacitor will take care of itself and you won't even know it's there. Now when the 1-wire device wishes to communicate with the controller it will pull the data bus low. At this point in time the 1-wire device will use the stored charge from the capacitor to power the circuit inside the 1-wire device. In our case it will power the DS1820B's temperature probe and logic.

You will notice that there is a resistor between Vdd and the data line. What's that for? That's the pull-up resistor. Its job is to grab the data bus line and pull it high at all times. This allows the 1-wire client device to pull the bus down when needed or to release the bus when not needed, thus letting the data bus be pulled up. In this chapter I will use a 1.0K ohm resistor. How did I come to this value? Well, I didn't: I read the data sheet of the DS18B20. From the data sheet I can work out this value. The value was picked to work well in parasitic mode and standard mode. If you wanted just standard mode I would recommend a 4.7K ohm or a 10K ohm resistor. Data sheets are your new friends as of this chapter. Find them, read them, and keep them handy! You will notice that a lot of 1-wire projects use the same value of the pull-up resistor as well. It's a fairly common value in 1-wire projects and will allow you to use a Vdd of 5.0 V or lower without a worry. For the Raspberry Pi you should be sticking with 3.3 V if you intend to keep the magic smoke in.

The 1-wire has one main thing you must keep in mind. You need to have direct hardware access. On a lot of other platforms like common computers, the 1-wire bus is controlled via the serial port. It's not a serial protocol in that sense. The 1-wire functionality makes use of the serial port and runs its own communication protocol over the underlying hardware. The 1-wire protocol pretty much hijacks the underlying hardware on your system. Lucky for you, the Raspberry Pi comes with the GPIO headers. Linux has a kernel module for the 1-wire protocol over GPIO. You just need to set it up and scan the micro LAN for devices.

By now I would have assumed that you can see the DS1820B has been the better solution for you under Linux. It's cheap, it's easy to run, and it's well supported within the Linux kernel. In this chapter I will mostly focus on setting up the 1-wire bus and the DS1820B. I will show you how you can use the DHT11 as well, just in case you have one lying around with no use. Let's get started with your first hardware project. I promise it will be simpler than you expect.

Building the Sensors

Here are the parts you are going to need:

- One DS1820B temperature sensor
- One 1K ohm resistor
- One 10K ohm resistor (only for the DHT11 section)
- One DHT11 sensor (only for the DHT11 section)
- Jumper and hook-up wire
- Breadboard

Let me show you the sensors you will be dealing with first. In Figure 3-6, you can see the small little black DS1820B and the blue square DHT11.

Figure 3-6. *The DS1820B and DHT11 side by side. Fight!*

Using the Little Black DS1820B

Here is how to use the DS1820B. In Figure 3-7 you can see the circuit schematic diagram. In this drawing I have included two drawings in the same figure. One is the standard wiring method and the other is the parasitic method. This will also show you how little the circuit will change between the two methods.

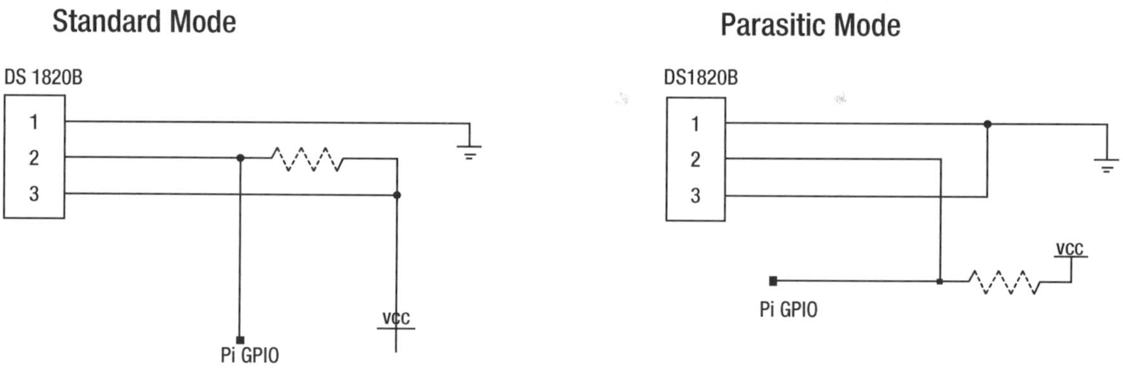

Figure 3-7. *Circuit schematics for the DS1820B*

As you know there are two ways in which you can connect the DS1820B to the Raspberry Pi. The first way has no special name and is thus called the standard mode; you're just connecting all the pins of the sensor to their respective type. This method is a good way to start, as sometimes using the sensor in parasitic mode can cause issues.

1. First, you need to know where pin 1 is on your DS1820B. Pick the sensor up and you'll notice it has two distinct sides. One side is curved and one side is flat with some text on it. The flat side with the text is the front of the device. When facing the flat side of the sensor, the pin on the left-hand side is the first. You should check your data sheet as well, remember them? Your new friends! Go take a look and check the pin out. If you do manage to insert the DS1820B in the wrong direction, don't worry it will get really hot but won't blow up. Take it out and let it cool down for some time; keep it still until it's cool enough to pick up.

2. Now that you have pin 1, insert the sensor into your breadboard. To make it easy for yourself, insert pin 1 into row 1 on the breadboard. You can see how I have inserted my sensor in row 1 at the top of the breadboard in Figure 3-8.

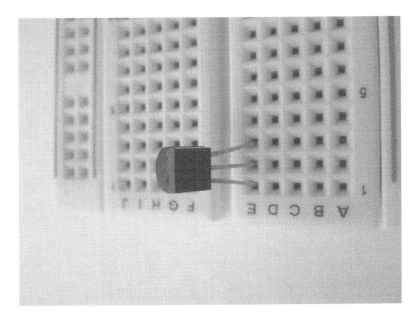

Figure 3-8. *The DS1820B inserted*

3. Breadboards make this type of prototyping work simple; they should be your second best friend (just don't let the data sheets know)! Next up, insert the jumper wire. In standard mode you need to feed the sensor power and provide a ground. So connect pin 1 to ground on the breadboard and connect pin 3 to your 3.3 V source. You can see how I have inserted my jumpers in Figure 3-9.

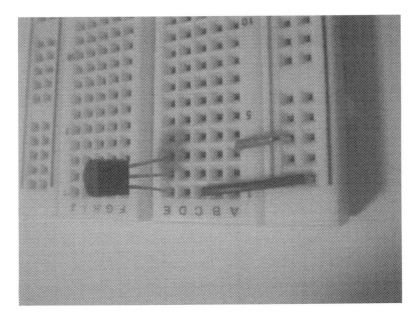

Figure 3-9. *Jumpers installed into the breadboard*

4. Now you need to install a resistor. This resistor is the pull-up resistor. You must insert it between pin 2 and pin 3. Place this close to the edge of the board. Have a look at Figure 3-10 for an example of a good placement. Why is that a good place? This is the pull-up resistor and it needs to follow the connection from the Raspberry Pi's GPIO pin. If you were to place the resistor before the connection your sensor won't work.

Figure 3-10. *Good resistor placement*

5. After this, you insert a hook-up wire from between the sensor and the resistor to P1-07 (GPIO-4) on the Raspberry Pi. In Figure 3-11 you can see the final connection. In Figure 3-11 you can see you have used all three pins (this is standard mode, remember). In a multidrop long-range deployment that would be a lot of wires! This is where the parasite mode comes in.

Figure 3-11. *The final connections in standard mode*

6. Now go ahead and pull everything but the DS1820B off your breadboard. Once again, start off by connecting your jumper wires. Connect pin 1 to ground as shown in Figure 3-11. Now place a jumper between pin 1 and pin 3. According to the data sheets for the DS1820B you must tie the Vdd line to the GND line. You're going to need to place a jumper wire out from pin 2 to a new row on the breadboard. Take a look at Figure 3-12: it will be much easier to see how I have done it.

Figure 3-12. *Jumpers for the parasite mode installed*

7. Remember the pull-up resistor? I hope you do! It is an important part of the 1-wire bus. You need to place this resistor in between the new row on your breadboard and your 3.3 V source. You then connect a hook-up wire from the opposite side of the row to P1-07 (GPIO-4) on your Raspberry Pi. Figure 3-13 will help you understand this.

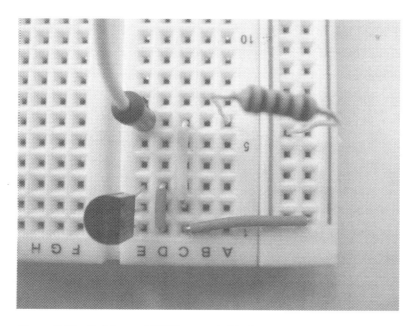

Figure 3-13. *Resistor and GPIO connected to the new row*

All the connections are made now. Turn on your Raspberry Pi and turn on the power source for your breadboard. You can connect the GPIO pins while the Raspberry Pi is powered on as well. You could also power the sensors from the Raspberry Pi itself if you wanted to. I tend to avoid this as a safety measure.

Reading the DS1820B on Linux

There is a very good reason why I picked P1-07 (GPIO-4) on the Raspberry Pi. I did not just randomly select it. Recall I spoke about the 1-wire protocol hijacking the serial port? You're going to do something similar with the GPIO. Lucky for us now, in the stock Raspberry Pi kernel (after August 2012) the w1_gpio module has coded GPIO-4 as the 1-wire bus. If this had not been done you would have needed to set this yourself in the source code for the w1_gpio module and rebuild your kernel. Lucky for us, you don't need to. First, you're going to need to load the 1-wire bus support because this module is not loaded by default. Run the following command to load the 1-wire bus:

```
# modprobe w1_gpio
```

When you do this, two things should happen if you've connected everything correctly. The first thing that will happen is two messages will be printed in dmesg (see Figure 3-14). You can see where the kernel loaded the 1-wire bus and where the 1-wire master controller found a device.

```
[ 1264.494483] Driver for 1-wire Dallas network protocol.
[ 1264.552585] w1_master_driver w1_bus_master1: Family 10 for 10.0008027e34ca.b4 is not registered.
```

Figure 3-14. *A 1-wire device is found*

The second thing that will happen is the creation of a new bus in the /sys/bus/w1/devices filesystem. Let's take a look at that now.

In Figure 3-15 you will see two devices. One has the 54-bit serial ID of your 1-wire device and the other will be the w1_bus_master, which is the Raspberry Pi. You are going to be more interested in the device attached, in my case the 10-0008027e34ca. If you take a look at that device you will notice there is not much you can do with it. Take a look at Figure 3-16 as an example.

```
[root@hobo ~]# ls -la /sys/bus/w1/devices/
total 0
drwxr-xr-x 2 root root 0 Feb 10 13:11 .
drwxr-xr-x 4 root root 0 Feb 10 13:11 ..
lrwxrwxrwx 1 root root 0 Feb 10 13:13 10-0008027e34ca -> ../../../devices/w1_bus_master1/10-0008027e34ca
lrwxrwxrwx 1 root root 0 Feb 10 13:11 w1_bus_master1 -> ../../../devices/w1_bus_master1
[root@hobo ~]# 
```

Figure 3-15. *The 1-wire device filesystem listing*

```
[root@hobo ~]# ls -la /sys/bus/w1/devices/10-0008027e34ca/
total 0
drwxr-xr-x 3 root root    0 Oct 17 17:53 .
drwxr-xr-x 4 root root    0 Oct 17 17:53 ..
lrwxrwxrwx 1 root root    0 Oct 17 17:59 driver -> ../../../bus/w1/drivers/w1_slave_driver
-r--r--r-- 1 root root 4096 Oct 17 17:59 id
-r--r--r-- 1 root root 4096 Oct 17 17:59 name
drwxr-xr-x 2 root root    0 Oct 17 17:59 power
-rw-r--r-- 1 root root 4096 Oct 17 17:59 rw
lrwxrwxrwx 1 root root    0 Oct 17 17:53 subsystem -> ../../../bus/w1
-rw-r--r-- 1 root root 4096 Oct 17 17:53 uevent
[root@hobo ~]# 
```

Figure 3-16. *Empty 1-wire client filesystem*

There is a good reason for this being empty. You have just loaded the kernel module that controls the bus and the bus master. Linux still has no idea what the device is. You're going to need to load another module. This one is called w1_therm:

```
# modprobe w1_therm
```

Nothing will be printed in dmesg this time. If you now take a look at your 1-wire device filesystem you will see a new entry called w1_slave. This is how you will access the temperature information from the DS1820B. Use cat to find the w1_slave file; if all is well it should print some information for you. There will be a short delay on your shell when you do this. Hopefully your output looks something like Figure 3-17.

```
[root@hobo ~]# cat /sys/bus/w1/devices/10-0008027e34ca/w1_slave
3c 00 4b 46 ff ff 0e 10 43 : crc=43 YES
3c 00 4b 46 ff ff 0e 10 43 t=29875
[root@hobo ~]# 
```

Figure 3-17. *Successful output from the DS1820B*

Let me show you what the two lines of text mean. Each line can be broken up into segments.

- The first segment of nine hex values is what is directly read from the device. You really don't need to pay attention to this value on either of the lines.

- The next segment on the first line is CRC=43. This is the checksum value of the data that has been read from the DS1820B. The last section on the first line is YES. This means the checksum matches and your data are valid. If you do encounter a NO value here you can no longer trust any of the information from the sensor and it would be wise to replace the sensor.

- On the second line you have the hex values, as in the first line.

- Then the second part of this is t=, which means temperature equals. Last up you have "29875" in my example. Since this is a high-precision device this measurement actually means 29.875°C. (It's a little warm sitting under my 30-inch LCD.)

Something simple like this will get you the temperature:

```
# cat /sys/bus/w1/devices/10-0008027e34ca/w1_slave  | grep t= | cut -c 30-31
```

This should just give you back the first two digits. Later on in this chapter I will show you a simple script to monitor the sensor or log the values to a file.

By default Linux won't autoload the w1_gpio and w1_therm modules. If you want your 1-wire device to automatically appear on reboot you're going to need to set up a module autoload file. This will be the same process you used in Chapter 2. Create a file called 1w-therm.modules in the /etc/sysconfig/modules directory. Enter the following into the file:

```
#!/bin/bash
lsmod | grep -q w1_gpio || /sbin/modprobe w1_gpio >/dev/null 2>&1
lsmod | grep -q w1_therm || /sbin/modprobe w1_therm >/dev/null 2>&1
```

Save the file and reboot. Now your 1-wire device will be detected on boot on the Raspberry Pi.

Using the Big Blue DHT11

Now you have seen what the DS1820B can do and how easy it is to use. I now want to show you how the DHT11 can be used. It's not as easy to use under Linux as the DS1820B but it can be done. Take a look at the electronic schematics in Figure 3-18. You'll notice it's a very simple connection for this sensor.

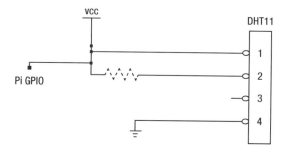

Figure 3-18. *Electronic schematics for the DHT11*

You can see that you still need a pull-up resistor. It's not a 1-wire device, but it works in a similar way in that the DHT11 expects the data line to be high at all times; it can then pull it low when required.

One of the nice things about the DHT11 is how simple it is to wire up. It also requires only one data line but you cannot use this device in parasitic mode. Take a close look at the back of your sensor or the data sheet if you can read it. My sensor has a voltage range from 3.6 to 6.6 V. It's a rather odd range; it also means you must use an external voltage source. I always do, but this time you must.

1. Place your DHT11 into your breadboard. I like to place it so that pin 1 is on row 1 of the breadboard. The front of the sensor has all the little square holes. When looking at the front of the sensor, pin 1 is on the left-hand side. Pin 1 is also the Vcc pin. Take a look at Figure 3-19 to see how I have placed the DHT11.

Figure 3-19. *DHT11 placement*

2. Like last time, it's best to install the jumpers next. Connect one jumper from pin 1 to your voltage source.

3. Connect pin 4 to your ground.

4. Also connect a jumper from pin 2 to a free row on the side of your breadboard. This allows a clear placement for the pull-up resistor. In Figure 3-20 you can see that my jumper is installed.

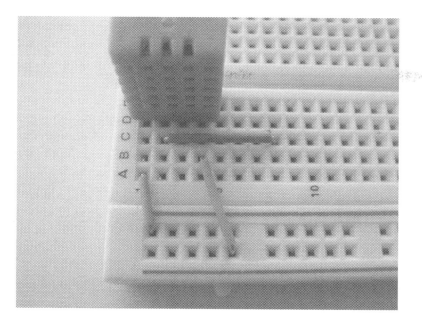

Figure 3-20. *Jumpers installed*

5. Insert your 10K ohm resistor between pin 2 and your voltage source. Place it from your voltage source across to the free row where you installed the jumper from pin 2.

6. Lastly, connect a hook-up wire from in front of the jumper wire on pin 2. This will connect to physical pin P1-11 on the Raspberry Pi. See Figure 3-21 for the final working breadboard.

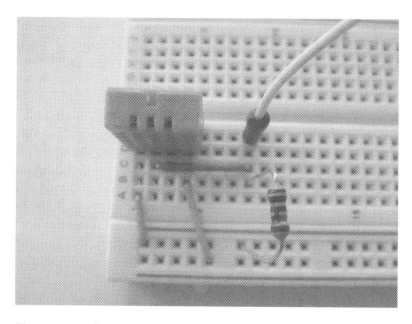

Figure 3-21. *All components installed and connected to your Pi*

Now you are all ready to let some software access it. Soon you will know just how hot and humid it is! Hong Kong is always very humid so for me this part may not be very useful. With that in mind it's time to move on to the software part.

Reading the DHT11 in Linux

With the DHT11 sensor connected, you're going to need a way to read it. You will recall from the start of this chapter that the DHT11 uses its own digital signaling. To enable you to use this sensor I have included some source code from the excellent Adafruit web site.

■ **Note** The application comes as source code. You're going to need to compile this on your Raspberry Pi. You can download the source code zip file from the Apress web site to get the required files, or you can visit `http://rpi.horan.hk` to get the source code.

Now that you have the source code unpacked, you will see three files:

- A make file
- `Adafruit_DHT.c`
- `Adafruit_DHT.o`

These three files are the source code, an object file, and a make file. Because all the hard work has been done for you, the main file you care about is the make file. This file tells the make application how to build the `Adafruit_DHT.c` source into an application. Go ahead and invoke the make application by running the following command in the project directory:

```
# make
```

You will quickly notice that it won't work:

```
-bash: /usr/bin/make: No such file or directory
```

Or something similar will appear. By default the Raspberry Pi Fedora image comes with no development tools. Go ahead and install make with this command:

```
# yum install -y make
```

Now that you have make installed, shouldn't it be fine?
Nope. You are now most likely getting this error:

```
make: gcc: Command not found
```

gcc is the tool you use to build c and other programs. Install gcc with this command:

```
# yum install -y gcc
```

gcc is quite big so this may be a good time to grab a nice beverage or two (in my case a tin of Tsing Tao).
Once gcc is installed you can type in make again. You will notice once again it has failed, this time with some cryptic message about the BCM2835 not being found. You can see the full error in Figure 3-22.

```
[root@hobo pi-dht11]# make
gcc -o Adafruit_DHT Adafruit_DHT.o -std=c99 -I. -lbcm2835
/usr/bin/ld: cannot find -lbcm2835
collect2: ld returned 1 exit status
make: *** [Adafruit_DHT] Error 1
[root@hobo pi-dht11]# 
```

Figure 3-22. *Link error for BCM2835 headers*

The BCM2835 is what powers the Raspberry Pi. If you also look at the error message you will notice that the build process is trying to link the BMC2835 header files. Exactly where do you get the header files from? They sure don't ship with Fedora. You can download the BCM2835 headers from http://rpi.horan.hk or the Apress web site. There is one thing to note: this project depends on version 1.8 of the BCM header files; newer headers will not work. Once you have this downloaded to the Raspberry Pi, extract the tarball. Now open the bcm2835-1.8 directory. Your next task is going to be to build and install this package. You're going to need to configure the build so it will know how to run make on your system. To do this, run the following command:

```
# ./configure
```

Take a look at Figure 3-23. You can see that the source has correctly been configured for my environment.

```
[root@hobo bcm2835-1.8]# ./configure
checking for a BSD-compatible install... /usr/bin/install -c
checking whether build environment is sane... yes
checking for a thread-safe mkdir -p... /bin/mkdir -p
checking for gawk... gawk
checking whether make sets $(MAKE)... yes
checking for doxygen... no
configure: WARNING: Doxygen not found - continuing without Doxygen support
checking for ranlib... ranlib
checking for gcc... gcc
checking whether the C compiler works... yes
checking for C compiler default output file name... a.out
checking for suffix of executables...
checking whether we are cross compiling... no
checking for suffix of object files... o
checking whether we are using the GNU C compiler... yes
checking whether gcc accepts -g... yes
checking for gcc option to accept ISO C89... none needed
checking for style of include used by make... GNU
checking dependency style of gcc... gcc3
configure: creating ./config.status
config.status: creating Makefile
config.status: creating src/Makefile
config.status: creating doc/Makefile
config.status: creating config.h
config.status: config.h is unchanged
config.status: executing depfiles commands
```

Figure 3-23. *The configure script runs successfully*

After this step you now need to build the application. Once again you use make to build the application. Type the following into the command prompt:

```
# make
```

That should finish quite quickly. Once it's done, type the following to install the files:

```
# make install
```

In Figure 3-24 you can see the whole process that ran on my Raspberry Pi.

```
[root@hobo bcm2835-1.8]# make
make  all-recursive
make[1]: Entering directory `/root/bcm2835-1.8'
Making all in src
make[2]: Entering directory `/root/bcm2835-1.8/src'
make[2]: Nothing to be done for `all'.
make[2]: Leaving directory `/root/bcm2835-1.8/src'
Making all in doc
make[2]: Entering directory `/root/bcm2835-1.8/doc'
make[2]: Nothing to be done for `all'.
make[2]: Leaving directory `/root/bcm2835-1.8/doc'
make[2]: Entering directory `/root/bcm2835-1.8'
make[2]: Leaving directory `/root/bcm2835-1.8'
make[1]: Leaving directory `/root/bcm2835-1.8'
[root@hobo bcm2835-1.8]# make install
Making install in src
make[1]: Entering directory `/root/bcm2835-1.8/src'
make[2]: Entering directory `/root/bcm2835-1.8/src'
test -z "/usr/local/lib" || /bin/mkdir -p "/usr/local/lib"
 /usr/bin/install -c -m 644  libbcm2835.a '/usr/local/lib'
 ( cd '/usr/local/lib' && ranlib libbcm2835.a )
test -z "/usr/local/include" || /bin/mkdir -p "/usr/local/include"
 /usr/bin/install -c -m 644 bcm2835.h '/usr/local/include'
make[2]: Leaving directory `/root/bcm2835-1.8/src'
make[1]: Leaving directory `/root/bcm2835-1.8/src'
Making install in doc
make[1]: Entering directory `/root/bcm2835-1.8/doc'
make[2]: Entering directory `/root/bcm2835-1.8/doc'
make[2]: Nothing to be done for `install-exec-am'.
make[2]: Nothing to be done for `install-data-am'.
make[2]: Leaving directory `/root/bcm2835-1.8/doc'
make[1]: Leaving directory `/root/bcm2835-1.8/doc'
make[1]: Entering directory `/root/bcm2835-1.8'
make[2]: Entering directory `/root/bcm2835-1.8'
make[2]: Nothing to be done for `install-exec-am'.
make[2]: Nothing to be done for `install-data-am'.
make[2]: Leaving directory `/root/bcm2835-1.8'
make[1]: Leaving directory `/root/bcm2835-1.8'
[root@hobo bcm2835-1.8]#
```

Figure 3-24. *The whole build and install process*

You've now got the tools and the headers installed, so head back into the source directory for the sensor build. This time when you run the make command you will get only one line of output. It will look something like the following with no errors:

```
[root@hobo pi-dht11]# make
```

```
gcc -o Adafruit_DHT Adafruit_DHT.o -std=c99 -I. -lbcm2835
```

```
[root@hobo pi-dht11]#
```

Do an `ls` on the current directory and you will now see an application called `Adafruit_DHT`, which is the application that will read from our sensor. The `Adafruit_DHT` application expects to receive two command-line options.

- The first option is what type of sensor it will be communicating with. In your case that will be the DHT11, so the first option will simply be 11.

- The last option the `Adafruit_DHT` application expects is the GPIO pin number. This is not the physical pin number but the logical GPIO pin reference number. Recall that you connected the data line of the DHT11 to pin P1-11: this is GPIO17.

Now that you have the required information to run the application, run it with the following command:

```
# ./Adafruit_DHT 11 17
```

This should produce something like what you see in Figure 3-25.

```
[root@hobo pi-dht11]# ./Adafruit_DHT 11 17
Using pin #17
Data (40): 0x1f 0x0 0x1d 0x0 0x3c
Temp = 29 *C, Hum = 31 %
[root@hobo pi-dht11]#
```

Figure 3-25. *Output of the Adafruit_DHT application*

The output of this application has three lines.

- The first line tells you what GPIO pin it's using.

- The second line is the raw data that the application received. The last line shows the important part: the temperature and humidity.

There is one odd thing you must remember about the DHT11. The sensor itself can only ever respond to a temperature and humidity reading request every two seconds or more. If you try to ask it more frequently you will get the output you see in Figure 3-26. It's not an error; there just are no data. You'll notice there is no third line. Give it a few seconds and ask again.

```
[root@hobo pi-dht11]# ./Adafruit_DHT 11 17
Using pin #17
Data (40): 0x1f 0x0 0x1d 0x0 0x1c
```

Figure 3-26. *No data received from the DHT11*

The `Adafruit_DHT` can be run anywhere on your Raspberry Pi. I personally like to move it to /usr/local/bin as this complies with the Unix filesystem layout, but feel free to place it wherever you want. Because /usr/local/bin is in your path you won't need to specify the full path to the binary when you run it. Here is a neat little one liner for placing the temperature and humidity readings on a separate line:

```
# Adafruit_DHT 11 17 | grep Temp | tr "," "\n"
```

This will give you the readouts on separate lines. Nice and pretty!

Scripting the Sensors

Now that you can read the sensors you may want a way to log the values or just to monitor them from a terminal screen. As you can see, the commands I gave you to read the two sensors are a little unfriendly to keep typing all the time. To solve this issue I will give you a little script that can read the DHT11 or the DS1820B. This script will poll the sensor at your given interval in seconds. The script has two modes of operation.

- You can run the script in monitor mode; this will just print the value of the sensor to the terminal.

- The other mode that the script supports is writing the value of the sensor to a log file.

In Listing 3-1 below you can see the code. The script has a few small assumptions. It assumes that the sensors are connected to the GPIO pins you used in this chapter and that the Adafruit_DHT binary file is in the same directory as the script itself.

Listing 3-1. A Script to Read/Log the Sensors

```
#!/bin/bash
# Description : A simple bash script to monitor or log the temp sensors
# Author : Brendan Horan
SLEEP=$2
LOG=$3
function ds1820_mon {
  echo Polling DS1820 every $SLEEP seconds.
    for (( ; ; ))
    do
      echo Temperature is :
      cat /sys/bus/w1/devices/10-0008027e34ca/w1_slave  | grep t= | cut -c 30-31
      sleep $SLEEP
    done
}
function dht11_mon {
  echo Polling DHT11 every $SLEEP seconds.
    for (( ; ; ))
    do
      echo Temperature and humidity is :
      ./Adafruit_DHT 11 17 | grep Temp | tr "," "\n"
      sleep $SLEEP
    done
}
function ds1820_log {
  echo Logging DS1820 to file every $SLEEP seconds. >> $LOG
    for (( ; ; ))
    do
      echo Temperature is : >> $LOG
      cat /sys/bus/w1/devices/10-0008027e34ca/w1_slave  | grep t= | cut -c 30-31 >> $LOG
      sleep $SLEEP
    done
}
function dht11_log {
  echo Logging DHT11 to file every $SLEEP seconds. >> $LOG
    for (( ; ; ))
```

```
         do
           echo Temperature and humidity is : >> $LOG
           ./Adafruit_DHT 11 17 | grep Temp | tr "," "\n" >> $LOG
           sleep $SLEEP
         done
}
case $1 in
  dht11_mon)
     dht11_mon
  ;;
  ds1820_mon)
     ds1820_mon
  ;;
  dht11_log)
     dht11_log
  ;;
  ds1820_log)
     ds1820_log
  ;;
  *)
     echo ------------------------------------------------------------------------------------------
--
     echo
     echo  DHT11/DS1820 tool syntax.
     echo  The tool has two modes, monitor and log.
     echo  Monitor will print to screen and log will log to a file.
     echo  Script assumes the Adafruit_DHT tool is in the same directory.
     echo ------------------------------------------------------------------------------------------
--
     echo    -- Monitor Mode --
     echo  Monitor mode accepts two variables the name of the sensor and the polling time in seconds.
     echo  To poll the ds1820 every 5 seconds the syntax would be :
     echo  "./sensor.sh ds1820_mon 5"
     echo
     echo  To poll the DHT11 every 5 seconds the syntax would be :
     echo  "./sensor.sh dht11_mon 5"
     echo ------------------------------------------------------------------------------------------
--
     echo    -- Log Mode --
     echo  Log mode accepts three variables the name of the sensor, polling time and the log file
name.
     echo  To log the ds1820 every 5 seconds to the syntax would be :
     echo  "./sensor.sh ds1820_log 5 /var/log/ds1820_temp &"
     echo
     echo  To log the DHT11 every 5 seconds the syntax would be :
     echo  "./sensor.sh dht11_log 5 /var/log/dht11_log &"
     echo ------------------------------------------------------------------------------------------
--
  ;;
esac

# END
```

The first time you run the script it would be a good idea to run it with no options:

```
# ./sensor.sh
```

By doing this you will be presented a help page on how to use the script. This help page will show you all the different options you can use.

For example if I wanted to monitor the DS1820B every five seconds my command would look like this:

```
# ./sensor.sh ds1820_mon 5
```

If I wanted to log the DHT11 sensor every five seconds to a log file my command would look like this:

```
# ./sensor.sh dht11_log 5 /var/log/dht11_sensor
```

Summary

In this chapter you received a detailed introduction to my love of data sheets and breadboards, starting off with how breadboards work and how they are laid out. I still suggest that you keep many breadboards around. I can guarantee you that sometimes you will have half-finished projects and pulling all the components off the board just to build something simple gets a little frustrating very quickly. This rule applies for jumper wire too. Even with a box of it I still find myself unable to find that exact cable or jumper I need. You also may have noticed my tendency to always refer you back to the data sheets when possible. I can't stress enough how important they are. Just quickly read over them: sometimes they will save you hours of frustration.

A good example of this is the DHT11 used in this chapter. You would expect it to run fine at 3.3 V; after all it's a very common voltage source. On the other hand 3.6 V is not common. I don't know why or how the DHT11 came to need that as a minimum voltage, but my point is that one quick glance at your data sheets would show you this right away. The voltage range was printed on the back of the DHT11, lucky enough, but that's not normal just like 3.6 V.

After all this I then explained the differences between the DS1820B and the DHT11. I still feel that the DS1820B is a better sensor in a lot of aspects. This is more so when you're talking about connecting it to the Raspberry Pi and not an Arduino. The DHT11 is just far too timing-critical to work well in Linux. Sure, we got it working but I would not pick it as a sensor for use with the Raspberry Pi.

With that in mind I showed you how to access the DS1820B via the 1-wire bus. I also showed you how to make use of parasitic power. I talked about how to load the modules for the 1-wire bus and what each of them did. Once we had kernel support for the 1-wire bus I showed you how to search for and access each one of the 1-wire slaves.

In the last part of this chapter I talked about the DHT11 and how you can access it under Linux. This proved to be a bit more involved than using the built-in 1-wire bus. You were required to install additional header files to support the application that reads the DHT11. In the end the sensor was up and working, giving you temperature and humidity readings every two or more seconds. This is a little slow compared with the DS1820B. It works fine if you need to use it. The only reason I have included it is that it's quite common to use the DHT11 with the Arduino. So you may have one lying around. Now that you have mastered data sheets and breadboards, in the next chapter you will connect a simple LCD. It will require more breadboard action and, of course, more reading of data sheets.

CHAPTER 4

Driving a Simple Character LCD

Character LCDs seem less of a craze and more of an old technology these days, although I've still got a soft spot for them (much like I do for valves and tubes). I can recall when everyone that was modding PCs wanted a small 18-by-2 character LCD modded into their case. I remember the details quite well: more often than not I was the one doing the wiring jobs for them. There were many nights spent cutting up parallel port cables and wiring them into the little LCDs. Then everyone watched in joy as I would write some simple characters to prove that the LCDs did in fact work. After all there was something "high-tech" about being able to display your CPU temperature or your current playing song or even something as simple as the time on a little LCD screen. You can see in Figure 4-1 a simple character LCD displaying the time. These LCDs are everywhere these days. You will find them in printers, vending machines and payphones, or, in my case, by the cabinetful in local electronics markets, of every shape and size. You may even be able to recycle one from a dead device you have lying around. It should be quite simple to desolder the LCD out of the broken device.

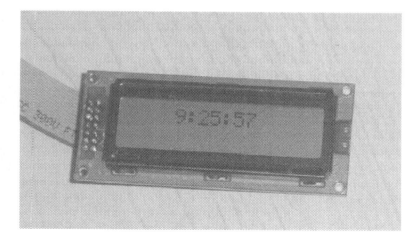

Figure 4-1. *A simple character LCD clock*

Given that an 18-by-2 LCD would also fit neatly into a 5.25-inch bay on your standard PC case, this may have been why such screens became so popular. Back then it was the Hitachi HD44780 and its clones that everyone was using. The stock size was 18 by 2 but screens do get much bigger. I did manage to get my hands on a 20-by-4 HD44780 clone and everyone I knew was most envious. I had four full lines of 20 characters that displayed the track listing, systems info, and, of course, the date and time. Given what your average mobile phone these days can achieve resolution-wise, 20 by 4 now seems a lot less impressive.

These days there are more clones of the HD44780 than the original Hitachi modules; not that it makes any difference because they all work exactly the same way. It's lucky for us that all the manufacturers followed this single standard. What else made the HD44780 so common? Well, it is simple to drive and has a well-established instruction set that is easy to program for. If you are looking online or wandering around your local electronics store you can easily spot the HD44780 and its clones by looking at the pin connectors. They will come in either two configurations: two rows of 7 solder pads, or one single row of 14 solder pads. You also need to check the data sheet if you can read it. The data sheet should mention the access mode being either four bits or eight bits. This refers to how many data lines are required to drive the display. You need more than just the data lines to drive the LCD though. I will show you what the other pins are used for later on.

The standard and most basic method to drive the LCD is the eight-bit mode. The four-bit mode is much more complicated but also uses fewer cables. Fewer cables must be better, right?

Well, you first need to understand the difference between four-bit and eight-bit mode before you can make this judgment. What exactly is the difference between these modes and why should you care?

Pulling Apart the HD44780 and the Clones

Let's take a look at the function of each pin on a standard HD44780. In Table 4-1 you can see the pin mapping for a generic HD44780 display. If you notice that your LCD is missing pins 15 and 16 this simply means your LCD has no backlight. Some of the HD44780s also move pins 15 and 16 to the edge of the LCD rather than on the same strip of pins as the data lines.

Table 4-1. *Pin listing for the HD44780*

Pin	Name	Function	Use
1	GND	Ground	Ground for logic board and LCD
2	VCC	Supply Voltage	Supply voltage for logic board and LCD
3	LCD DRIVE	Contrast Voltage	Sets the voltage range that controls the contrast on the LCD
4	RS	Register Select	Sets the mode; if you pull it high, the LCD expects data to display, and if you pull it low the LCD expects an instruction to control the LCD
5	R/W	Read or Write Select	Is used to read from the LCD
6	EN	Start Data Read/Write	Sets up when the LCD can expect a data or instruction command
7	DB0	Data Bit 0	First data line
8	DB1	Data Bit 1	Second data line
9	DB2	Data Bit 2	Third data line
10	DB3	Data Bit 3	Fourth data line
11	DB4	Data Bit 4	Fifth data line (first data line in four-bit mode)
12	DB5	Data Bit 5	Sixth data line (second data line in four-bit mode)
13	DB6	Data Bit 6	Seventh data line (third data line in four-bit mode)
14	DB7	Data Bit 7	Eighth data line (fourth data line in four-bit mode)
15	BL VCC	Backlight Supply Voltage	Supply voltage for LCD backlight
16	BL GND	Backlight Ground	Ground for the LCD backlight

On my LCD, as you can see in Figure 4-2, I have both pins 15 and 16 as well as anode and cathode solder pads on the side solder pad for the backlight (you can see this on the left-hand side on the white pad). The pad configuration on my LCD is one single row, which makes it quite easy to solder a pin header on.

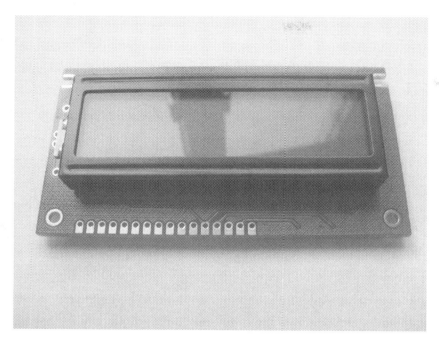

Figure 4-2. *The front of a generic HD44780 display*

If I flip the LCD over and take a look at the back of the printed circuit board (PCB), it appears that pins 15 and 16 may be connected to the anode and cathode of the LCD backlight. Now, you don't want to just guess it's connected, do you? That's a perfect way to let the magic smoke out. This is where the ohm setting on your multimeter comes in real handy. Remember that ohms are the measure of resistance. If you set your multimeter to the ohms setting and touch the two probes together, what happens? You get a reading of zero. That means there is no resistance between each probe. If you move the probes away, you will see the value rising back to a positive integer. This is called continuity testing. With this in mind you can use continuity testing to measure the resistance between pins 15 and 16 and the anode and cathode. Take a look at Figure 4-3: you can see the pin out listing including pins 15 and 16. You will notice that pins 15 and 16 have no label; I had to use my multimeter to figure out what they were connected to.

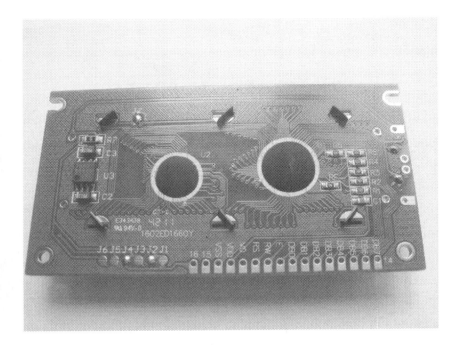

Figure 4-3. *The rear of my generic HD44780*

Now place a probe on pin 15 and the anode pad. You will notice the multimeter reads zero, which means that the two pins are connected to each other. If you try measuring from pin 16 to the anode you will notice that your meter reads a large positive integer, which indicates they are not connected. Now that you have all the pins mapped out, make a reference somewhere as you will need this information later on when you connect the jumper cables to the LCD. If you're really lucky your handy data sheet will have all this information already for you.

Next up it's a good idea to understand what happens when you send an instruction to the LCD. Take a look at Table 4-2; you can see what the clear display instruction looks like in eight-bit mode.

Table 4-2. *The clear display instruction in eight-bit mode*

Data Bus	DB7	DB6	DB5	DB4	DB3	DB2	DB1	DB0
Binary	0	0	0	0	0	0	0	1
Timing	200-µs wait							

In this mode all eight data lines are used to send the one instruction, whereas in four-bit mode only the high four data lines are used. The high data lines are DB4, DB5, DB6, and DB7. If you wanted to send the same clear display instruction as above, you would now need to split the same eight-bit instruction into two separate sets of data with timing in between. This is what makes the four-bit mode harder to program than the eight-bit mode. In Table 4-3 you can see the exact same instruction but provided in the four-bit mode.

Table 4-3. *The clear display instruction in four-bit mode*

Data Bit	DB7	DB6	DB5	DB4
Binary	0	0	0	0
Timing	200-μs wait			
Data Bit	DB7	DB6	DB5	DB4
Binary	0	0	0	1

You can see now that you need to set up timing in between each set of bits also before and after each data write. Note that the timing will not matter for you as the software I will be using will take care of that for you.

Now you are going to need to find something that has a minimum of four data lines. I bet if you take a look at any newer PC or your laptop you would be hard-pressed to find anything that has more than four separate data lines. This was not always the case. Back when LCDs were all the rage pretty much every PC came with a parallel port. The parallel port was perfect for driving the LCD. It could easily support all the data lines needed and was simple to interface with. Given the ease of programming in eight-bit mode and the abundance of parallel ports it's easy to see why this method of interfacing was selected by PC hobbyists.

Preparing the Hardware

Hang on: the Raspberry Pi has no parallel port! No, but it has GPIO: remember that all you need are data lines and a few control lines. So how are you going to connect this magic little LCD to the Raspberry Pi? That's what I am going to show you in this section. First, let's prep the LCD so it's easy to work with.

LCD Prep Work

If you take a look at your LCD you'll see the little holes and solder pads. While it's possible to solder and desolder wires to the LCD more than once you do risk the potential of damaging the solder pads if you do this. They are not designed to be heated up all the time. If you did heat the solder pad too much, you may cause the pad to lift from the PCB. If this happens you can no longer use the solder pad and you may not be able to use the LCD. You can repair a broken pad but it's neither simple nor easy. It's much better if you just respect the solder pad to start with and ensure that you don't break it. Given this, you need a way to easily connect the LCD to any board you may have. By looking at the LCD the first thing that may come to mind is soldering some wire to the LCD solder pads and leaving them hanging. This is fine and would work without any issues. Unfortunately it has some downsides. You may want to remove or add data lines in the future. For example, if you move from eight-bit mode to four-bit mode you need to add or remove four wires. This once again brings us back to the solder pad issue. Also, having a bunch of wires hanging off your LCD looks messy for a nonpermanent installation. So now what? If you look closely at the solder pads you may notice that each pad has the same spacing between each pad (in this case 2 mm).

In electronics there are normally three standards of spacing for headers:

- The most common spacing you will find is 2.54 mm.

- The next most common is 2 mm.

- Lastly there is 1.27-mm spacing. I have yet to see anything that uses the 1.27-mm spacing but I am sure they are out there.

With this in mind you can buy pin headers. They come in many forms; you will need a single row of 16 pins. In Figure 4-4 you can see the pin header I used.

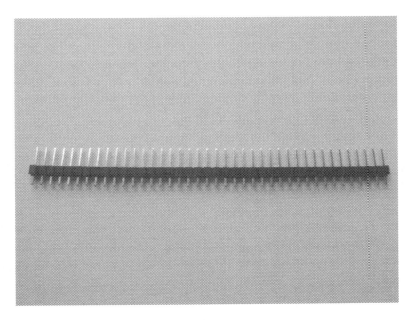

Figure 4-4. *My pin header with 2-mm spacing*

If your pin header is too long, just cut the extra pins off. The key thing to remember is that you need a single row rather than a double row. The pin headers won't be much use unless you solder them on. Strangely enough they won't do much sitting on your desk. If you take a look at your LCD you will see that the solder pads may only be on one side of the PCB. On most of the LCDs I have seen, they are on the top. In my case they are on the top and bottom. This is important so that you know what side to face the pin headers on. I will face my pin headers upward and make use of the solder pads on the back of the LCD. In Figure 4-5 you can see the pin headers in place, before soldering has started and in Figure 4-6 you can see the finished result. In the book's introduction I mentioned jumper cables; this is where they will come in handy. You can now connect any of the pins easily and without any possibility of damaging the solder pads. It also looks a lot nicer. There is nothing worse than messy cabling or bad soldering jobs.

Figure 4-5. *Pin headers that are ready to solder in*

Figure 4-6. *Pin headers soldered in*

Solder the outer two pins first. Then work from the middle outward. This will hold your pin headers in nicely.

Shift Registers

Now you have your LCD ready to use and you've got your breadboard out and your Raspberry Pi on. So what's next, you ask? It should be simple: just connect all the data lines to the GPIO. Yeah, but not quite. That will work but you need to write your own driver and that defeats one of the key points of the HD44780 and its clones. Let's keep this simple and make use of years of work done by other people for these LCDs. I will talk more about the software after we connect the LCD to the Raspberry Pi. There is no use in having software when your hardware is not even connected. You may wonder how you are going to connect all the data lines to the Raspberry Pi. If so, that's a good thing; you won't be connecting any of the data lines to the Raspberry Pi directly.

Wait, what? How can you drive the LCD if it's not connected to the Raspberry Pi? Well, the LCD will be connected to another chip called a shift register. Why use this magic shift register? Because you have very few GPIO pins on the Raspberry Pi. If you were to connect this LCD and use all the data lines you would not have much room for any other projects that need access to the GPIO pins. You want to save as many of the GPIO pins as possible. This is where your new friend, the shift register, will come in.

Shift register? This all sounds a little shifty. What exactly is a shift register? Shift registers, or serial in parallel out (SIPO) or parallel in serial out (PISO) as they are also known, are a handy way of turning a serial data stream into a parallel data stream or the other way around. I will use a SIPO shift register to drive the LCD.

Let me explain how they work. In our case the shift register will take an input of serial data and output that into parallel data. How this works is the Raspberry Pi will send bits of data across the I2C bus (explained in detail in the next section). Each bit of data will be separated by a clock pulse. When the shift register receives this data, it will shift each bit of data into one of the data output lines. As soon as it receives another string of data the previous bits of data will be shifted out of the data output lines. This cycle will keep going as long as the shift register receives data input. Take a look at Figure 4-7. On the left you have the serial data input from the I2C bus and also the clock signal from the I2C bus; these are the inputs. Data will be clocked in via the serial data input line. In this example the shift register is four bits wide. So when you clock the four bits of serial data into the shift register you will have the same four bits of data available on the four parallel data outputs.

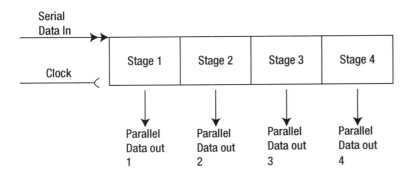

Figure 4-7. *A logic diagram of a shift register*

Pretty cool stuff! Now exactly how will the shift register get its data?

The I2C Bus

That's where the I2C bus comes in. I will use the I2C bus to feed the shift register. What's this I2C bus? It sounds like a bad instant messaging client. Well, not quite, but it will transfer messages. The I2C bus is used to exchange messages between low-speed devices. I2C was invented by Philips in 1982 and its main goal was to link low-speed computer peripherals together with a common bus and protocol. Because the I2C bus has been around for some time now, there are a few versions of it. The version on the Raspberry Pi is version 2.1, which is pretty much just a bug fix for version 2.0. The 2.0 version is a little dated now, having been first introduced in 1998. It runs at 3.4 mHz and is often referred to as high-speed mode. High-speed mode is capable of transferring 3.4 Mbit/s so it's no slouch for simple devices. Do keep in mind that the 3.4 Mbit/s includes protocol overhead too. I can't see a character LCD streaming 3 Mbit/s of data at any one time.

Physical Layout

So what makes up the I2C bus? The I2C bus is a serial protocol that consists of two physical wires that can operate in both directions. These two lines are known as the serial data line (SDA) and the serial clock line (SCL). These two lines normally operate at 3.3 V or 5 V. Although the I2C standards do permit other voltages, they are not widely seen.

- The SDA is where the transmission of data to and from the slaves/master occurs.

- The SCL's job is to set the timing on the bus. It's also used to set flow control for the data on the SDA.

By default the SDA and SCL are pulled high via a pull-up resistor (recall that we also learned about a pull-up resistor in Chapter 3).

Raspberry Pi Tolerance and High-Level Voltage Input

One big thing to keep in mind when selecting I2C devices for the Raspberry Pi is that the I2C bus is not tolerant of 5 V. So what's that mean to you exactly? It means you are limited to what devices you can safely put on the I2C bus of the Raspberry Pi without letting the magic smoke out. For this you're going to need to read your friendly data sheet. I love data sheets and you should too: they have very useful information.

The data sheet for your I2C device will contain an all importation value called "Vih," or high-level voltage input. This key value tells you what the I2C slave device will attempt to pull the SDA up to when it needs to place the line high. Most of the time the Vih is a range expressed as a percentage above and below the supply voltage of the I2C slave device. Some devices have a wide range for the Vih and others don't. If your device has a voltage source of 5 V and the Vih of 4 to 5.5 V it will never be able to pull the SDA high on the Raspberry Pi. In short it won't work and may damage your Raspberry Pi. So please do read the data sheets and try and avoid letting the magic smoke out. Choose 3.3-V devices to be safe or at least check the data sheet to ensure that the Vih can go down to 3.3 V.

Pull-Up Resisters and Open Drains

Another important part of the I2C bus is the need for pull-up resistors. On the SDA and SCL you need to have a resistor to pull each line to a known high state. In the case of the Raspberry Pi, it has 1.8K ohm resistors already. Don't try and add external pull-up resistors to any of your I2C projects. Why do you need to pull up the lines? The design of the I2C bus is that of an open drain. Sounds fancy? It's a simple concept, really. Just think of your kitchen sink drain. You can only place things down the drain. Normally things should not come out of the drain; if they do you have issues. It's the same for the I2C bus; it's always pulled to a low state. The low state is a drain and cannot without external assistance go to a high state. This is where the pull-up resistors come into play. They pull up the line to high by default. Now when a slave device needs to access the line it can pull the line down. When it's done, the line will return to high as the resistors are pulling the line up. In the case of the Raspberry Pi the I2C bus is pulled up to 3.3 V.

Now what happens when you use the bus? When a slave device wants to use the bus it will pull the SDA low; once the SDA is pulled low the slave device will then pull the SCL low to indicate to other slave devices that the bus is in use. Once the slave has finished transmitting or receiving data it will let the SDA go high to signal the end of transmission. It will then let the SCL go high to indicate the bus is no longer in use.

Addressing I2C Devices

So how will the I2C bus know which device to communicate with? Each slave device will have either a seven-bit or ten-bit address. This address should be unique on the given I2C bus. On most slave devices you can set the address or at least some bits of the address. The Raspberry Pi can address either seven-bit or ten-bit devices. Given this large address space, that's a lot of I2C devices you can support on just two wires! The ten-bit addressing method is backward-compatible with the seven-bit addressing method. So you can mix ten-bit and seven-bit devices on the same single bus. In Figure 4-8 you can see what a typical seven-bit address will look like on the bus.

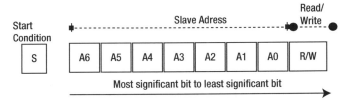

Figure 4-8. *An example of a seven-bit I2C address*

The I2C bus has a few distinct advantages that make it a good candidate for your projects. First, as you now know, it's a two-wire bus, and you will be saving the precious GPIO pins on the Raspberry Pi. Second, as the name implies, I2C is a bus topology. Let's talk more about this bus.

The Bus Itself

The I2C bus is a multimaster bus, meaning you can have more than one master device on the bus and many slave devices. The master in our case is the Raspberry Pi. In addition to this the master and slave roles can be reversed if requested by the slave and master. In Figure 4-9 you can see an I2C bus with two slave devices. For our use you will have only one master.

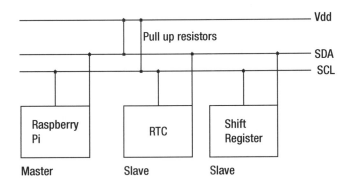

Figure 4-9. *An I2C bus with two slaves and one master*

Putting It All Together

The I2C bus is not that hard to work with, as you can see. With the above knowledge in mind let's connect that LCD to the Raspberry Pi. You're going to need only a few parts for this project. I did tell you the I2C bus was simple. Here is a listing of parts you will need:

- At least 12 pieces of hook-up wire
- One breadboard and some jumper wire
- One shift register (I use the Texas Instruments PCF8574AN)
- A 5-V source and 3.3-V source
- One HD44780 or clone character LCD
- Pin headers for your LCD (optional)

In Figure 4-10 you can see what the finished project breadboard should look like. I have used my handy USB power source to give me 3.3 V and 5 V on each side of the breadboard. Now that you can see what it should look like, let's take a look at the schematic version of this. In Figure 4-11 you can see the electronic wiring schematic for this project.

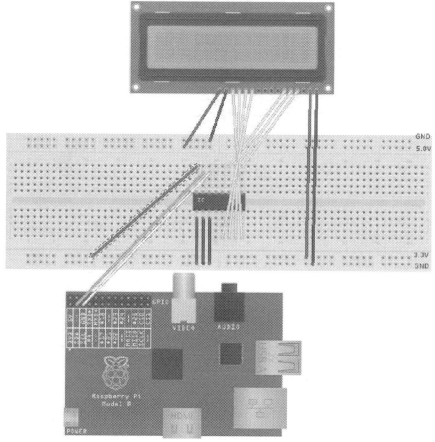

Figure 4-10. *A mockup of the finished breadboard*

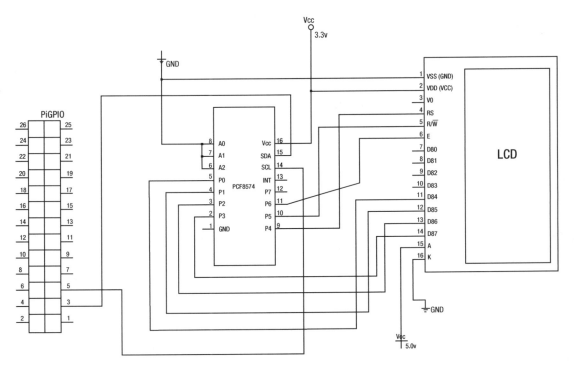

Figure 4-11. *Circuit schematic diagram*

▓ **Warning**   Figure 4.11 is accurate according to the components I have used. Please read your data sheets and cross-check all connections. For example your register select pad on the LCD may be in a different location than mine. Check your data sheets! It takes only a small glance to feel safe in the knowledge that you have made the right connections.

You now have all the information you need to start work! This is the fun part.

1.   Get your breadboard out and insert the PCF8574AN shift register into the center of the board. You can see this neatly done in Figure 4-12. Remember that the half-moon crescent on the package indicates the top/pin1.

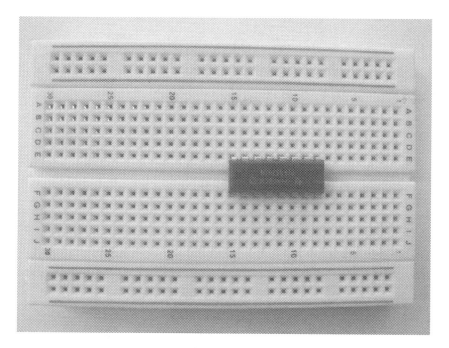

Figure 4-12. *Shift register inserted*

2. I then like to lay out my jumper wire. If you look closely at Figure 4-13 you can see that I have tied pins 1, 2, and 3 to ground.

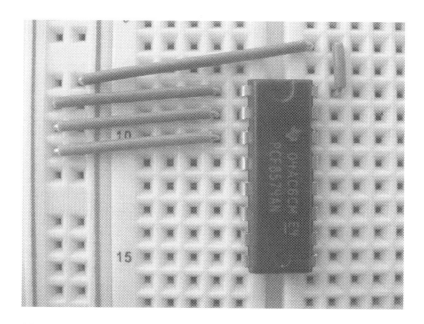

Figure 4-13. *Breadboard jumper wire installed*

■ **Note** Pins 1, 2, and 3 are not ground pins at all. These three pins select the I2C address. You can configure part of the address of the I2C device using these pins. As I am only going to have one device on my I2C bus at the moment, I will tie all the address pins to ground. This has the effect of pulling them down. The result is a low bit address. There would be nothing stopping me tying them to the 3.3-V Vcc. This would have the effect of pulling all address bits high. You could also mix high and low on each address pin.

3. Let's move on from the address selection pins. You can see that I have connected pin 16 to the 3.3-V Vcc on the breadboard. Next up in Figure 4-14 I have added my power source and connected the hook-up wire to the 3.3-V source for the LCD logic and the 5-V source for the LCD backlight. In Figure 4-14 the power rails closest to the USB port are set to 3.3 V and the rails on the other side are set to 5 V.

Figure 4-14. *Power source added to the breadboard*

4. Lastly, in Figure 4-15 I add in the hook-up wire for the I2C lines and the lines for the LCD.

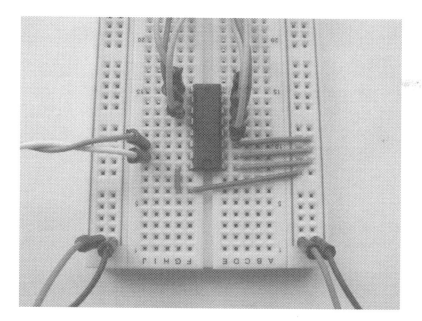

Figure 4-15. *Finished breadboard*

5. Now as per the data sheet of your LCD, or if you're lucky in my case the markings on the back of the LCD, connect the shift register pins to the LCD as listed in Table 4-4.

Table 4-4. *Mapping of PCF8574AN pins to LCD pins*

PCF8574AN Pin	LCD Pin
P0	DB4
P1	DB5
P2	DB6
P3	DB7
P4	RS
P5	RW
P6	E

6. Don't forget to connect the LCD's logic Vcc and GND. If your LCD has a backlight don't forget that too. In my case the backlight is 5 V and can be accessed via pins 15 and 16.

7. As long as the power is off to the LCD and the shift register you can connect it to the Raspberry Pi's I2C bus. Connect pin 15 (SDA) on the PCF8574AN to the Raspberry Pi's P1-03 header and connect pin 14 (SCL) on the PCF8574AN to the Raspberry Pi's P1-05 header. If you are worried about letting the magic smoke out of the Raspberry Pi, just power it down while you make the connection.

8. Now it's a very good time to double-check all your connections.

9. Once the connection has been made, turn on the power to the shift register and the LCD. If all has gone well you should see that the top row of your LCD has been filled out by blocks. This is part of the startup sequence on all HD44780s and clones. This is a good sign. If you don't see anything, go back and check your connections. Remember that things don't often work the first time. If you have managed to let the magic smoke out, then off to the shops for you: I guess you forgot to check your connections first!

You do want more than just a magic set of blocks on the LCD, right? This is where our next section comes in. I will be using an open source application called lcdproc to drive the LCD.

Finding Your I2C Device

So the magic smoke is in and you're all ready to use the LCD. It's now time to access the I2C bus within Linux. By default you may not have the I2C bus module loaded. To quickly check if you have I2C support loaded, run the following command:

```
# ls /dev/i2c-*
```

This should return a listing of at least /dev/i2c-0. In my case it listed nothing. Fedora will not autoload the I2C kernel module. You can fix this in two ways. For a temporary fix you may just want to load the I2C kernel module. You can do this via the following command:

```
# modprob i2c-dev
```

If you want Fedora to autoload the module on each boot, create a file in the /etc/sysconfig/modules/ directory called i2c-dev.modules. Enter Listing 4-1 as shown.

Listing 4-1. Autoload Code for i2c-dev modules

```
#!/bin/bash
lsmod | grep -q i2c-dev || /sbin/modprobe i2c-dev  >/dev/null 2>&1
```

Save the file and reboot your Raspberry Pi to check that the module was loaded. You now have access to the I2C bus. Exciting times are ahead! How do you go about finding the LCD now that you have access to the bus? Recall that it's connected to a bus with the address we set by pulling the address pins low. I did not calculate the address at that time; I just pulled the address bits low. This seems like a bit of an issue if you cannot find the LCD. It might be on another platform like the Arduino or another embedded device; lucky for you that you are running Linux. You can use a handy command called i2cdetect to discover all I2C devices on a given bus. To be able to use this handy tool, you're going to need to install the i2c-tools package.

To do this, simply run the following command:

```
# yum install -y i2c-tools
```

This package will install a few different tools; the main two we will be concerned with are i2cdetect and i2cset. Ensure that you are the root user when you run the i2c-tools command as it needs access to the raw devices.

The first tool I want to show you is i2cdetect. This tool accepts an I2C bus as an input. It will then scan that bus and report back any devices it finds. If you take a look at the output of the following command you should see /dev/i2c-0.

```
# ls /dev/i2c-*
```

This is our first I2C bus; it's also the one connected to the GPIO pins. Another way to find your I2C bus is to scan for all I2C buses on the system; you do this via the i2cdetect command. Run the following to list all available I2C buses on your system:

```
# i2cdetect -l
```

I prefer to list the dev tree nodes but both tools will give you a similar output. Now that you have the bus ID let's scan the bus before we turn on the LCD. The syntax for i2cdetect will be quite simple if you just wish to scan the bus. Depending on the model of the Raspberry Pi you have you may need to use /dev/i2c-0 or /dev/i2c-1; it's safe to scan both buses. Run the following command to scan the /dev/i2c-0 bus:

```
# i2cdetect 0
```

Answer yes when prompted to scan the address range. If you don't see your device, try to scan the next bus until you see your device. In Figure 4-16 you can see the scan has run and no devices are detected.

```
[root@hobo /]# i2cdetect 0
WARNING! This program can confuse your I2C bus, cause data loss and worse!
I will probe file /dev/i2c-0.
I will probe address range 0x03-0x77.
Continue? [Y/n] y
     0  1  2  3  4  5  6  7  8  9  a  b  c  d  e  f
00:          -- -- -- -- -- -- -- -- -- -- -- --
10: -- -- -- -- -- -- -- -- -- -- -- -- -- -- -- --
20: -- -- -- -- -- -- -- -- -- -- -- -- -- -- -- --
30: -- -- -- -- -- -- -- -- -- -- -- -- -- -- -- --
40: -- -- -- -- -- -- -- -- -- -- -- -- -- -- -- --
50: -- -- -- -- -- -- -- -- -- -- -- -- -- -- -- --
60: -- -- -- -- -- -- -- -- -- -- -- -- -- -- -- --
70: -- -- -- -- -- -- -- --
[root@hobo /]# []
```

Figure 4-16. *Nothing found on the I2C bus*

Now turn on the LCD and the shift register. Let's run the exact same scan again. How exciting that something was found! If you take a look at Figure 4-17 you can see at address 0x38 that the scan found a device.

```
[root@hobo /]# i2cdetect 0
WARNING! This program can confuse your I2C bus, cause data loss and worse!
I will probe file /dev/i2c-0.
I will probe address range 0x03-0x77.
Continue? [Y/n] y
     0  1  2  3  4  5  6  7  8  9  a  b  c  d  e  f
00:          -- -- -- -- -- -- -- -- -- -- -- --
10: -- -- -- -- -- -- -- -- -- -- -- -- -- -- -- --
20: -- -- -- -- -- -- -- -- -- -- -- -- -- -- -- --
30: -- -- -- -- -- -- -- -- 38 -- -- -- -- -- -- --
40: -- -- -- -- -- -- -- -- -- -- -- -- -- -- -- --
50: -- -- -- -- -- -- -- -- -- -- -- -- -- -- -- --
60: -- -- -- -- -- -- -- -- -- -- -- -- -- -- -- --
70: -- -- -- -- -- -- -- --
[root@hobo /]# []
```

Figure 4-17. *An I2C slave found at 0×38*

This is our shift register's address in hex. This indicates that you have successfully detected an I2C device on the bus. If you don't get this far, go back and check your connections. More than likely you have something wrong and I would suggest checking the address pins. You'll notice that the first three addresses are not present on the output of the i2cdetect utility. This is because they are part of the reserved address space according to the I2C specification.

Now that you have found something what should you do? Simply probe it! You want to see if your I2C device can communicate back with the bus correctly before you try and use it at a software level. This is where our good friend i2cset comes into play. You can use the i2cset command to send a simple write command to the device you found. Let's do that now. Run the following command:

```
# i2cset 0 0x38 255
```

Does this make sense? Unlikely, so let me explain the command.

- First up we have the tool i2cset; its main function in life is to set an I2C register.

- The first option to this command is 0, which indicates the bus: in your case /dev/i2c-0 is specified as bus 0. If your device was detected on a different bus in the previous step, change this value to the value you found your device at. This should be 0 or 1.

- You have the bus, so the next part of the string is the address in hex of the device. The output of i2cdetect makes this part very easy. Find the two-digit number and prefix it with 0x. So 38 on the table would be expressed as 0x38.

- The last part of this command writes the byte value of 255 to the I2C device. This value of 255 is not super important: it's just a random register on the device. You could use 254 and it would work just as well. You are just testing the communication between the master and slave.

Now let's run the command and see what happens. If the I2C device is responding correctly you should get nothing back from the command. If something is wrong you will get some form of error. The most common error will be "Write failed". If you do get this error, check that you turned on the LCD and the shift register. Don't laugh; it happens a lot, just like not turning on your soldering iron. So in Figure 4-18 you can see that the i2cset tool has successfully ran and we got no response. No response means no error, so it's all good.

```
[root@hobo /]# i2cset 0 0x38 255
WARNING! This program can confuse your I2C bus, cause data loss and worse!
I will write to device file /dev/i2c-0, chip address 0x38, data address
0xff, no data.
Continue? [Y/n] y
[root@hobo /]#
```

Figure 4-18. *The i2cset tool as run successfully*

If this tool gives you any error back, you have a problem. Go back and check your connections again. Keep trying until this tool gives no feedback. Now that you have confirmed you can communicate without error to your I2C slave device it's time you did something with it.

Software and LCD Clients

lcdproc is a client/server application. You can find it by going to http://lcdproc.org. One of the main reasons I selected lcdproc is that it supports a wide range of displays connected in many different methods. This is important as you are making use of the I2C bus to connect the LCD rather than the more common parallel port or USB methods. Don't be too concerned about the project's slow release cycle; there are not many changes in the character LCD world. Another reason why I like lcdproc is that it comes in the client/server model; you will see why that's a good thing later on. Let's install the application for now. To install lcdproc, run the following command:

```
# yum install -y lcdproc
```

This will install the LCDd server and a client called lcdproc. Your first step should be to set up the LCDd server, because no matter what client you end up using you must have the server running.

Server Configuration

The first thing you're going to need to configure is the LCDd.conf file: you can find it at /etc/sysconfig/lcdproc/LCDd.conf.example. This file is just an example; I like to make a copy of it and strip all the unnecessary parts out so that the LCDd.conf file matches my particular LCD. I will now go over all the options I have in my LCDd.conf file. Some will be optional, some will have different settings, and some are mandatory for the LCD you are using. You can see in Figure 4-19 a minimal config file that I use to run my LCD. You can also download a copy of the configuration file from http://rpi.horan.hk.

```
[root@hobo lcdproc]# cat /etc/sysconfig/lcdproc/LCDd.conf
[server]
DriverPath=/usr/lib/lcdproc/
Driver=hd44780
Bind=192.168.0.199
Port=13666
ReportLevel=3
ReportToSyslog=yes
User=nobody
Foreground=no
WaitTime=5

[menu]

[HD44780]
ConnectionType=i2c
Device=/dev/i2c-0
Port=0x38
Backlight=yes
Size=18x2
DelayBus=false
DelayMult=1
Keypad=no
[root@hobo lcdproc]#
```

Figure 4-19. *My LCDd config file*

Let's take a moment to understand what each of the config lines mean and what their effect is. You will also notice that the config file has two main types of lines. One starts with a square bracket; these are section headings. The other type is an option, then an equal sign followed by the setting. In Table 4-5 you can see what each setting in the first section called [server] will do.

Table 4-5. *[server] section config options*

Option	Setting	Effect
DriverPath	/usr/lib/lcdproc/	Where LCDd will find the LCD drivers; the default path should be correct
Driver	hd44780	Set this to hd44780, because you are driving an HD44780 or clone LCD
Bind	192.168.0.199	IP address to bind to; you can use 127.0.0.1 too but it should be an IP address that belongs to the Raspberry Pi
Port	13666	Port to bind to
ReportLevel	3	Syslog report level
ReportToSyslog	yes	Report to syslog enable/disable
User	nobody	What user to run as
Foreground	no	Fork the process to background or let it run in the foreground
WaitTime	5	Pause time between each screen

The next section is not very important for your current LCD. This section is called [menu] and its main use is if your LCD has a set of buttons. You can use this section to create a menu that is driven by the buttons on the front of the LCD.

The last section is the driver you will be using. You can see it's called [HD44780] as that's the LCD you are using or one of the clones. Take a look at Table 4-6 to see what each option will do.

Table 4-6. *A list of settings for the [driver] section*

Option	Setting	Effect
ConnectionType	i2c	How the LCD is connected
Device	/dev/i2c-0	What bus to use in the case of I2C
Port	0x38	The address of the port expander found via i2cdetect
Size	18x2	Screen size of the LCD
DelayBus	false	Delays messages to the bus and may be useful under a high load
DelayMult	1	The multiplier for the above setting
Keypad	no	Indicates whether your LCD has a keypad

Testing the Server

Now it's time to test the server. Save the above configuration file as /etc/sysconfig/lcdproc/LCDd.conf and test the server by starting it on the command line with the foreground flag:

```
# LCDd -f
```

If this has worked you should see only the program's license print to the screen with no errors printed to your terminal. Now take a look at your LCD: you should see a welcome message followed by the client and server count being displayed. If you don't see this, you have errors; revisit your config file. If no errors appeared, kill the process and start it as a service:

```
# service LCDd start
```

Don't forget to run the following if you want the service to start on boot:

```
# chkconfig LCDd on
```

Alright, the server is up and running. Now what? How can you make it do something? This is one of the best features of lcdproc. You now have many choices for clients and where that client will run. You recall from the LCDd.conf file that you configured an IP address and this sets up LCDd to listen on the set IP and port. This allows you to run your LCD client from anywhere on the same subnet. You could run it on the Raspberry Pi or you could run it on another desktop. You can even sample data from the client running on the remote machine and send it to the Raspberry Pi's LCDd server to display.

Running a Client

For a quick test I will use the built-in client called lcdproc; you can find its configuration file at /etc/sysconfig/lcdproc/lcdproc.conf. This file has a similar style as the LCDd.conf file you configured before. This file is broken up into two main sections:

- One is called [lcdproc].

- The other sections are all called screens. A screen is what will appear on the physical LCD when you run the client; it may look like [cpu], for example.

You're going to need to set only one option to allow the lcdproc client to communicate with the LCDd server. In the [lcdproc] section, search for the option called server and change this to be the host where LCDd is running. In my case I set this IP address to be the IP of the Raspberry Pi. Do note that localhost won't work in this scenario as you have bound the LCDd server to a set IP address rather than localhost or the wildcard address.

Take a look at the screens section next. Each screen may or may not have configuration options; read though the comments to see what each option will do for each screen. There is one setting that is common across all screens and that setting is called Active. If the screen has the Active setting set to True, the LCDd server will display this screen on your LCD. If you set this value to Active=false, the screen will no longer be displayed on your LCD. Now that you have a basic lcdproc.conf file set up, it's a wise idea to test it. Ensure that LCDd is running; if it's not, lcdproc will throw an error about not being able to connect to the specified host. To test the lcdproc client, run the following command:

```
# lcdproc -f
```

This should give you no feedback if it's working correctly. Now take a look at your LCD; you can see the screens you defined in the lcdproc.conf file scrolling across the LCD. You can now start this as a service if you like. Or if you feel the default lcdproc client is a little limited, then take a look at a list of clients on http://lcdproc.org/clients.php3. If none of the clients are suitable, you may want to write your own.

▒ **Note** The LCDd server protocol accepts clear text messages; take a look at the development guide at http://lcdproc.sourceforge.net/docs/lcdproc-0-5-5-dev.html. This guide will show you how to write a client. It's not as hard as it sounds; like I said, the LCDd server speaks in clear text.

If you use Telnet with your Raspberry Pi on port 13666 you should get a connection. The server is now waiting for a command. Be nice and issue the hello command to your LCDd server. You can see in Figure 4-20 where I have said hello to my LCDd server and the server responds back with the version and the dimensions of the LCD.

```
brendan@pcb / $ telnet 192.168.0.199 13666
Trying 192.168.0.199...
Connected to 192.168.0.199.
Escape character is '^]'.
hello
connect LCDproc 0.5.3 protocol 0.3 lcd wid 18 hgt 2 cellwid 5 cellhgt 8
^]quit

telnet> quit
Connection closed.
brendan@pcb / $ █
```

Figure 4-20. *Saying hello to your new friend*

Displaying Text

It's quite simple to communicate with the LCDd server. I am now going to show you how to use Ruby to write a small script that will display text on your LCD. This script will communicate with the LCDd server and send it a simple text message. You can execute this script anywhere on the same subnet as the Raspberry Pi that is running the LCDd. It will stay connected until you terminate the script. Once you run it, check the syslog on the Raspberry Pi for connection messages that the new client generates. Take a look at the script in Listing 4-2; you can see my simple example to write a text string to the LCD.

Listing 4-2. A Simple LCDd Client in Ruby

```ruby
#!/usr/bin/ruby
# Description : A simple script to talk to the LCDd server
# Author : Brendan Horan

# Use the net telnet functions
require 'net/telnet'

# Trap ctrl-c nicely
trap("INT") { puts " Shutting down client."; exit}

# Create a new connection to the Pi
  pilcd = Net::Telnet::new(

    # Change this IP to your Pi's IP
    "Host" => "192.168.0.199",
    "Port" => 13666,

    # We are not a real telnet client
    "Telnetmode" => false,
```

```
      # Don't time out we don't care about responses
      "Timeout" => false)

# Send the hello command to start communicating
pilcd.puts("hello")

# Add a screen and set it to foreground
pilcd.puts("screen_add s1")
pilcd.puts("screen_set s1 -priority 1")

# Create two widgets for each row
pilcd.puts("widget_add s1 w1 title")
pilcd.puts("widget_add s1 w2 string")


# Write to each widget to each row of the LCD
pilcd.puts("widget_set s1 w1 {I2C LCD}")
pilcd.cmd("widget_set s1 w2 4 2 {MOAR Pi !}") { |c| print c }
```

Let me talk you through the parts of the code that interact with the LCDd server. The rest of the code is basic Ruby.

The code will start off with the hello command: this tells the server you want to talk to it. Then you need to add a screen; remember the screens in lcdproc? This is no different; it's just our very own screen that I have called s1. How exciting! As I only have one screen, I want it to always be displayed on the LCD; this is where the following line comes in:

```
screen_set s1 -priority 1
```

Without this line LCDd would scroll though all your defined screens. Now that you have an active screen it's time to define two widgets. A widget is a container for text and formatting that will end up on each line of the physical LCD when you run the client. The first widget is called w1 and is a title widget; this gives the nice square block effect you see in Figure 4-21. The second widget is called w2 and is just your everyday boring string type. So your widgets and screens are done: now what? Now you should set the widgets on the screen. I set w1 on s1 and then wrote the text "I2C LCD." As this is a title for the widget, you don't set the location on the screen as it will take up the whole top row (it's a title, remember?). The second widget, w2, is also set on s1 but this time you need to set the location. You start off with the X axis; ask for the first character to start on the fourth LCD block. Then set the Y axis as 2, which means the second row of the physical LCD. After that, you are just feeding it the string of "MOAR Pi!" In Figure 4-21 you can see the LCD working and printing the text we asked for.

Figure 4-21. *A fully functional LCD*

Simple enough: your grandmother could do it while making pie! Now run this script and you should see the following output as seen in Figure 4-22, if it works.

```
$ ./pi-client.rb
connect LCDproc 0.5.3 protocol 0.3 lcd wid 18 hgt 2 cellwid 5 cellhgt 8
success
success
success
success
success
success
listen s1
^C Shutting down client.
$
```

Figure 4-22. *Ruby client script output*

The output of the script may look a little odd so let me explain it. This is the first message you see:

```
connect LCDproc 0.5.3 protocol 0.3 lcd wid 18 hgt 2 cellwid 5 cellhgt 8
```

This is your client saying hello to the LCDd server. From then on you receive a "success" message for each command that executes on the LCDd server without error. If you do have a syntax error the LCDd server will print a line that starts with "huh?" Lastly you can see where I have hit Ctrl+C and terminated the application:

```
^C Shutting down client.
```

Summary

In this chapter you got to use the I2C bus, one of the many buses on the Raspberry Pi. I started off with the simple character LCD that you used throughout the chapter: the cheap and plentiful HD44780 or one of its many clones. I would expect you could find or scavenge one of these LCDs from anywhere; they turn up in a lot more places than you would think.

Up next was the I2C bus; this older bus is still widely used in today's technology. It's not the fastest bus in the world but you don't really need a PCI bus to drive a character LCD. You also found out that you can chain more than one device off the I2C bus, making it an even better value for the Raspberry Pi.

After that it was time to bust out the breadboard and dig into some chips. In this chapter you used the PCF8574AN shift register as the workhorse for converting the serial signal on the I2C bus to a parallel signal. Shift registers are pretty cool when you think about them. After this chapter you could in theory use most parallel devices on your Raspberry Pi, without the need to have a parallel port or to use up valuable GPIO pins.

Of course, what good is all this hardware if you don't have any software to use on it? In the last part of this chapter I showed you how to set up lcdproc and how to make use of the generic lcdproc client. Then I showed you how easy it can be to write your own lcdproc client by using a simple Ruby script. You can now use your LCD for anything you may think of. Or you may want to use it in Chapter 7 when you set up XBMC on your Raspberry Pi.

CHAPTER 5

■ ■ ■

Security Monitoring Device

The Raspberry Pi can be used for a lot of different projects, two of which you have seen so far. There was one application for the Raspberry Pi that I overlooked because I originally assumed it may be too complicated. This would be how handy the Raspberry Pi would be to use to make a small home security system. This idea was given to me by a close friend and the first thing I did was question him on the fact that I thought security systems were complex. However, the devices used inside the systems at a very basic level are quite simple. A good example of this is when I prompted my friend about pressure sensor pads and the lack of documentation I could find on them. He then explained to me that the pad is just two contact points that touch when pressure is applied; simply put, the pad is a normally open circuit. The idea of using the Raspberry Pi as a security monitoring device was then born.

I spent several hours thinking about how and what devices I could attach to the Raspberry Pi. In most common security systems you may have come across, you may have noticed that they use more than one type of sensor for monitoring. For example, a lot of motion sensors are a combination of a passive infrared sensor and an ultrasonic motion detector. After all you don't want a false alarm resulting from something like your window curtain gently moving.

The Raspberry Pi makes a wonderful little security device: you can place it anywhere in your home and it's easy to keep out of sight. If you have Model B you can also take advantage of the Ethernet port to send remote alerts when someone has tripped one of your alarms. You could also use the LCD screen (discussed in Chapter 4) to display alerts if a zone has been breached. Or you may want to trigger another GPIO on the Raspberry Pi to do something when a zone is breached. The fact that the Raspberry Pi is running Linux gives you so many opportunities for this project compared to Arduino or a similar microcontroller. After all it's quite simple to add an Internet connection to the Raspberry Pi so it can keep you up to date about the sensors. Or you may want to log how many people walk past your house every day. Whatever your reasons are to use the Raspberry Pi as a security device, it's a very good choice.

In this chapter I will explore two of the most common devices you may come across in a security system:

- A pressure mat

- A passive infrared sensor

These two devices are easy to use and indicate a breached zone very well. By using the pressure mat you will see how easy it is to use and it will also provide knowledge on how to use some other basic devices like tilt switches. I am sure you are all waiting on the edges of your seats to find out how to use these two devices.

First up, you need to understand how these devices work. Only then will you see how simple they are in fact to use. This also brings me to another point. Modern security systems have a lot of extra circuits and a lot of extra components to ensure that they cannot be altered or tampered with. For the sake of showing you how the basic devices can be interfaced I have left this side of the security devices alone. It would be very simple to tamper with the way I have configured the devices in this chapter so by no means is the Raspberry Pi a full replacement for your security system but it could make a good zone-watching device and would be perfect for all your home data center needs.

Introduction to the PIR

Let's take a look at the passive infrared sensor, or PIR for short. Let's get one thing straight first: PIRs do not detect motion. What do they detect then? To answer that I first need to talk about how they work. The first step to understanding how these sensors work is to understand that everything above zero kelvin or absolute zero emits some form of heat. This heat can be seen as infrared radiation. This radiation is commonly known as infrared light, and humans cannot see this light wavelength. Figure 5-1 shows a large spectrum of wavelengths that humans cannot see.

Figure 5-1. *Figure showing some available wavelengths*

Each segment in Figure 5-1 if broken down further would contain many types of wavelengths. The easiest way to think about this is with the visible wavelength. If you were to break this group down, each frequency between infrared and ultraviolet would be a color you can see with your eyes. The PIR is no different to humans in this regard; it can see only a certain range of frequencies. The range of frequencies that the PIR can see is infrared. The PIR is unable to see anything in the visible frequency range just as much as humans are unable to see anything in the infrared range.

That has still not answered exactly how the sensor detects motion. When active, the PIR will detect all the current heat sources in a given space by using a photosensitive receiver. These receivers are similar to the remote control for your TV. Within seven seconds of its initial powering on, the PIR will have built up a map of heat sources in your given area. What PIR you have governs what happens next; the PIR you have I would hope is of the digital type and not of the analog output type. The analog version will just send back a voltage difference and the Raspberry Pi has no analog inputs to sense this.

So then how will your digital PIR work? This is a two-step process that all happens inside the PIR itself.

1. The first step is to amplify the signal detected by the photoelectric sensor to a level that can be easily worked with by other semiconductors. This step happens in both the analog and digital versions of the PIR. In the analog version the signal is sent out of the sensor and on to another external device.

2. Because we're concerned with the digital version of the PIR, the signal is sent over to another small chip that lives inside the PIR. This little chip is from a family of circuits called a comparator. You would mostly find a comparator inside an analog-to-digital converter, just like your PIR. A comparator's sole job is to compare two voltages or currents and then switch an output to indicate which is larger. Figure 5-2 is a diagram of how a comparator will work.

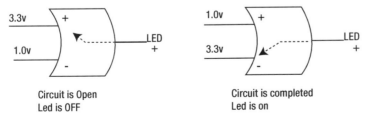

Figure 5-2. *A very basic comparator circuit*

As you can see, when the voltage on the negative side is higher the circuit is completed and the LED turns on; DC current flows from one side of the circuit to the other. When the voltage is higher on the positive side, the circuit is broken because current cannot flow from the positive side of the LED to the positive side of the comparator. This is our analog-to-digital converter, converting an analog signal into a digital on/off state.

Now that you know all the parts inside your PIR, I will tell you exactly how they all work together to give you a nice digital on/off signal. When your PIR has its map of temperature built up, the voltage across the photoelectric sensor will not change. As soon as the infrared heat profile of your area changes, this will generate a small charge inside the photoelectric sensor. This small charge is then amplified by the internal amplifier inside the PIR; this will then be handed off to the comparator. The comparator will detect there is a larger voltage and will switch on the output signal of the PIR or send the output high. Once the charge inside the PIR has gone away, the comparator sets the output back to low. This digital signal is what the Raspberry Pi can read via its GPIO pins. This signal will look something like what you see in Figure 5-3 to the Raspberry Pi.

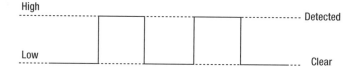

Figure 5-3. *The digital output of the PIR sensor*

As you can see, the PIR takes care of most of the hard work and gives you a nice clean digital output to work with and that's perfect for the Raspberry Pi.

Introducing the Pressure Mat

The next device, your common pressure sensing mat, is far simpler than the PIR but just as useful for detecting motion. I personally often thought of these devices as some form of high-tech equipment that would be hard to interface with. I was very wrong on this fact. If you were to vertically cut your pressure mat in half it would look something like Figure 5-4.

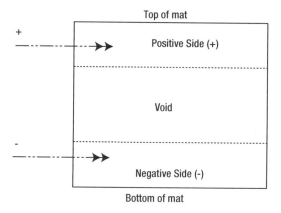

Figure 5-4. *A diagram of a common pressure mat*

Pressure mats are not polarity-sensitive, although I have used positive and negative indications in Figure 5-4 to help you understand how they work. A pressure mat is a type of circuit called normally open, or NO for short. This type of circuit is expected to be open and an alarm will be triggered when the circuit is closed. Looking at Figure 5-4, you can see three distinct parts of the pressure mat.

- On the top side of the mat you will see the positive contact.

- On the bottom of the mat you will see the negative contact.

Separating them is the section called void and this is simply just an air gap wide enough to stop the positive and negative sides from touching when there is no pressure. Because the pressure mat is made of porous material, when you step on it the air is expelled from the void and the positive and negative sides make contact. The circuit is now closed and the alarm will trigger. When you remove the pressure from the mat the sides separate again and the circuit is broken.

Some security mats also come with an additional two or more wires. These wires are often in place to act as a tamper loop, most often in a normally closed circuit. I won't use them in this chapter as I only want to demonstrate the use of the mat itself. Now I want to show you the full circuit schematic for the mat; you will soon see how simple it really is. In Figure 5-5 you can see the two loops. The pressure loop is the loop you will be interfacing with: as you can see it's a normally open circuit. It will work just like a big switch.

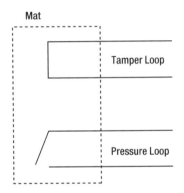

Figure 5-5. *A typical pressure mat circuit diagram*

Don't worry about the tamper loop: you won't be using it but you can see that it's a normally closed circuit. If you did want to use the tamper loop it would be the exact opposite circuit from the pressure loop. This type of tamper loop prevents someone from cutting the mat open and jamming the pressure loop into an open state. If you were to cut the mat, you would cut though the normally closed tamper loop circuit and the alarm would trigger.

Assembling the Devices

Now that you know more about the pressure mat and the PIR sensor, let's make them work. For this chapter you're going to need the following items:

- Pressure mat

- PIR sensor (I used a Panasonic AMN31111)

- 39K ohm resistor

- 100K ohm resistor

- 10K ohm resistor

- Some wire

As you can see you don't need many components for this chapter. First up I will show you how to use the pressure mat.

The Pressure Mat

The first thing you need to understand about the GPIO pins for this part of the project is that they don't have a known state to the operating system. You can drive it high or low, but you won't know the original voltage level. This is because the GPIO pins are in a floating state. Just like with the I2C bus you need to pull up the GPIO pin to give it a fixed value. This is where the 10K ohm resistor comes into the picture. I will use this resistor to pull up the GPIO pin to a known voltage of 3.3 V. The circuit I will use to interface with the pressure mat could be used on any number of switch-style inputs including mercury tilt switches and magnetic door sensors. It's now time to take a look at the circuit schematic. In Figure 5-6 you can see the circuit diagram and exactly how simple it is!

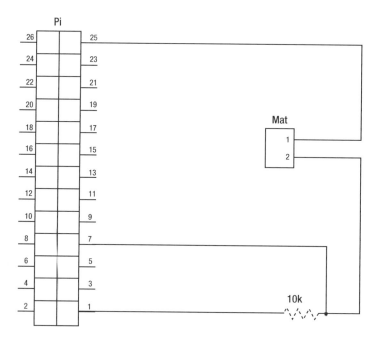

Figure 5-6. *The pressure mat circuit schematic*

Because this circuit is so simple I haven't included a breadboard image of the completed circuit. The first thing I did was solder an extension cable and some breadboard pin headers onto the pressure mat (I cut a hook-up wire in half for this job). You can see in Figure 5-7 the finished mat and the two unused tamper loop wires.

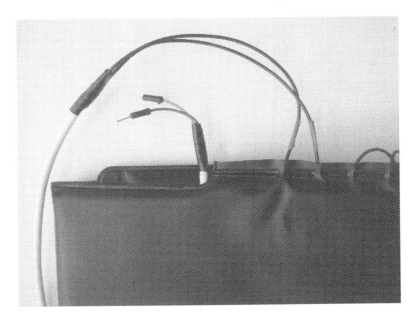

Figure 5-7. *The pressure mat is ready*

Now, you make the first and only set of connections. You can safely power the pressure mat from the Raspberry Pi; after all, it's just a big switch. Also, the pressure mat has no polarity so it's quite simple to work with.

1. First, connect any ground pin from the Raspberry Pi to your breadboard's ground rail on the side. I have selected GPIO pin P1-25 but you are free to use any of the ground pins.

2. Do the same for the 3.3-V rail by connecting GPIO pin P1-01 to your breadboard's positive power rail.

3. Take the two wires from the pressure mat and connect them to separate rows on the breadboard.

4. Take a jumper wire from the ground rail and connect it to one of the rows from the pressure mat. Halfway there!

5. Install the GPIO cable: place the hook-up wire directly in front of the other row from the pressure mat. Connect this GPIO cable to P1-07 (GPIO-04) on the Raspberry Pi.

6. Connect your 10K ohm resistor from the positive power rail so that it is in front of the GPIO cable. If you get this last part wrong, your mat won't work because you're not pulling up the GPIO pin voltage correctly.

Take a look at Figure 5-8 to see the finished breadboard.

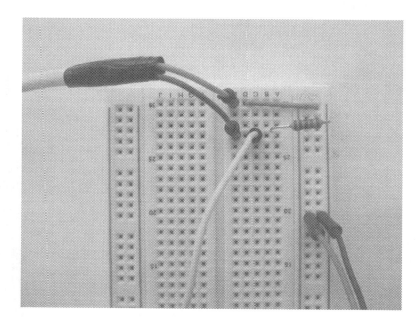

Figure 5-8. *The finished circuit on my breadboard*

That's it! Turn on your Raspberry Pi and wait for nothing to happen. After all, there is nothing for the Raspberry Pi to detect: the pressure mat is just a big switch.

Using the GPIO Pins

To use the GPIO pins with the pressure mat, you're going to need to log in to your Raspberry Pi as root. Where are the GPIO pins? I can't see them under /sys/class/gpio/ in Figure 5-9.

```
[root@hobo ~]# ls -la /sys/class/gpio/
total 0
drwxr-xr-x  2 root root    0 Jan  1 1970 .
drwxr-xr-x 29 root root    0 Jan  1 1970 ..
--w-------  1 root root 4096 Jan  1 1970 export
lrwxrwxrwx  1 root root    0 Jan  1 1970 gpiochip0 -> ../../devices/virtual/gpio/gpiochip0
--w-------  1 root root 4096 Jan  1 1970 unexport
[root@hobo ~]# 
```

Figure 5-9. *Where are my GPIO pins?*

By default the GPIO support that is built into the kernel will not export any GPIO pins to the operating system. After all there is no way for Linux to know what you have connected to each pin. So you are going to need to export your GPIO pin before you can work on it. This is simple: first, you need the number of the GPIO pin (not the physical pin number but the logical GPIO number); in your case this will be GPIO-04. In Figure 5-9 you can see two special writable files called export and unexport. You're going to need to use the export device. The syntax for this special device is just to echo the pin number into it. You will need to run this command to export GPIO-04:

```
# echo 4 > /sys/class/gpio/export
```

Now take a look at /sys/class/gpio again. You should now see a directory called gpio4. This directory is how you will control the GPIO pin. Take a look at Figure 5-10 and you can see the contents of my GPIO-04 directory.

```
[root@hobo ~]# ls -la /sys/class/gpio/gpio4/
total 0
drwxr-xr-x 3 root root    0 Dec  4 14:38 .
drwxr-xr-x 4 root root    0 Jan  1  1970 ..
-rw-r--r-- 1 root root 4096 Dec  4 14:43 active_low
-rw-r--r-- 1 root root 4096 Dec  4 14:43 direction
-rw-r--r-- 1 root root 4096 Dec  4 14:43 edge
drwxr-xr-x 2 root root    0 Dec  4 14:43 power
lrwxrwxrwx 1 root root    0 Dec  4 14:38 subsystem -> ../../../../class/gpio
-rw-r--r-- 1 root root 4096 Dec  4 14:38 uevent
-rw-r--r-- 1 root root 4096 Dec  4 14:43 value
[root@hobo ~]#
```

Figure 5-10. *The contents of my GPIO-04 directory*

You can now work on doing something with your GPIO pin. This directory contains the real business end of the GPIO subsystem. I what to give you a quick overview of each of the main special files in this directory and what value types they may accept. Table 5-1 contains the descriptions of some of the most useful special files.

Table 5-1. *A listing of the most useful special files*

Name	Accepted Value	Description/Use
Direction	In (Input), out (Output)	Sets the GPIO pin as input or output
Value	0 (low), 1 (high)	Sets the initial pin state high or low and reads the current state
Edge	none, rising, falling	Sets the signal edge type
Active_low	0 (false), 1 (true)	Indicates whether the pin is active when driven low

Given that you need to sense the GPIO pin's state, you're going to need to set it up as an input. From Table 5-1 you can easily see that you need to use the direction special file. To set the direction, run this command:

```
# echo in > /sys/class/gpio/gpio4/direction
```

Once you have done that, you can read the state of the GPIO pin. Once again by looking at Table 5-1 you can see that you may want to take a look at the value special file. You can do this if you run the following command:

```
# cat /sys/class/gpio/gpio4/value
```

Now if all has gone well this should echo "1" to the terminal. Why 1? Take a look at Table 5-1 again and remember that if the GPIO pin is high its value will be 1. The GPIO pin is high because you have the pull-up resistor pulling the pin up to a high state. Now when you step on your pressure mat you complete the circuit and the GPIO pin is brought into a low state or "0". Take a look at Figure 5-11. In the first reading of the value file you can see it is outputting 1 because you are not standing on the mat. Then stand on the mat and re-read the value file: now you can see it's outputting 0.

```
[root@hobo ~]# cat /sys/class/gpio/gpio4/value
1
[root@hobo ~]# cat /sys/class/gpio/gpio4/value
0
[root@hobo ~]#
```

Figure 5-11. *The pressure mat in operation*

A Script for Your Mat Status

Now that you know your pressure mat is working correctly and your Raspberry Pi can read its value correctly, it might be a good idea to write a simple script to poll the GPIO pin to warn you if someone steps on the mat. Take a look at Listing 5-1 to see a simple bash script that I wrote to poll the GPIO and print a message to your terminal if someone steps on the mat.

Listing 5-1. A Simple Bash Script to Poll the Mat

```bash
#!/bin/bash
# Description : A simple bash script to read the pressure mat status
# Author : Brendan Horan

# Start a loop that can't end
while true; do

# Get the value of the GPIO Pin
MATSTAT='cat /sys/class/gpio/gpio4/value'

if [ $MATSTAT == 1 ]
then
# Sleep for 2 seconds if status=1
sleep 2
else
# Echo out text if status=0
echo "Ouch! Don't step on me!!"
fi

done
```

To use this simple script, create a file in /usr/local/bin and call it mat.sh. Then put the contents of Listing 5-1 into the file and ensure that it's set to be executable. Run the mat.sh script and step on the mat. You will now see your console fill up with lines printing "Ouch! Don't step on me!!"

This exact same circuit and code could be used on devices like tilt switches and magnetic door switches too. Now that you have the pressure sensor set up, it's a good idea to use another method to detect if your area has been breached. This is where the PIR will do its job.

Connecting the PIR

I will now show you how to connect and use the PIR. I'm sure you will notice a lot of similarities with the pressure mat.

▓ **Caution**   You may have noticed that your PIR came well wrapped and even stuck into some antistatic foam (well, I hope it did anyways). Unlike other sensors throughout this book, the PIR is quite sensitive to static. As you may know by now humans are very good at retaining a high amount of static electricity so be careful.

There is not a lot to the PIR circuit; in fact it's just two resistors. For this project I recommend that you either solder a length of wire to the PIR or mount it on a secondary breadboard because to test the PIR you're going to need to do two things at once:

- Being in front of it

- Typing on your keyboard

This leads to the PIR always detecting you and as such you also need a good way to hide the PIR from yourself. With that in mind let me show you the electronic schematic for the PIR. In Figure 5-12 you can see how simple the circuit really is. Maybe this should have been the first chapter: it's that simple!

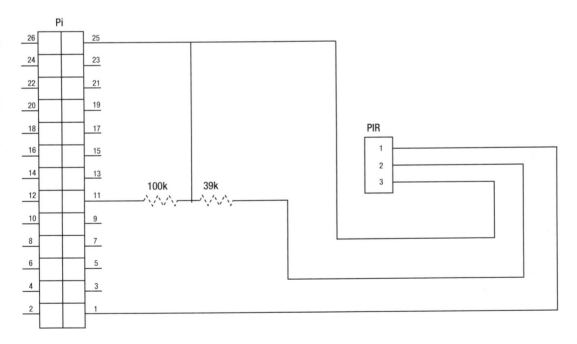

Figure 5-12. *The PIR schematic*

Now I have taken the approach to use two breadboards to build the sensor for testing purposes; obviously you would need a length of wire attached to the PIR when you build this for real.

1. The resistor placement for this sensor is quite critical: if you get it wrong, your sensor just won't work although you are unlikely to damage it: Install a 100K ohm resistor between ground and one row of the breadboard. It's a good idea to place this on a slight angle as you will need to access the holes on each side of the row.

2. Next install the 39K ohm resistor on the inner side of the breadboard and place the other leg of the resistor into a brand-new row.

3. Connect the out pin of the PIR sensor to the same new row into which you placed the other leg of the 39K ohm resistor.

4. Now connect the Raspberry Pi's P1-11 GPIO to the power rail side of the 100K ohm resistor. Take a look at Figure 5-13 for a close-up image of the resistor and GPIO pin connections.

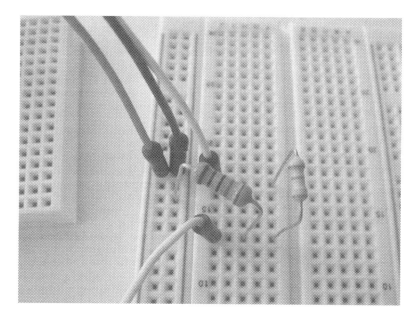

Figure 5-13. *A close-up of the resistor placement*

5. Once that is done, connect your power rail to the Raspberry Pi's P1-01 3.3-V power and connect the ground rail to the Raspberry Pi's P1-25 ground connector.

6. Then place the PIR sensor on a small breadboard and extend the GPIO wire and the two power rails to the PIR. Make sure you get the pins correct on the PIR. Check your data sheet for how you should connect your sensor. In the case of the Panasonic AMN31111 you can see the pin outs in Figure 5-14.

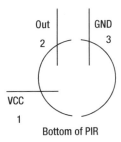

Figure 5-14. *The pin outs of the AMN31111*

Whether or not you are using the AMN31111 make sure you check your data sheet: you may find something interesting. Once the finial connections have been made, your breadboards should look like Figure 5-15.

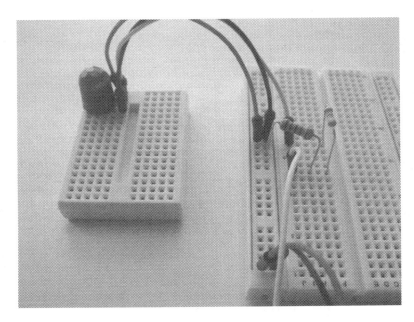

Figure 5-15. *Finished breadboards*

Next up, you would need to access the sensor from the Raspberry Pi. This is achieved in a very similar way to the pressure mat. First, export the GPIO pin that is working with P1-11 (GPIO-17):

```
# echo 17 > /sys/class/gpio/export
```

Next, set the type of the GPIO pin with this code:

```
# echo in > /sys/class/gpio/gpio17/direction
```

Now if you cat the value file you should see "1," meaning that the sensor has detected someone. If you're seeing "0," wave your hand in front of the sensor; if that fails you have an error somewhere.

Now you're back to what to do with the output of this `value` special file. You can't sit there all day and `cat` the file. You could modify the code in Listing 5-1. If you wanted to, you could edit the following line:

```
MATSTAT='cat /sys/class/gpio/gpio4/value'
```

Replace `gpio4` with `gpio17`. Of course, this brings up another issue now that you have two sensors on your Raspberry Pi: you would need to use SSH with the Raspberry Pi twice to see what's going on, and this is not exactly a good idea. I am going to show you how to write a simple web server in Ruby to solve this problem.

Bring Forth the WEBrick

Why Ruby? That's an easy question to answer. For a start it's already on the Fedora remix. Second, I like Ruby: it's simple and powerful. I am not a fan of Perl so please don't ask.

Just to be safe, check that Ruby works with this simple command:

```
# ruby -v
```

This should output the version of Ruby running on your system. Where is the web server? I won't be using any type of big web server like Apache or Nginx. It's not because they are bad or would not do what you need; it's more that they are both very heavy if you are just reading two system files. This is another feature of Ruby I have come to like: the ability to create a simple web server anywhere.

Welcome WEBrick

I am not sure where the name WEBrick comes from and I have a bad habit of reading the name as "web brick", mostly because under a high load the server responds about as well as a brick. WEBrick was not designed for heavy loads or big amounts of data: it's a simple HTTP and HTTPS server built inside of Ruby. The best part about WEBrick is how easy it is to use with a few lines of code; you can serve up a directory or just a simple HTML page. It's quite powerful for small applications or admin pages for your personal applications, but don't go and run a big commercial site on it. When it comes to system resources, it's quite light as long as what you are serving up is also quite light. This makes it perfect for serving up an HTML page to display the status of the GPIO ports. With around six lines of Ruby code you could have a fully functional web server. Let's use WEBrick now.

Split your very basic application into two files:

- The first one is called `security-server.rb` (see Listing 5-2). This script is the one you will run. It has two main functions: the first and most important function is to create the WEBrick instance with the given options inside the file.

- The second function is to launch and clean up the helper script called `reader-loop.rb`.

The `reader-loop.rb` script is where the real work happens (see Listing 5-3). This script will read the gpio4 and gpio17 value files every second and generate an HTML file called `index.htm`. This HTML file is what WEBrick serves up. I have included an HTML element that will refresh the page automatically every one second as well. This allows you to leave the page on a monitoring screen and watch to see who has breached your sensors. When you start the script for the first time it will create an `index.html` file and an `access.log` so you can keep track of who has accessed your site.

There are three small notes about setting up this simple application. It must be run as root in order to access the GPIO pins. It expects the two Ruby scripts to be in the same directory. You must have already exported your GPIO pins and set their mode. Take a look at Figure 5-16 to see how I have installed the scripts. You may have noticed they are under /root/; because they must be run as root and it's a demo application I can't see any issue with this.

```
[root@hobo security-page]# ls -la /root/security-page/
total 16
drwxr-xr-x   2 root root 4096 Dec  5 14:53 .
dr-xr-x---. 14 root root 4096 Dec  5 14:49 ..
-rwxr-xr-x   1 root root  950 Dec  5 14:40 reader-loop.rb
-rwxr-xr-x   1 root root  903 Dec  5 14:42 security-server.rb
[root@hobo security-page]#
```

Figure 5-16. *The directory layout of the security server*

The Security Application Code

Listing 5-2 displays the security-server.rb code.

Listing 5-2. The Main security-server.rb Code

```ruby
#!/usr/bin/ruby
# Description : Ruby webrick html server and reader loop
#   this app will run out of one directory self contained
#   ensure security-server.rb and reader-loop.rb are in the same dir
# Author : Brendan Horan

# Include
require 'webrick'
include WEBrick

# Set up the webrick
  dir = Dir::pwd
  port = "80"
  access_log_stream = File.open('access.log', 'w')
  access_log = [ [ access_log_stream, AccessLog::COMBINED_LOG_FORMAT ] ]

  puts "Access at :-"
  puts "URL: http://#{Socket.gethostname}:#{port}"

# Start the background reader loop
  puts "Starting Reader Loop on pid :-"
  pipe = IO.popen("./reader-loop.rb")
  puts pipe.pid

server = HTTPServer.new(
  :Port            => port,
  :DocumentRoot    => dir,
  :AccessLog       => access_log
)

# trap exit safely and start the webrick
  trap("INT"){ server.shutdown }
  puts "Running.. Hit Ctrl+c to stop."
  server.start
```

As you can see from the code you will be running an HTTP server on port 80 and binding on all addresses. You may have also noticed this line:

```
access_log = [ [ access_log_stream, AccessLog::COMBINED_LOG_FORMAT ] ]
```

This line sets up the access log to the exact same format of the Apache server access logs. This is very handy for any Apache log parsing scripts you may already have; WEBrick will just seem like another Apache server log. You also will notice that everything, including the log files, will be contained in one directory. This is not a really good practice but it's okay for this code demonstration. A very important line is the following:

```
pipe = IO.popen("./reader-loop.rb")
```

This line will spawn the reader-loop.rb script and the best part of using the popen function is that when the security-server.rb script is terminated it will also terminate the spawned child script.

Listing 5-3. The reader-loop.rb Code

```ruby
#!/usr/bin/ruby
# Description : Ruby webrick html server and reader loop
#  this app will run out of one directory self contained
# Author : Brendan Horan

# Start a loop that should not end
  while true do

# Open index.html for writing and the two value files for reading
  index = File.new("index.html", "w+")
  mat = File.open("/sys/class/gpio/gpio4/value")
  pir = File.open("/sys/class/gpio/gpio17/value")

# Set the html page to auto refresh every second
  index.puts "<HTML><HEAD> <meta http-equiv='refresh' content='1'></HEAD>"

# get the status of the pressure mat
  while line = mat.gets do
    index.puts "<p>Mat status :-</p>"
    index.puts line
  end
  mat.close

# get the status of the PIR
  while line = pir.gets do
    index.puts "<p>PIR status :-</p>"
    index.puts line
  end
  pir.close

# Close index.html and sleep to allow security-server.rb to read
  index.close
  sleep 2
  end
```

In this script you can see first that I created an endless loop that will keep running as long as the parent security-server.rb is running. You can then see that I created the index.html file and opened the two special value files for reading. I then have two loops that read from the special file and output to index.html. After this I closed off all the files and have the system sleep for two seconds to allow the parent script to read the index.html file and refresh the web page.

Running the Security Application

Now it's time to run it: how exciting! Ensure that security-server.rb and reader-loop.rb have their execute bit set and then launch the application from the directory you created like this:

```
# ./security-server.rb
```

You then should see output similar to Figure 5-17.

```
[root@hobo security-page]# ./security-server.rb
Acess at :-
URL: http://hobo:80
Starting Reader Loop on pid :-
2872
[2012-12-05 14:57:44] INFO  WEBrick 1.3.1
[2012-12-05 14:57:44] INFO  ruby 1.8.7 (2011-06-30) [arm-linux]
[2012-12-05 14:57:44] WARN  TCPServer Error: Address already in use - bind(2)
Running.. Hit Ctrl+c to stop.
[2012-12-05 14:57:44] INFO  WEBrick::HTTPServer#start: pid=2871 port=80
```

Figure 5-17. *Starting the security-server.rb application*

You now will also see two files in your directory: index.html and access.log. Go to your Raspberry Pi's IP address and you should see something like Figure 5-18.

Mat status :-

1

PIR status :-

0

Figure 5-18. *The view from a web browser*

You can see from Figure 5-18 that I am warm and moving because the PIR has a status of "0" and the pressure mat has a status of "1"; the mat has a status of "1" because I am currently sitting down and not standing on the mat. If you were to check back on WEBrick you may notice it was giving you an error that looks like this:

```
[2012-12-05 15:11:34] ERROR '/favicon.ico' not found
```

That is because your web browser expects to find a little file called favicon.ico for every web site you go to. The quick and dirty fix for this is to run the following command in the same directory that the Ruby scripts are in:

```
# touch  favicon.ico
```

You can now also see that your access.log file has entries in it now. When you are done with the WEBrick server, just hit Ctrl+C; I have trapped this exit code so that my scripts will clean themselves up nicely when you hit Ctrl+C. Congratulations! You now have a very simple security system.

Summary

In this chapter you gained an understanding of how simple a pressure mat is and that it is not some mystical security device. Next up you learned about the PIR and that it's an infrared heat-wave sensor and not a motion sensor. After the basics of the two devices in question, I gave you the methods to connect them to the Raspberry Pi; in turn you also gained the knowledge of how to use other similar devices like tilt switches and magnetic door switches.

This was also the first time you manipulated the Raspberry Pi's GPIO pins at the command line. There are a lot of other tools and scripts that can do this as well. You could use Python or the WiringPi tools; the latter can be found at https://projects.drogon.net/raspberry-pi/wiringpi/.

You then wrote a small and simple (but effective) shell script to detect movement on the pressure mat. After connecting the PIR you faced the issue of how to monitor more than one device on the Raspberry Pi: reading the output of a special file would no longer cut it. Ruby once again saves the day with WEBrick. In this last section you created an HTTP web server inside Ruby that polled the special GPIO value files and displayed the output on a very simple web page.

■ ■ ■

## CHAPTER 6

Cross Compile Environment

Unfortunately this chapter will not contain any electronics work, and it will not really contain much work on your Raspberry Pi. In fact you will spend most of this chapter on a host machine and most likely it will be an x86 system. Most systems available today are using an x86 processor type. This is an evolution from the original Intel 8086, and all consumer-grade CPUs from Intel and AMD use the x86 architecture. On that note I also hope your host system has a lot more power than your Raspberry Pi. I don't want you using that spare Celeron 733-MHz system you may have hidden in the cupboard. At this point I hope you're a little bit confused as to why I am talking about everything but the Raspberry Pi. There is a good reason for this. This chapter is going to need a lot of resources on what will be referred to as your host system.

This chapter is written for a host system that runs Linux, and any Linux distribution is fine. It may be possible to do this under Cygwin in Windows but I have not tried nor will be trying that. So what has this host system got to do with a Raspberry Pi? To better answer that, you need to think about how any distribution for the Raspberry Pi is put together. Recall in Chapter 2 that you used a tool to install Fedora: where did that tarball come from? Did someone sit down one day and compile a whole distribution on a Raspberry Pi? Given the Raspberry Pi's limited resources, I would assume not. I know firsthand how much goes into compiling your own Linux distribution. Armed with this knowledge I can assume that someone cross compiled the Fedora remix on a more powerful machine, rather than doing it by hand slowly on the Raspberry Pi. If you're interested, take a look at the Linux From Scratch project at http://linuxfromscratch.org. This will give you an idea about how to compile your own distribution. It will not only teach you a lot about Linux but also show you why someone did not do this style of work on the Raspberry Pi.

In this chapter you won't be building a whole distribution so don't feel too worried! By the end of this chapter you will have set up a basic cross compile environment that is capable of building binary applications for your Raspberry Pi. You will do this without even using a single CPU cycle on the Raspberry Pi. How amazing is that? You will be using your desktop machine to build an application that can be run on your Raspberry Pi, in anticipation of Chapter 7 where you will need to do just that.

Introducing Cross Compiling

So how did you end up with a Linux distribution for your Raspberry Pi? This is where your host machine comes back in with a concept called cross compiling. Cross compiling is where you compile an application for a different machine type than your host system. In this chapter the host will be a 64-bit x86 machine and the target machine will be your little Raspberry Pi, a 32-bit ARM machine.

▓ **Note** When I use the term "machine type," I'm talking about the type of CPU the machine uses. For example, your desktop machine type is an x86 whereas the Raspberry Pi's machine type is ARM. It's just a simple way to know which type of CPU the machine has. The terms "32-bit" and "64-bit" refer to the width of the instruction that the machine type can process. The Raspberry Pi and some older desktops are 32-bit machines and newer CPUs from AMD and Intel are each 64 bits. For the cross compile it really won't matter if your desktop machine is 32 bit or 64 bit as you will be compiling for the Raspberry Pi.

Cross compiling has a few uses and the main one is to compile an application for an embedded or a very resource-limited machine. A secondary use is for a process called bootstrapping, where you compile an application for a new machine type that doesn't have tools to compile its own applications yet (in other words, you'll have to compile the compiler). There are also two methods of cross compiling:

- The first one and the most widely used method is where you have one host architecture and one target architecture. This is the type of cross compile you will be performing.

- The second type of cross compiling is called Canadian Cross. The Canadian Cross will always involve a minimum of three systems, as you can see in Figure 6-1.

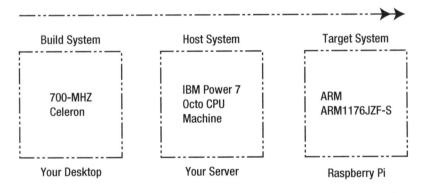

Figure 6-1. *An example of a Canadian Cross build environment*

The build system will build a cross compile environment for the second machine called the host system. The host system will then use this cross compile environment to cross compile an application for the third machine known as the target. The target would be where you expect the final application to run. The only machine that will be able to run the final binary would be the target. Setting up a Canadian Cross environment is not needed for this chapter nor will it bring you any advantage. A Canadian cross compile environment would be of value when your build host and your target are very slow machines. For example you have a 700-MHz Celeron as a desktop and you wish to compile for the Raspberry Pi. You could use a powerful middle machine to build the binaries for the target machine. Given that most current desktops are at least five times faster than the Raspberry Pi there is not much gain in this method for you.

This chapter will cover the methods and tools that you need to set up a generic cross compiling environment. Many Linux distributions have their own methods of cross compiling. This is especially true for Gentoo, given the wide range of machine architecture types it supports. I will avoid doing anything distribution-specific. This should allow you to create the cross compile environment on any Linux machine you may have.

Cross compiling may be a new concept for you. This may be your first non-x86 machine. That's very exciting! Personally I have over six different architectures of machines in my house and they all run Linux. So I am more than used to cross compiling. Not that it makes it any easier: there are always new and interesting errors to be found. Lucky for you I will be using the most common architecture in my collection: the x86. Let's talk about that next.

The Host

You're going to need a Linux machine. This can be a physical machine or a virtual machine. You may be able to apply the instructions in this chapter to the OSX as it is based on the Berkeley Software Distribution, and getting a working copy of the GNU Compiler Collection (GCC) should not be a hard task. You may be able to get this to work under Cygwin but I do not have the knowledge of Windows to do this. My home contains no Windows or OSX machines so I will be using Linux. You should also use a reasonably fast machine. Some applications such as LibreOffice and GCC itself are very memory- and processor-intensive to compile; they also require a large amount of temporary disk space. GCC will require well over 5 GB of disk just to compile. You're also going to find out very quickly that cross compiling an application is not a simple process: it will fail and you may need to start the build from scratch. Do you really want to do that on a low-powered machine?

To build a cross compiling environment you're going to need some basic tools. The most important tool you're going to need is GCC. If you're using Gentoo, then you already have a working installation of GCC. More than likely you are not using Gentoo but one of the more common distributions like Fedora or Ubuntu. These distributions by default do not come with GCC installed. You're going to need to use your distributions package manager to install GCC. To install GCC in Fedora use this command:

```
# yum groupinstall "Development Tools"
```

For Ubuntu you can use this command:

```
# apt-get install build-essential
```

Now you should have a working GCC version. It's a wise idea to test GCC to confirm it's alive and working. First, check that you can execute GCC. A simple test is to run the `gcc -v` command. This command will list the version and build information about GCC. In Figure 6-2 you can see the output of this command on my machine.

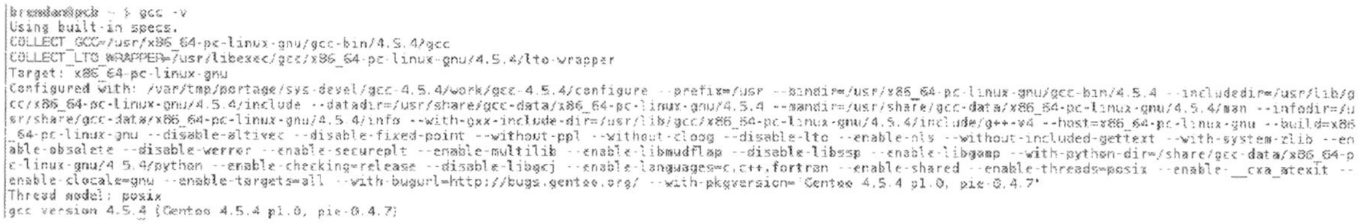

Figure 6-2. *The output of the gcc -v command*

It is very important that this command execute successfully. If you try and do any part of this chapter without a working GCC you're never going to get anywhere. Moving on from GCC, you're going to make use of an open source project called crosstool-NG.

Crosstool-NG

The crosstool-NG project aims to provide a stable, easy-to-build tool chain. A tool chain is a set of tools, including GCC, that allows you to build an application for a different architecture than the one you are building on. As part of crosstool-NG it will take care of downloading and configuring parts of the tool chain for your selected architecture. The tool chain will include the `binutils` tool and some C libraries that are specific to your target architecture. Crosstool-NG also has a very nice ncurses menu system that will easily allow you to build a tool chain.

With that in mind, it's time to download and configure this tool. Open up your browser and go to `http://crosstool-ng.org/download/crosstool-ng/`. It's best to sort the file listing by the "Last Modified" field because you want the latest package. You will see a file at the top of this directory that indicates the current version: in my case, that is 1.16.0. You can see in Figure 6-3 the latest version at the time of writing and the download file named crosstool-ng-1.16.0.tar.bz2. I use wget to download files as I spend a lot of time at the command line. I have used the following command to download the file:

```
# wget http://crosstool-ng.org/download/crosstool-ng/crosstool-ng-1.16.0.tar.bz2
```

Index of /download/crosstool-ng/

Name	Last Modified	Size	Type
Parent Directory/			Directory
01-fixes/	2012-Aug-04 22:08:03	--	Directory
00-LATEST-is-1.16.0	2012-Sep-04 11:09:58	0.00B	0 File
crosstool-ng-1.16.0.tar.bz2	2012-Aug-04 22:08:59	1.87MB	BZ2 File
crosstool-ng-1.16.0.tar.bz2.md5	2012-Aug-04 22:08:00	62.00B	MD5 File
crosstool-ng-1.16.0.tar.bz2.sha1	2012-Aug-04 22:08:00	70.00B	SHA1 File
crosstool-ng-1.16.0.tar.bz2.sha512	2012-Aug-04 22:08:00	158.00B	SHA512 File

Figure 6-3. *The crosstool-NG download site*

Download the file to a clean directory. The next steps will configure and build the tool. Extract the tarball with this command:

```
# tar -xvf crosstool-ng-1.16.0.tar.bz2
```

Now that you have extracted the tarball, put it into the crosstool-NG directory.

■ **Note** Crosstool-NG by default will install into /usr/local/. You may want to change that, depending on your preference. I already have a version of crosstool-NG in /usr/local/bin/ so I will change the install path to /usr/local/crosstool/. This will keep the install a little neater and make exporting crosstool-NG's path easier for me. If you don't have anything installed in /usr/local/ then by all means leave the install path as the default.

In Figure 6-4 you can see my extracted crosstool-NG directory that is ready to be built.

```
drwxr-xr-x 4 brendan brendan  4096 Nov  2 09:45 .
drwxr-xr-x 4 brendan brendan  4096 Nov  1 11:39 ..
drwxr-xr-x 6 brendan brendan  4096 Nov  2 09:45 .build
-rw-r--r-- 1 brendan brendan 54174 Nov  2 09:49 build.log
lrwxrwxrwx 1 brendan brendan    44 Nov  1 11:42 config -> /usr/local/crosstool/lib/ct-ng.1.16.0/config
-rw-r--r-- 1 brendan brendan 10718 Nov  2 09:36 .config
-rw-r--r-- 1 brendan brendan 10728 Nov  2 09:45 .config.2
drwxr-xr-x 2 brendan brendan  4096 Nov  1 11:42 config.gen
-rw-r--r-- 1 brendan brendan 10707 Nov  2 09:24 .config.old
```

Figure 6-4. *The crosstool-NG directory extracted*

The next step is to run the configure script. This is where I will tell the crosstool-NG build where crosstool-NG will end up being installed on the system. If you don't need to set the install directory, then just run the configure command by itself:

```
#./configure
```

The ./configure command will configure all defaults and install into /usr/local. If you wanted to install into a different path, say, for example, /usr/local/crosstool, you can use the –prefix option to tell the configure tool to install into /usr/local/crosstool. The full command would be this:

```
#./configure –prefix=/usr/local/crosstool
```

Just ensure that the directory exists before you run the configure script because the configure tool will not create it for you.

This process must exit cleanly; if there are any errors, fix them before you make the build. If you do get missing build components, ensure that you have installed the install build-essential group for Ubuntu or, under the Fedora install, the "Development Tools" group; of course, if you are a Gentoo user all the tools will already be present. In Figure 6-5 you can see the command I used and the end result of a successful configure. There is a lot of output in between but I have removed it as long as the exit status is clean.

```
brendan@pcb $ ./configure --prefix=/usr/local/crosstool/
checking build system type... x86_64-unknown-linux-gnu
checking host system type... x86_64-unknown-linux-gnu
checking for library containing initscr... -lncursesw
configure: creating ./config.status
config.status: creating Makefile
brendan@pcb $ echo $?
0
brendan@pcb $
```

Figure 6-5. *Running the configure script*

Why am I echoing $?? Exactly what is the $?? The $? is the numeric exit code of the previously run command on the bash shell. Once the configure stage has run, I echoed the exit code of the configure state to the running terminal. As you can see it has an exit code of zero, so all is well: anything above zero would indicate a problem.

Once you have successfully generated the make file with the configure tool, it's time to build and install crosstool-NG. The next step is to run the make command. make will read the make file generated by the configure script and will build the install. You can run make as a regular user. make should also exit with no errors. The make process should be pretty quick. Once it's done, the next step is to install crosstool-NG. This is what the make install command will do. You need to have root privileges for this step. If you're on Ubuntu or Fedora you may need to use the sudo tool to run make install. Because I am using Gentoo I will become the root user and run the make install command:

```
# make
```

Once this has finished, run the following command:

```
# make install
```

In Figure 6-6 you can see that my install of the crosstool-NG was a success.

```
    crosstool-ng-1.16.0 # make install
  GEN     'config/configure.in'
  GEN     'paths.mk'
  GEN     'paths.sh'
  MKDIR   '/usr/local/crosstool/bin/'
  INST    'ct-ng'
  RMDIR   '/usr/local/crosstool/lib/ct-ng.1.16.0/'
  MKDIR   '/usr/local/crosstool/lib/ct-ng.1.16.0/'
  INSTDIR 'config/'
  INSTDIR 'contrib/'
  INSTDIR 'patches/'
  INSTDIR 'scripts/'
  INST    'steps.mk'
  INST    'paths'
  INSTDIR 'samples/'
  INST    'kconfig/'
  MKDIR   '/usr/local/crosstool/share/doc/crosstool-ng/ct-ng.1.16.0/'
  INST    'docs/*.txt'
  MKDIR   '/usr/local/crosstool/share/man/man1/'
  INST    'ct-ng.1.gz'

For auto-completion, do not forget to install 'ct-ng.comp' into
your bash completion directory (usually /etc/bash_completion.d)
    crosstool-ng-1.16.0 # ▮
```

Figure 6-6. *A successful install*

You only need root privileges to run the make install command; crosstool-NG has no requirement to be run as root. It's always wise in Linux and Unix to use the fewest number of privileges so please don't build as root unless your package needs it. Now that you have the tool installed, you need to set up your environment to run crosstool-NG. Depending on how you configured crosstool-NG and depending on your system's path settings, you may need to add the crosstool-NG bin path to your path variable. I have installed crosstool-NG into /usr/local/crosstool, so I will need to append its bin path to my own path. Because I won't be running crosstool-NG every day, I just do the export command each time I want to run the tool. The path option is a similar concept to the library path I showed you in Chapter 2.

```
# export PATH="${PATH}:/usr/local/crosstool/bin"
```

The next step you must do before running the crosstool-NG application is to create a working directory for your project. This directory can be anything you like. I would suggest it be inside your home directory and it's best to be a new clean directory. For example, I created the working directory of /home/brendan/ct/rpi/.

Once you have created your working directory, change into it and try and run the crosstool-NG binary called ct-ng. If you have done everything correctly, you will receive the crosstool-NG help page. Please read the help page; help pages are the data sheets of the application world and you know how much I like data sheets. You should notice after you have read the help page that the command that you need is ct-ng menuconfig. Run this command and you should be presented with a nice ncurses screen as you see in Figure 6-7. If you get an error that contains "Unable to find the ncurses libraries," then you need to install the ncurses libraries. In Fedora you will need to install the ncurses package and the ncurses-devel package. If you are using Ubuntu the ncurses-devel package is simply called ncurses-dev. If you're using Gentoo you won't need to do a thing!

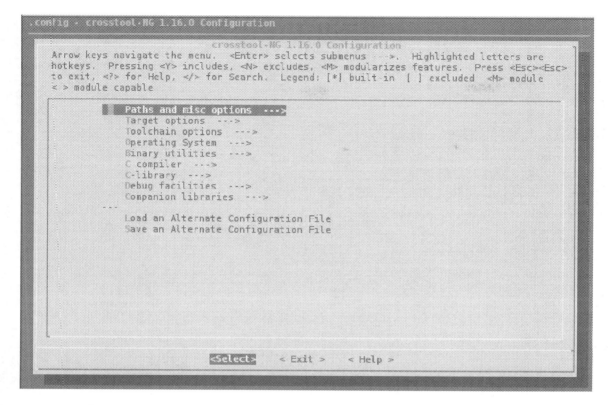

Figure 6-7. The crosstool-NG running

This is a nice-looking tool but what do you do with it? I shall show you how to configure the crosstool-NG tool in the next section. In case you're not familiar with ncurses, here is a quick rundown on how to use it.

- First, use the arrow keys on your keyboard to navigate up, down, and left or right.

- Use Enter to select a menu item and the spacebar to toggle between options.

- You will notice three buttons at the bottom of the screen: Select, Exit, and Help. You can select each one of these by using the Tab key or you may have noticed that a letter in each word is red. The red letter indicates that it is a hotkey. Pressing "H" when you have selected an item will bring you to the help screen.

Configuring crosstool-NG

There are a lot of menus and options in crosstool-NG. A lot of them you won't need to worry about, so don't feel too intimidated by the sheer number of options.

Paths and Misc Options

The first menu item, "Paths and Misc Options," and its suboptions mainly look after the way the crosstool-NG works and how to control its behavior. You should not need to change anything in this section. Feel free to take a look in this section but it's not wise to change any of the options unless you have a good reason to do so.

Target Options

The next section is called "Target Options." This section is much more relevant. If you recall early on in this chapter I talked about the target being the Raspberry Pi. This section contains the options that are applied to the application that will end up running on the target. Select the menu and I will discuss the suboptions that you need to use (you can see in Figure 6-8 all the options I have selected for the "Target Options" screen).

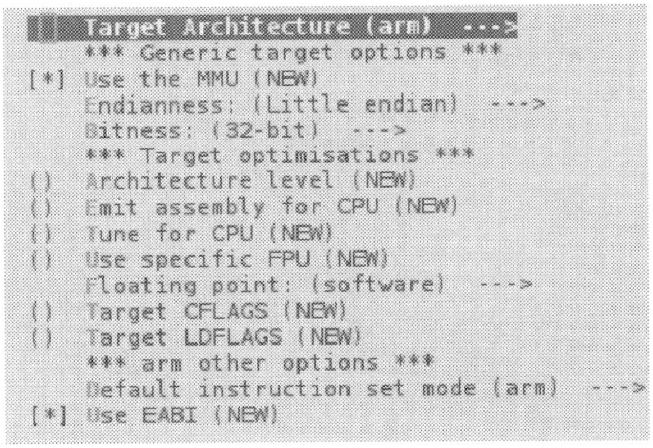

Figure 6-8. *The Target Options screen*

- The first item, "Target Architecture," should be an easy guess for you. This needs to be set to "ARM" as our target is the Raspberry Pi.

- Make sure you select "Use the MMU": the Raspberry Pi's SoC contains a memory management unit (MMU).

- The next option on the list is the "Endianness" that you will build for. The ARM11 is bi-endian but the default is little endian. Most of the distributions for the Raspberry Pi use little endian. Little endian will be the easiest to cross compile for and the most widely used. So select "Little endian" for this option. The next option should be obvious as well: "Bitness" has to be 32-bit. You have no choice, as the ARM11 is a 32-bit CPU.

- There is one last option on this screen that you must take care of and that is the type of floating point. This option will depend on the distribution installed on your Raspberry Pi. For example, the Fedora 14 distribution still uses the soft-float option, whereas OpenELEC uses the hard-float option. I would suggest following your installed distribution; because I am using Fedora 14 I will select software.

- The rest of the options on this screen can be left at their defaults.

Tool-Chain Options

The next screen of options labeled "Toolchain Options" displays options related to the tool-chain build process. You don't need to configure any of them and the defaults are fine. Feel free to take a look though the submenus if you want.

Operating System

The next menu item you will see is "Operating System." This one is important; by default crosstool-NG will default to "bare-metal" as an operating-system type. This selection would be perfect if you were trying to cross compile a boot loader. I won't be and I am pretty sure you won't be as well, so let's change it to "Linux." Now you will see a whole submenu unfold. There is only one option that you need to select and that's the "Linux kernel version."

This option can seem a little misleading. You won't find every kernel version in this menu, so how can you select the exact kernel on your Raspberry Pi? If you are wondering what kernel version you have on your Raspberry Pi just type the following command and it will print your kernel version:

```
# uname -r
```

Well, you can't. The Linux kernel number is made up of three parts: for example, 3.2.25. The first number (3) indicates the kernel version number, the section number (2) indicates the major revision of the kernel, and the third number (25) indicates the minor number. When selecting a version in this option you must match the kernel version number. Then pick as close as you can for the kernel revision number and the minor revision is not really that important. Leave all the rest of the options on their default settings.

In Figure 6-9 you can see my selection. I have selected kernel version 3.2.25 as my Raspberry Pi is running 3.2.27.

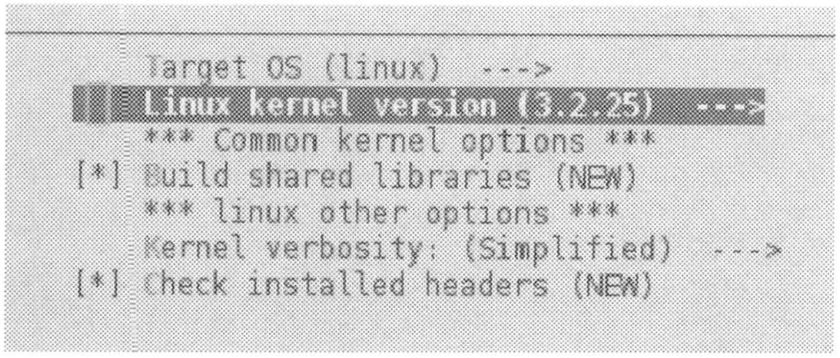

Figure 6-9. *The operating-system menu options*

Binary Utilities

The next menu item on your list is "Binary Utilities." This is where you can configure your binutils version and your linker options. Where possible I like to use the latest binutils version; at the time of writing that was 2.21.1a. Leave the linker as ld; there are other linkers you can use but I strongly recommend you stick with the generic ld linker for the time being. Nothing else needs to be done for this section.

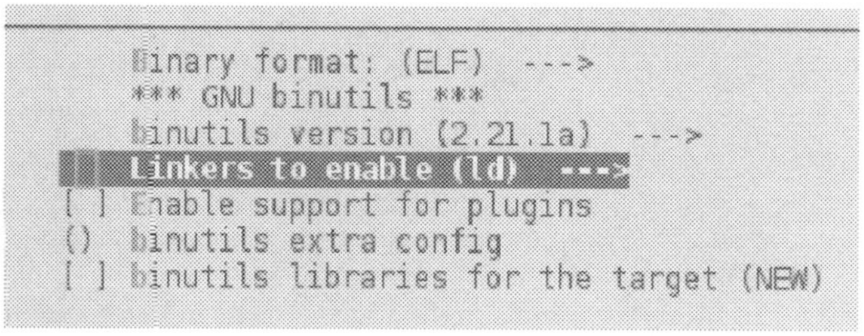

Figure 6-10. *The Binary Utilities menu*

C Compiler

The "C Compiler" menu is next. This gets down to the business end of crosstool-NG. You can really break your build or you can really get some good optimization done. As a general rule I like to keep this section generic for my first build. Recall earlier on that I said that building a cross compiled tool chain is a complicated task, so for the moment it's best to keep it simple. Leave your "C compiler" set to gcc.

Once again select the latest version of GCC; at the time of writing that version was 4.6.3. Make sure that you enable the "C++" option. Most of the user land applications that you will be building will quite often be built using C++ so it's wise to include support for C++; it can't hurt even if none of your applications will use it. The section named "Flags to pass to --enable-cxx-flags" can be used to optimize your cross compile tool chain later on. For the moment, leave it empty and leave the rest of the options at their defaults (I'll cover optimization later in this chapter). Figure 6-11 shows the options I have used at this stage. They are quite safe.

```
     C compiler (gcc)   --->
     gcc version (4.6.3)   --->
     *** Additional supported languages: ***
 [*] C++
 [ ] Fortran (NEW)
 [ ] Java (NEW)
     *** gcc other options ***
 () Flags to pass to --enable-cxx-flags
 () Core gcc extra config
 () gcc extra config (NEW)
 [*] Link libstdc++ statically into the gcc binary
     *** Optimisation features ***
 [*] Enable GRAPHITE loop optimisations
 [*] Enable LTO
     *** Settings for libraries running on target ***
 [*] Optimize gcc libs for size
 [ ] Compile libmudflap
 [ ] Compile libgomp
 [ ] Compile libssp
 [ ] Compile libquadmath
     *** Misc. obscure options. ***
 [*] Use __cxa_atexit (NEW)
 [ ] Do not build PCH
 <M> Use sjlj for exceptions (NEW)
 <M> Enable 128-bit long doubles
 [ ] Enable build-id
```

Figure 6-11. *The C Compiler page*

C Library

Of course, because you're using a C compiler you're going to need a C library. Take a look at the next menu called "C Library." The first option is called "C library" and this lets you select what C library will be used alongside GCC in the cross compile environment. I have selected "eglibc." eglibc stands for Embedded GLIBC. Its goals are to be small and feature-rich in a cross compiling environment. It's designed for use on embedded systems where size matters.

There are two other options in this submenu: uClibc and generic old glibc. If you're having issues with eglibc then give uClibc a shot; it has been used extensively in embedded environments as well but is a little less optimized than eglibc. Stay well away from the generic glibc: it's far from ideal for an embedded or small system. I also selected 2_13 as my version because this is the same version that the Fedora remix uses. I suggest you check to see what your distribution uses. Finding your glib version is also quite simple. Just run the following command:

```
# ldd --version
```

Now look for the line that looks like the following, which is your glib version right there:

```
ldd (GNU libc) 2.13
```

There are also a lot of options to optimize your tool chain. For your initial build the only option I recommend is the "optimize eglibc for size (-Os)". By selecting this, your tool chain may be able to produce smaller binary files. Less to execute and less in memory is always a good thing when you are resource-limited. This option will make your compile times longer: no free lunch, remember. Leave the rest of the options at their defaults (see Figure 6-12).

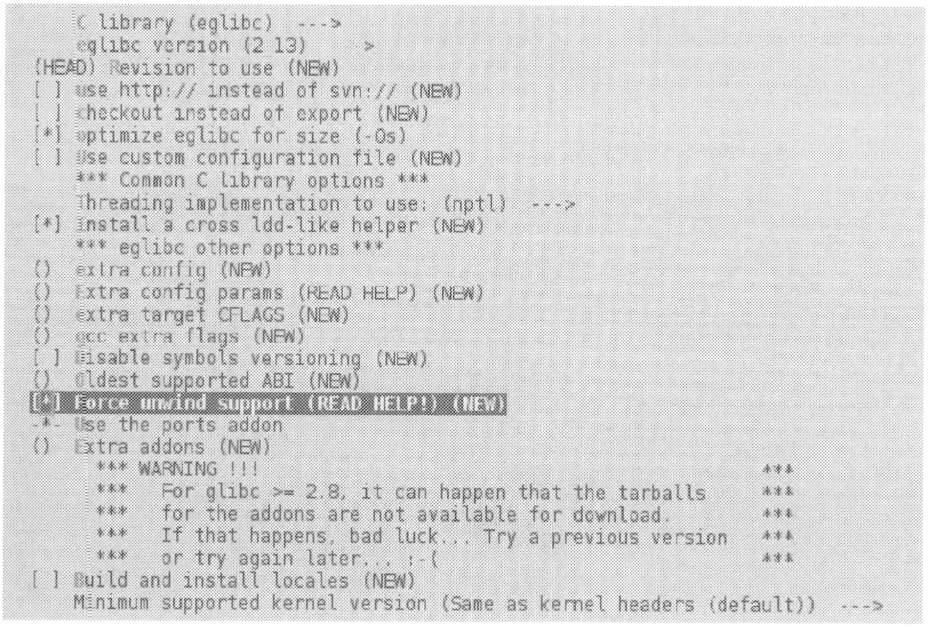

Figure 6-12. *The C Library page settings*

Debug Facilities

There is only one other menu you should configure. That is the "Debug Facilities" page. On this page, select gdb and strace; you should not need the other tools for basic debugging. Don't worry about configuring any suboptions for either of the tools. The default options for each tool will be fine.

Building the Tool Chain

Now you're all done with the configuration tool. Use the Tab key to select "Exit" from the bottom menu. Make sure you select "Yes" to save your new configuration, otherwise you will be redoing all your settings again. Next up it's time to build your cross compiled tool chain. There are fun times ahead and a lot of waiting. Use the following command to start the build process:

```
# ct-ng build
```

At this point in time it's a good idea to walk away and go get some food or a beer or two. You're going to need your energy when it's done. The tool has a lot of work to do. It must download all the sources for the tools and their libraries. It then must build a working copy of these tools using the host's build tools. This is called the first pass; once crosstool-NG has a working set of tools it will then use the tools it has just built to rebuild the exact same version for your target architecture. This is called the second pass. After this you should have a working cross compile tool chain. Now if you think about that in detail that's a lot of compile time (maybe you should grab two beers).

You may come back to find that your build failed. In my case I expected it to fail as computers have a habit of not working for me or maybe that's computers in general. Take a look at Figure 6-13. crosstool-NG has pretty good error screens.

```
brendan@pcb $ ct-ng build
[INFO ]  Performing some trivial sanity checks
[INFO ]  Build started 20121102.094542
[INFO ]  Building environment variables
[INFO ]  =================================================================
[INFO ]  Retrieving needed toolchain components' tarballs
[ERROR]
[ERROR]  >>
[ERROR]  >>  Build failed in step 'Retrieving needed toolchain components' tarballs'
[ERROR]  >>        called in step '(top-level)'
[ERROR]  >>
[ERROR]  >>  Error happened in: do_debug_strace_get[scripts/build/debug/500-strace.sh@592]
[ERROR]  >>        called from: do_debug_get[scripts/build/debug.sh@21]
[ERROR]  >>        called from: main[scripts/crosstool-NG.sh@540]
[ERROR]  >>
[ERROR]  >>  For more info on this error, look at the file: 'build.log'
[ERROR]  >>  There is a list of known issues, some with workarounds, in:
[ERROR]  >>      '/usr/local/crosstool/share/doc/crosstool-ng/ct-ng.1.16.0/B - Known issues.txt'
[ERROR]
[ERROR]  (elapsed: 3:51.74)
[03:52] / make: *** [build] Error 1
```

Figure 6-13. *The build has failed!*

It gives you a lot of information and even a file to read about common errors. More importantly, it has a build log file. This file is called build.log and this can be found in the working directory that you created. Taking a look at this log shows me that for some reason crosstool-NG cannot download the strace tarball. This is a simple fix. All you need to do if you get this type of error is find where to download the tarball and place it into the .build/tarballs directory in your working directory. In the case of the strace example you can download the strace file from http://sourceforge.net/projects/strace/files/strace/. Once you have this downloaded, copy it into the .build/tarballs directory that you had extracted the initial crosstool-NG build into (in my case, this is /home/brendan/ct/rpi/.build/tarballs). Once you have placed any missing tarballs into the sources directory you can resume the build and wait for more errors. crosstool-NG will log what it's doing to your currently running terminal (standard out). Once it's done you should see a "finishing installation" message. You can see in Figure 6-14 an example of this.

```
[INFO ]   Cleaning-up the toolchain's directory
[INFO ]     Stripping all toolchain executables
[INFO ]   Cleaning-up the toolchain's directory: done in 1.15s (at 13:54)
[INFO ]   Build completed at 20121102.104832
[INFO ]   (elapsed: 13:53.41)
[INFO ]   Finishing installation (may take a few seconds)...
```

Figure 6-14. *crosstool-NG has finished building the tool chain*

Preconfigured Tool Chains

Now that you have gone through every menu and all the suboptions I will show you the easy way to use crosstool-NG. If you had read the help screen for crosstool-NG you would have noticed a section on preconfigured tool chains. A really good feature of crosstool-NG that I have purposely not told you about is that it includes sample configurations to build many different tool chains. You can get a list of all preconfigured tool chains by running the following command:

```
# ct-ng list-samples
```

This will produce a list of available cross compiler tool chains. You will notice a set of letters in square brackets. These indicate where the profile is stored and its status. I would advise you not to use any tool chains that have a broken status. If you wish to opt for the easy way to build the tool chain that you have just finished manually building you can run the following command:

```
# ct-ng arm-unknown-linux-gnueabin
```

This will use a set of predefined and tested options to build the tool chain. Once you have told crosstool-NG what profile to use, you can run the normal build step to build and install the cross compile tool chain. There is a good reason I put this method at the end of the manual process: I am trying to show you what exactly is involved with configuring a cross compile environment because it's really important that you start to understand the environment and architecture that you are developing for. This way you can optimize your tool chain and produce better binary files for your Raspberry Pi. You can also optimize your applications better if you know where and how to do so. The predefined profiles won't give you this ability. Now that you have built a tool chain, what can you do with it? You can cross compile an application, of course.

Your First Cross Compile

The first thing you're going to need to know is where did your tool chain get installed? It's not in /usr/local/crosstool, so where is it? When you run the build steps for crosstool-NG the last step creates a directory called x-tools in your home directory. In this directory there will be a subdirectory for each tool chain you build. In my case the full path to the tool chain I had just created will be /home/brendan/x-tools/arm-unknown-linux-gnueabi. Inside the arm-unknown-linux-gnueabi directory will be the usual directories for a Linux application and a copy of the build log. Given the way that modern make and configure scripts work, you're going to need to update your path so that the scripts can find where the ARM tool chain has been installed.

This should be a simple case of running the following command:

```
# export PATH=$PATH:$HOME/x-tools/arm-unknown-linux-gnueabi/bin
```

This will append the tool-chain bin path to your existing path variable. To test that your tool chain is fully working I recommend that you cross compile a simple well-known application. For this I use the GNU hello application. I am sure you can guess what this application will do. Connect to the following web site to find the latest version of the GNU hello application: http://ftp.gnu.org/gnu/hello/. For me, it was version 2.8. Download a copy of the application and extract it to any directory you want. I like to create a build directory for each architecture I will be cross compiling for; this will help you later on when you have applications with many dependencies. The GNU hello application requires a configure step and then a make step; this is quite normal.

You're going to need two pieces of information for the configure stage to succeed. First, you need to update the CC variable, which will ensure that the configure script uses the correct GCC version. This must be specified as the full name of the ARM tool chain. In your case this will be arm-unknown-linux-gnueabi-gcc. You can easily work this out by looking into the bin directory of the tool chain to see the full name of the GCC binary. You can see in Listing 6-1 the full name of my ARM tool-chain GCC binary.

Listing 6-1. The Real GCC Location

```
/home/brendan/x-tools/arm-unknown-linux-gnueabi/bin/arm-unknown-linux-gnueabi-cc->
arm-unknown-linux-gnueabi-gcc
```

As you can see it's a symlink to the CC application. Now that you know the full name of your application you can move on to the configure script parameters. It's always wise to run the configure script with the –help option the first time:

```
# ./configure -help
```

This will print all of the options that the configure script supports for the GNU hello application. There should be one option that stands out right away if you have taken the time to read the output. That option is the --host=HOST option. This option sets what host architecture you will build for. This is not simply ARM. After all, ARM is a very vague term. This is where you come back to the full path of the CC application. This full path can be broken up into five sections. See Table 6-1 for the breakdown.

Table 6-1. *The full name breakdown*

Section	Meaning
arm	Main architecture type
unknown	Subarchitecture type
linux	Operating system
gnueabi	Application binary interface (ABI) type
gcc	Binary application name

With this information it is quite simple now to work out what your host should be set to. You should use the name of the application up to the last section. For you this will be arm-unknown-linux-gnueabi. You now have the two critical pieces of information for cross compiling any application. You may in the future need more configure options but you will not get away with any less than these two. With that in mind, the full command to configure the GNU hello application is the following:

```
# CC=arm-unknown-linux-gnueabi-gcc ./configure -host=arm-unknown-linux-gnueabi
```

This should complete quickly with no errors; if you have errors you need to fix them. The best thing about using configure scripts is that it lessens the amount of options for make. The make file now knows that you're doing a cross compile and for what architecture and with what tool chain. Make files will become another good friend of yours. Go ahead and run make:

```
# make
```

This should also produce no errors. Normally the next step would be to run make install but that won't be very helpful. Change into the src directory and run the file command:

```
# file hello
```

Now take a look at Figure 6-15 and you can see why it's not helpful.

```
brendan@pcb /working/book-work/ch5/build/hello-2.7/src $ file hello
hello: ELF 32-bit LSB executable, ARM, version 1 (SYSV), dynamically linked (uses shared libs), for GNU/Linux 3.2.25, not stripped
```

Figure 6-15. *Why running make install would be bad*

It's now quite clear why make install would not go as planned. It's always a good idea to run the file tool across your cross compiled binary files: this will make sure that you have in fact cross compiled the application and not just used the local version of GCC. Now copy the hello application across to your Raspberry Pi by whatever means fits best. I like to use scp to copy the file from my build machine to my Raspberry Pi. You could also insert the SD card back into your host machine if you wanted to. Now it's time to see if it really worked. Run the hello application. The GNU hello application supports a few options; in Figure 6-16 you can see my favorite option and its output.

```
[root@hobo tmp]# ./hello -g "MOAR, Pi"
MOAR, Pi
[root@hobo tmp]# □
```

Figure 6-16. *The output of the GNU hello application*

Congratulations! You have your first cross compiled application. Unfortunately, GNU hello is not very useful. I do use it to test my tool chains; after all, I know the source code is in a well-maintained and working state.

Now that you have tested your tool chain, try and compile a small simple application. I will show you another example for the application called netcat. You will be surprised at how easy it is. Listing 6-2 shows the build process.

Listing 6-2. Commands to Build netcat

```
# CC=arm-unknown-linux-gnueabi-gcc ./configure --host=arm-unknown-linux-gnueabi
# make
```

Look familiar? Those are the exact same commands you used to build the hello application. It's not hard to cross compile a program if that program depends on nothing else. What would happen if you wanted to compile a more complex program when you can't use the system library files (after all, they are compiled for an x86 architecture)?

Cross Compiling with Dependencies

A good example of a program that uses system library files is nmap, which depends on the pcap library files. For you to be able to build nmap you're going to need to build libpcap for the ARM architecture first.

The first step will be to download libpcap into your build directory. You can download libpcap from http://www.tcpdump.org/. I will be using libpcap-1.3.0. Extract the source once the download is finished. I like to keep the source tarballs as well just in case I make a mess of the compile and install. In Figure 6-17 you can see the source and its tarballs in my build directory.

```
brendan@pcb /working/book-work/ch6/build $ ls -la
total 23624
drwxr-xr-x  7 brendan brendan     4096 Nov  6 13:09 .
drwxr-xr-x  5 brendan brendan     4096 Nov  5 19:29 ..
drwxr-xr-x 10 brendan brendan     4096 Nov  6 21:37 hello-2.7
-rw-r--r--  1 brendan brendan   599680 Mar 29 2011 hello-2.7.tar.gz
drwxr-xr-x 14 brendan brendan    12288 Feb 11 10:07 libpcap-1.3.0
-rw-r--r--  1 brendan brendan   608967 Nov  6 09:41 libpcap-1.3.0.tar.gz
drwxr-xr-x  7 brendan brendan     4096 Nov  5 21:51 netcat-0.7.1
-rw-r--r--  1 brendan brendan   398872 Jan 12 2004 netcat-0.7.1.tar.gz
drwxr-xr-x 22 brendan brendan     4096 Nov  6 13:45 nmap-6.01
-rw-r--r--  1 brendan brendan 21640157 Jun 17 2012 nmap-6.01.tar.bz2
drwxr-xr-x  7 brendan brendan    12288 Nov  6 10:57 tcpdump-4.3.0
-rw-r--r--  1 brendan brendan   887619 Jun 13 2012 tcpdump-4.3.0.tar.gz
```

Figure 6-17. *My populated build directory*

There is a good reason why I am showing you my build directory. When you compile more applications that have more dependencies, you need a clean way to find them all. Change into the libpcap directory; it's now time to start the build. Because I won't be installing libpcap onto this machine I like to create a build directory: this way I can use the make install tool. I have called this directory rpi-build; you will need to create this directory under the libpcap directory. Once you have done that it's time to run the configure command again. The full command looks something like this:

```
# CC=arm-unknown-linux-gnueabi-gcc ./configure --host=arm-unknown-linux-gnueabi --with-pcap=linux
--prefix=/'pwd'/rpi-build
```

Let me explain the new options.

- The first new option, --with-pcap=linux, tells libpcap what target operating system you are building for. After all, you may be cross compiling libpcap to run on AIX, for example.

- The last option you see, prefix=/'pwd'/rpi-build, tells the configure tool where you want to install the binary files and libraries when you run make install.

The configure process for libpcap should run pretty quickly.

Once again, you cannot allow errors in this stage. When you are certain your configure stage is error-free, run the make tool to build the source files. There is not much to be built for libpcap so this step should be quick. Lastly, install the build into the rpi-build directory you created. You can do this with the make install command; note that if you had not used the prefix option above, your build would be installed into your host system, which is not a good thing:

```
# make install
```

Take a look at Figure 6-18 for an example of a finished build of libpcap.

```
brendan@pcb /working/book-work/ch6/build/libpcap-1.3.0 $ ls -la rpi-build/
total 32
drwxr-xr-x  6 brendan brendan  4096 Nov  6 12:14 .
drwxr-xr-x 14 brendan brendan 12288 Feb 11 10:07 ..
drwxr-xr-x  2 brendan brendan  4096 Feb 11 10:07 bin
drwxr-xr-x  3 brendan brendan  4096 Feb 11 10:07 include
drwxr-xr-x  2 brendan brendan  4096 Feb 11 10:07 lib
drwxr-xr-x  3 brendan brendan  4096 Nov  6 12:14 share
```

Figure 6-18. *Libpcap installed into the rpi-build directory*

Now that you have built nmap's dependencies, it's time to retrieve nmap and build it. Open your web browser and go to the nmap download page at http://nmap.org/dist/. For this example, please use the 6.01 version of nmap (nmap-6.01.tar.bz2), because the current version at the time of writing has issues building without liblua. Save the nmap-6.01.tar.bz2 file into the build directory. Next extract the files into this directory.

Now change into the nmap source directory and create an rpi-build directory again. The configure stage for nmap is a little more complicated. For a start, I don't want to build certain parts of nmap. For example, I do not want the zenmap front end nor do I want to compile in netcat, for example. You now also need to tell nmap's configure tool where to find libpcap's ARM install; this is why having a decent build directory layout will save you a lot of pain. Here is the full command to run the configuration for nmap:

```
# CC=arm-unknown-linux-gnueabi-gcc ./configure --host=arm-unknown-linux-gnueabi --without-ndiff
--without-zenmap --without-liblua --without-ncat --with-pcap=linux --with-libpcap=/working/book-
work/ch7/build/libpcap-1.3.0/rpi-build -prefix=/'pwd'/rpi-build
```

There are a lot of new options, though a lot of them are just disabling parts I do not want. They are --without-ndiff, --without-zenmap, --without-liblua, and --without-ncat; these lines just disable parts of nmap. The only other new option is the --with-libpcap option, which tells nmap where to find libpcap.

Don't try to be clever by using a relative path; it will cause you untold pain. Always use the full path, as make won't care what your relative path is.

RELATIVE PATH VERSUS FULL PATH

A relative path is a path on your system that won't take its parent path into consideration. For example, if you wanted to make an empty file in the directory /home/brendan, you could cd into the /home/brendan directory and then create the empty file like this:

```
touch empty-file
```

The file named empty-file is relative to your current location in the filesystem. This is called using the relative path. If you wanted to create the empty file using a full path you would need to use the following command:

```
touch /home/brendan/empty-file
```

This is the full system path to the empty file.

Configuring nmap takes a little longer than libpcap but you get a cool fire-breathing dragon at the end so it must be worth it. Once you're done with the configure stage and the dragon, it's time to move on to the make stages. This time I am going to add an extra parameter for make. This parameter is called static; by using this option you will create a binary that will not depend on shared libraries.

What are shared libraries, I hear you ask? A shared library is a shared group of functions that any program on your system can use. This saves having many copies of the same library on your system. For example, the tcpdump application and Wireshark both use the shared pcap library files. When you statically link all the libraries at build time, your application won't depend on any shared libraries on the system. This can be good and bad.

- It's bad because the size of your application on disk and in memory will increase.

- It's good when you need an application working at a very early stage in your boot process. Early in the boot process, the system's shared libraries may not be available yet. Another good use for static libraries is if you have an application that depends on some old version of a library. You can statically link the application to the old library and your system will still use the newer shared libraries.

I am also doing this so I can demonstrate another tool: there are only a few applications that really should be built as static. So now run the following to build the statically linked binary files:

```
#make static
```

Once that has completed without error, run this command:

```
# make install
```

Just like with libpcap you will see a new directory structure under the rpi-build directory. It's a good idea to check if your binary files are compiled for the correct architecture. In Figure 6-19 you can see the listing of the binary files.

```
brendangpcb ~/working/book-work/ch6/build/nmap-6.01/rpi-build/bin $ file *
nmap:  ELF 32-bit LSB executable, ARM, version 1 (SYSV), statically linked, for GNU/Linux 3.2.25, stripped
nping: ELF 32-bit LSB executable, ARM, version 1 (SYSV), statically_linked, for GNU/Linux 3.2.25, stripped
```

Figure 6-19. *Running the file command on the binary files*

Looking at the output, you will notice first that the files are a little larger because you have statically linked them. You will also notice right at the end it says "not stripped." What exactly does that mean? By default, when you compile a binary you will add in a lot of symbols. Some of these symbols, such as debugging symbols, may be useful. Other symbols may be of no use and just add unnecessary space. Now I'll show you how to strip out all unneeded symbols; however, this will prevent you from debugging the application on the Raspberry Pi. Stripping an application may also break the application like a lot of things: in the cross compiling world it's a matter of trial and error.

Now you can't just use your system's strip tool: after all, it won't be able to read an ARM binary file. The cross compiled version of strip lives in the bin directory of your x-tools install. On my system this would be /home/brendan/x-tools/arm-unknown-linux-gnueabi/arm-unknown-linux-gnueabi/bin/strip. To strip all symbols from the two binary files, run the strip command with the -s option and an * to select all files:

```
strip -s *
```

You will now notice that the binary file is a little smaller. Run the file tool back across the two files and you will see they are now marked as "stripped" rather than "not stripped." Copy the nmap binary across to your Raspberry Pi. I like to place the binary into /usr/local/bin but it will work anywhere you want. In Figure 6-20 you can see nmap running on the Raspberry Pi and showing you the compile time options:

```
[root@hobo ~]# nmap -V

Nmap version 6.01 ( http://nmap.org )
Platform: arm-unknown-linux-gnueabi
Compiled with: nmap-libpcre-7.6 libpcap-1.3.0 nmap-libdnet-1.12 ipv6
Compiled without: liblua openssl
[root@hobo ~]#
```

Figure 6-20. *Compile time and version numbers from nmap on the Raspberry Pi*

With this basic knowledge and the crosstool-NG tool chain you can build anything from the Linux kernel to LibreOffice. The two main concepts will apply to pretty much every main build process out there. Cross compiling applications can be a painful process at the best of times. You may have hours of building only to see seconds of failure. As my fiancée sometimes says, you need to take a step back and look at it with a clear head.

Optimization

If by now you still want to do more with your tool chain or make your code possibly run faster, then this is the section that will give you more details about that. These optimizations may break some applications or may not even work on all distributions. This section also will require you to read and understand the architecture white papers and the GCC manuals. I will provide some examples but you really should read at least the ARM1176 process architecture white paper and the GCC ARM options page for your version of GCC. The first page I open whenever I am going to look at optimizations is the GCC manual. In particular, look at section 3.17.2 on "ARM Options."

It's best to get the manual for the exact version of GCC you are using. The link you need is http://gcc.gnu.org/onlinedocs/gcc-4.6.3/gcc/ARM-Options.html#ARM-Options. The good people who work on GCC do a very good job on documentation. You should be happy that there are walls of text for you to read, unlike some other larger OSS projects that have only around four lines of text within their manuals. The GCC manual, while it is very good, is only half the documents that you need. All the options in GCC will be pretty useless if you don't know what your CPU can support. The ARM is also quite good about supplying decent levels of documentation. Take a look at the following web page: http://arm.com/products/processors/classic/arm11/arm1176.php.

The main page gives a good brief overview of the ARM1176 processor family but you could guess by now you're going to need more detail. Select the "Resources" tab and find the link called "ARM1176JZF Development Chip Technical Reference Manual"; this will bring you to an online version of the manual. With the ARM and GCC manuals you can now start to work out what you can do with GCC. It's a good idea to read the whole thing. Now let's get some optimization happening. Change back into your crosstool-NG working directory (in my case this was /home/brendan/ct/rpi). Ensure that you update your path setting and then launch the ct-ng menu:

```
ct-ng makemenuconfig
```

Select the "Target Options" menu. The first thing you should set is the "Architecture level" option, which is the equivalent of the GCC -march option. There are many choices for this but the best choice is armv6j. This sets the architecture type to ARMV6-J; this is the closest fit to the ARM1176JZF-S CPU.

Now that you have set the family of the CPU you should also set the subfamily type. For the "Tune for CPU" option, enter arm1176jzf-s as that's what the Raspberry Pi uses.

Next up is the value of the floating point unit. You should know by now that the ARM1176JZF-S uses a vector floating point unit. Set this option to vpf. The next option you will see is the one everyone is talking about: the magical hard or soft float. For the best performance you should select "hardware (FPU)"; if your distribution is still using a soft float it's best to use the "software" option here.

The last option for this section is "CFLAGS." A lot of people get carried away with adding as many CFLAGS as they can find in the GCC manual but this is not a good idea. The thing with CFLAGS is that, depending on your workload type, they may make your code run much more slowly. On the flip side, if you can see why a certain CFLAG may help your workload, then by all means do use it. Once again you need to read the manuals and really understand your workload to make CFLAGS of any use. Please don't just add random CFLAGS. With that warning in mind I will heed my own advice and not add any. In Figure 6-21 you can see my final options. Once you're done, exit and save because there is no need to edit anything else in crosstool-NG.

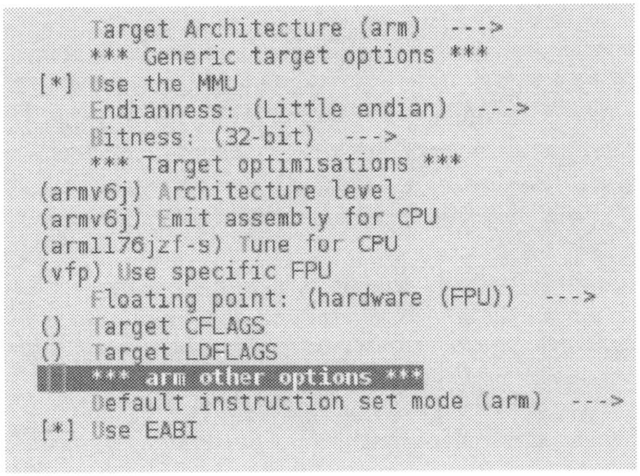

```
    Target Architecture (arm) --->
    *** Generic target options ***
[*] Use the MMU
    Endianness: (Little endian) --->
    Bitness: (32-bit) --->
    *** Target optimisations ***
(armv6j) Architecture level
(armv6j) Emit assembly for CPU
(arm1176jzf-s) Tune for CPU
(vfp) Use specific FPU
    Floating point: (hardware (FPU)) --->
() Target CFLAGS
() Target LDFLAGS
    *** arm other options ***
    Default instruction set mode (arm) --->
[*] Use EABI
```

Figure 6-21. *The optimized crosstool-NG build*

I like to move my old tool chain to a backup location before I make the new one. I will just rename the arm-unknown-linux-gnueabi directory under the x-tools directory to arm-unknown-linux-gnueabi.old. Once that's done, it's time to build the tool chain again. When this is done you must recompile your applications that you have already compiled for the new tool chain. Always keep in mind when optimizing the tool chain that there is a lot of potential for things to bake even the same application but a newer or older version may not compile the same way. Reading the manuals and understanding the features is key.

Summary

This chapter has focused heavily on tools that do not directly run on the Raspberry Pi. I have done my best to make this as distribution-free as possible. The steps and tools have all been built from sources using only your distributions and GCC to bootstrap the initial process. You started this chapter by reading about what a cross compile environment is. After all, you may not have a lot of different types of architectures. I hope by reading this that you have found a need or a good reason to consider using a cross compiler. After discovering what a cross compiler can do, I talked about GCC and its many roles in the cross compiling environment. Next up, I introduced you to one of my favorite tools: crosstool-NG. Many years ago I used to do the two stages (GCC and dependency build) by hand; back then it was for a MIPS 64-bit architecture and not an ARM architecture. This process was painful and getting to a working tool-chain stage took weeks of work (and many errors, a lot of foul language, and many beers).

None of that happens anymore; as you saw from the friendly menus in crosstool-NG, you can manage to get a tool-chain build done very quickly and with little pain. Once you had built a very basic tool chain for the Raspberry Pi, the next task was to cross compile your first application. After that I showed you how to build an application with no external dependencies. Lastly I demonstrated how to build a simple application with one dependent application. These steps are building blocks for all cross compiling. It's just a matter of using configure flags and dependencies from now on. Dependencies will become a lot harder to manage with bigger projects. Lastly I showed you some settings for optimizing the build. More important, I showed you how you can use the hardware's white papers and the GCC manuals to understand what the GCC is going to do.

CHAPTER 7

■ ■ ■

Mini Media Center

So far, you have spent most of your time on the command line. Not that that is a bad thing: the Raspberry Pi makes for a good little server. It's also my favorite way to use the Raspberry Pi. However, it is capable of so much more than what you have seen in the previous chapters. In this chapter you will learn how to set up a media center that can drive a 1080p display. It's pretty impressive to think that something less than the size of your standard DVD case can play back high-definition content. Only a few years back, you needed a dedicated video card to achieve this feat. And many years ago you needed a decent video card and an MPEG accelerator card installed in your PC just to be able to play back an ordinary DVD. Now you can do all of that with the Raspberry Pi, and with just one connection to the TV as well.

Given the Raspberry Pi's size you could attach your media center behind a wall-mounted TV. Impress your friends with a media center that cannot be seen. No more bulky PC to sit next to your TV! The HDMI connection will also bring you the benefit of surround sound and high fidelity audio. This media center can even play back programming from radio stations: perfect for that outdoor jukebox. There are endless ideas for such a small powerful media center. With the addition of USB ports, the media center can be tasked to do a whole new range of functions related to media from recording live TV to storing your music collection, for example. In addition to installing the media center software I will also guide you through how to purchase the VC-1 and MPEG-2 licenses that enable hardware-level decoding of the two formats. The installation of the licensed codecs is optional but they are a low-cost addition that will add a lot of power to your Raspberry Pi.

The main subject of this chapter is a particular open source project that has had my attention for many years now. Back in 2003 I was at an IT conference and they had a drawing for all attendees. The prize was the original Xbox. The drawing was free to enter but I am not a gamer by any stretch of the term. Nonetheless I entered; after all, it was free. To my surprise a few weeks later I was notified that I was in fact the proud winner of a new Xbox gaming console. I think I was the least impressed winner in the entire world, going so far as to hang up on the caller the first time, thinking it was a joke. A few weeks passed and I received the Xbox. I got it home and looked at it with a puzzled expression but decided to try it out. I played the bundled game for about one hour before I got bored (or I should say before the desire to bust open the Xbox got the better of me).

With that thought in mind, I reached for the Torx-head screwdriver (Torx-head screws are those annoying hex-shaped screws). I removed the extra-long screws from the base of the unit, along with my warranty. Now this was much more fun! After finally getting the case off, I noticed the 16-pin row where a pin header could be fitted. Not knowing anything about the modding community or even what this pin header was used for, I set out in search of what I could do with it. This little group of pin headers was in fact Intel's LPC bus, and a lot of importation devices hang off this bus in the original Xbox design. This is how I found out about modding the Xbox and the open source project called "Xbox Media Player." Hang on, don't you mean Xbox Media Center (XBMC)? In a way, yes, the original project name for XBMC was Xbox Media Player back in 2003. XBMC no longer works on the original Xbox and is now available for a large range of systems, including Linux. This is the media center software that I will use on the Raspberry Pi. This chapter will also indicate a change away from the Fedora distribution to the distribution called OpenELEC. OpenELEC Stands for Open Embedded Linux Entertainment Center. The main reason why I have selected this distribution over Fedora is that OpenELEC has poured a lot of effort into creating an extremely lightweight Linux distribution for running XBMC. That is the sole goal and function of OpenELEC: to run XBMC. It's a much better fit for this purpose than, say, Fedora would be. Fedora would work but you would need to build XBMC by hand or cross compile it from another machine. Now that you know what to use I will talk about why to use it.

Why OpenELEC?

I want to show you some of the features that make OpenELEC perfect for our media center.

First, it fully supports the hard float, and all parts of the operating system and application stack are compiled with hard-float support where possible. I talked about the benefits of a hard float in Chapter 1 so I won't go over it again. The optimization does not stop with just a hard float. The OpenELEC team has included three other optimizations that will greatly help the Raspberry Pi keep up with the challenge of playing back your most demanding media titles.

The first two optimizations are related to the GNU Compiler Collection (GCC). They are the -Ofast optimization level and the link-time optimization (LTO). The third is related to the GCC linker.

I want to make it crystal clear that any optimization may have adverse effects or may stop you from debugging an application or system crash. You won't get anything for free; there will always be a trade-off. With this in mind I want to talk about the first optimization and that is -Ofast.

Using the -Ofast Optimization

To understand what -Ofast is and its benefits or pitfalls you need to take a step back and look at the three main optimization levels. The main three levels are -O3, -O2, and -O1. These optimization levels are accumulative and they start off at -O1. In other words, level 3 optimization will enable all of level 2 and all of level 1.

- At the third level of optimization a lot of applications and even the kernel itself cannot be fully debugged anymore. In addition to this it will enable a lot of compile-time options that may lead to some programs being unstable. This is the price you pay for running at such a high level of optimization. What, did you expect this magic -O3 to be a free lunch? This is where -O2 comes in. -O2 is also known as safe by most applications. At this level the GCC won't make any optimizations that may have a possibly large negative impact. You can still debug some applications at this level. This level is what most of the applications you use every day are compiled with, assuming that you use Linux.

- The last of the main three levels is -O1. At this level the GCC will only perform optimizations that don't end up taking a large amount of additional compile time. This level is very safe for applications.

So where will -Ofast fit into this? Way after -O3! In fact -Ofast can and will disregard compliance to any form of standards if it provides a performance benefit. It will enable all level -O3 optimizations. On top of that it will enable optimizations that have been known to break certain applications. It's designed to get the most out of your code on that given architecture. You can also forget about debugging anything at this level. If you start getting unexpected results or failed GCC builds, this optimization level may be a good place to start looking. Wow, that sounds bad so why would you want to do this? It's only bad if you've not tested everything you write at that level of optimization. If you recall, the original XBMC was made to run on a very resource-limited machine to start with: the original Xbox. You do remember the original Xbox was a 733-MHz Intel Celeron, don't you?

This gives XBMC a good ability to handle such high optimization levels. If you would like to see what compile-time options the GCC will apply when the application is built at a set optimization level I recommend you take a read of the GCC manual; in particular, you should check out this page on optimizations: http://gcc.gnu.org/onlinedocs/gcc/Optimize-Options.html. It will outline what gets done at each level and the possible benefits or pitfalls.

Next up, you have the LTO.

Using the LTO

No matter how much I read it, I can't help but think of LTO as "Linear Tape-Open:" lucky for you it has nothing to do with tapes. It has a lot to do with how the above optimizations are applied. For the moment I want you to think about an LTO tape (if you're not sure what an LTO tape is, think of an old cassette tape and if you're not sure what this is, ask your parents). Cassette tapes, or LTOs, are stream devices and by definition they are very horrible for random access. The reason for this is that a stream device starts at the start and plays through until the end. They have no issues with reading or writing a stream of constant data or playing back an entire album, for example. If you owned a portable cassette-tape music player you would know firsthand that it's not an easy task to skip a track or go back a track, unlike with a CD player where you can just jump forward or backward with ease; there is no holding down the rewind or fast-forward button. Tapes work more efficiently with one set of data rather than smaller chunks of data. So what has a tape drive got to do with the GCC and LTO function? For that, you need to understand how the optimization levels are applied and when they are applied.

Without LTO, the GCC will do its best to apply the given optimizations to each object file that it finds in the application you are building. Now you need to keep in mind that some optimization may be valid only for the GCC to apply if it knew about another object file. Going back to the tape drive example this is as inefficient as seeking the tape to access data randomly rather than in a stream. Sure, it works fine but it's not efficient. With LTO, the optimization levels are applied in a very different way. LTO will try its hardest not to apply any optimization until the final linker stage. At this point the GCC will apply the given level of optimization across the whole application instead of the individual object files. Let's go back to the tape-drive example again. This mode of optimization is now like writing or reading to the tape drive as a stream of data rather than random access. The GCC knows about the whole application and as such it will be able to optimize better.

Using Symbols as Needed

The last optimization is passed to the GNU linker application, rather than to the GCC. It is called --as-needed. Without this option, the ld linker tool runs to link your application and will link in whatever shared libraries your application thinks it needs. A lot of the time, this will link in symbols that your application has no direct dependency on. It's quite likely an indirect dependency or just unnecessary. This is where the --as-needed option comes in. This option will do its best to only link in symbols that your application directly depends on. Simple enough, really. This simple optimization gives you two main benefits.

- The first benefit is that the application's size on disk is reduced. This has the added benefit for the Raspberry Pi in fewer read/write cycles to the SD card.

- The second benefit of --as-needed is that the amount of shared libraries that are loaded with the application could be decreased. Now on a system with limited resources, like the Raspberry Pi, this is a huge benefit to your CPU and memory space, which can be lowered by each application running.

Two Final Advantages

Lastly, OpenELEC has a very small disk footprint weighing in at less than 130 MB. Not that it matters much: OpenELEC can support pretty much any type of remote filesystem. Now that you know why OpenELEC is so good, it's time to move on to the installation.

Installing OpenELEC

OpenELEC is distributed as a zipped tarball. Unlike the Fedora installer it has no pretty UI tool for installing the image to the SD. You're going to need to use the command line to create the SD card. Fun times going back to the command line! Because the Raspberry Pi build of OpenELEC is still under heavy development, OpenELEC is releasing frequent releases of the build. It's a wise idea to download the latest one; this won't mean it's bug free though. Sometimes the latest build may have a bug that affects you or you're installing OpenELEC from a Mac or Windows machine; then you're going to want to use the prebuilt images. You can find the prebuilt images at http://openelec.thestateofme.com/.

Once you have downloaded an image, extract and write it the same way you wrote the Fedora image in Chapter 2. If you want to use the latest build, then you're going to need to point your browser to http://sources.openelec.tv/tmp/image/ and find the latest release. The file names have the date in them so it's easy to identify which is the newest release. You can see what the download site looks like in Figure 7-1.

Index of /tmp/image

- Parent Directory
- .upload/
- OpenELEC-ATV.i386-devel-20121117111053-r12493.tar.bz2
- OpenELEC-ATV.i386-devel-20121124030318-r12577.tar.bz2
- OpenELEC-Fusion.x86_64-devel-20121124032211-r12577.tar.bz2
- OpenELEC-Fusion.x86_64-devel-20121126224411-r12603.tar.bz2
- OpenELEC-Generic.i386-devel-20121128132353-r12604.tar.bz2
- OpenELEC-Generic.i386-devel-20121206004145-r12662.tar.bz2
- OpenELEC-Generic_OSS.i386-devel-20121117111652-r12493.tar.bz2
- OpenELEC-Generic_OSS.i386-devel-20121124030823-r12577.tar.bz2
- OpenELEC-ION.i386-devel-20121117112136-r12493.tar.bz2
- OpenELEC-ION.i386-devel-20121124031227-r12577.tar.bz2
- OpenELEC-ION.x86_64-devel-20121117112337-r12493.tar.bz2
- OpenELEC-ION.x86_64-devel-20121124031757-r12577.tar.bz2
- OpenELEC-Intel.i386-devel-20121117111917-r12493.tar.bz2
- OpenELEC-Intel.i386-devel-20121124031029-r12577.tar.bz2
- OpenELEC-Intel.x86_64-devel-20121117113151-r12493.tar.bz2
- OpenELEC-Intel.x86_64-devel-20121124032609-r12577.tar.bz2
- OpenELEC-RPi.arm-devel-20121118220355-r12500.tar.bz2
- OpenELEC-RPi.arm-devel-20121124031454-r12577.tar.bz2

Figure 7-1. *The download site for OpenELEC*

Download the latest release and extract it. It's simple to extract the tarball as you can see in Figure 7-2.

```
$ bunzip2 OpenELEC-RPi.arm-devel-20121008083232-r12055.tar.bz2
$ tar -xf OpenELEC-RPi.arm-devel-20121008083232-r12055.tar
$ ls
OpenELEC-RPi.arm-devel-20121008083232-r12055
$
```

Figure 7-2. *Extracting the tarball*

The install script for OpenELEC has some very small dependencies and it's more than likely your distribution already has the needed tools. The dependencies are parted, mkfs.vfat, md5sum, and partprobe. If any of them are missing, the install script will warn you and quit. To install OpenELEC to your SD card you need to do the following:

1. Insert your blank SD card into the machine where you extracted the tarball.

2. Find the SD card device via dmesg or your other favorite tool. I like to look in dmesg after I insert the SD card. In Figure 7-3 you can see that my SD card is 8 GB in size and is the device named sde.

```
899311.816853]  sd 10:0:0:0: [sde] 15523840 512-byte logical blocks: (7.94 GB/7.40 GiB)
899311.822469]  sd 10:0:0:0: [sde] No Caching mode page present
899311.822473]  sd 10:0:0:0: [sde] Assuming drive cache: write through
899311.832691]  sd 10:0:0:0: [sde] No Caching mode page present
899311.832693]  sd 10:0:0:0: [sde] Assuming drive cache: write through
899311.840568]   sde: sde1
```

Figure 7-3. *My 8-GB SD card*

3. The next step is very simple: change into the directory where you extracted OpenELEC and then run the create_sdcard script. This script only accepts one option and that is the name of the raw device to install to. In my case, it is /dev/sde. So here is the full command I would run:

```
# ./create_sdcard /dev/sde
```

As expected, this fails for me, because a lot of things tend to fail the first time around. I got this strange error when trying to use the install script:

```
Could not start /dev/sde2 --- No such file or directory
```

Wonderful! I can only assume this was my system causing this issue as I can't find anyone else complain about this issue.

4. I noticed that the partprobe command on my machine seems to take a while to finish. I made this small change to the create_sdcard script. In Listing 7-1 you can see the code snippet where I added the sleep 15 line.

Listing 7-1. My Change to the create_sdcard Script

```
# tell kernel we have a new partition table echo "telling kernel we have a new partition
table..."

partprobe "$DISK"

sleep 40
```

5. In addition to this I had an issue with udisks trying to do silly things with the way the system was mounting the SD card. To stop udisks polling the SD card, I ran the following command:

```
# udisks --inhibit
```

In Listing 7-2 you can see the full process of creating the SD card.

Listing 7-2. Creating the OpenELEC SD Card

```
#########################################################
#                                                       #
#           OpenELEC.tv USB Installer                   #
#                                                       #
#########################################################
#                                                       #
#    This will wipe any data off your chosen drive      #
# Please read the instructions and use very carefully.. #
#                                                       #
#########################################################
```

```
checking MD5 sum...
target/KERNEL: OK
target/SYSTEM: OK
umount: /dev/sde: not mounted
writing new disklabel on /dev/sde (removing all partitions)...
creating partitions on /dev/sde...
marking partition active...
telling kernel we have a new partition table...
creating filesystem on /dev/sde1...
mkfs.vfat 3.0.13 (30 Jun 2012)
creating filesystem on /dev/sde2...
mke2fs 1.42 (29-Nov-2011)
Filesystem label=Storage
OS type: Linux
Block size=4096 (log=2)
Fragment size=4096 (log=2)
Stride=0 blocks, Stripe width=0 blocks
476720 inodes, 1904128 blocks
95206 blocks (5.00%) reserved for the super user
First data block=0
Maximum filesystem blocks=1950351360
59 block groups
32768 blocks per group, 32768 fragments per group
8080 inodes per group
Superblock backups stored on blocks:
        32768, 98304, 163840, 229376, 294912, 819200, 884736, 1605632
Allocating group tables: done
Writing inode tables: done
Creating journal (32768 blocks): done
Writing superblocks and filesystem accounting information: done
mounting partition /dev/sde1 ...
creating bootloader configuration...
copying files to /dev/shm/openelec_install...
syncing disk...
unmounting partition /dev/shm/openelec_install ...
cleaning tempdir...
...installation finished
```

You may not need to edit the script or inhibit udisks on your system. I needed to and I have listed what had to be done in case you encounter the same issues. After all, the script should just work. Now you have an SD card loaded with OpenELEC. Do take note that the second partition is empty, and this is correct. The root filesystem is in a squashfs container on the first partition. The squashfs filesystem is called SYSTEM. Now that you have an SD card ready you want to add the MPEG-2 and VC-1 licenses to the SD card you just made.

Decode Licenses

Getting the licenses is simple for the end user. On the Raspberry Pi Foundation's side, it is still a manual process to generate the keys; someone at the foundation still needs to generate the keys by hand and then e-mail them to you. This step is completely optional: OpenELEC does not need the MPEG-2 and VC-1 keys to run at all. The two licenses in question enable hardware decoding for the MPEG-2 and VC-1 codecs. This will be a massive performance improvement for you if you use the two codecs in question. The MPEG-2 codec is mostly used by DVD playback or digital TV, and the VC-1 is used by Windows-created videos that have extensions like ".WMV." I hope you don't have too many WMV files around, but if you do, VC-1 will help you out.

There is one main prerequisite to buying the license and that is having your CPU's serial number. It's not the serial number printed anywhere on your board. The quickest way to get your serial number is booting into Linux and running this command:

```
# cat /proc/cpuinfo
```

The last line of this output should be your serial number. You can see my serial number in Figure 7-4 on the last line that says "Serial: 00000000e1a985d1." This is the number that you need to enter on the foundation's web site in the next step.

```
[root@hobo ~]# cat /proc/cpuinfo
Processor       : ARMv6-compatible processor rev 7 (v6l)
BogoMIPS        : 697.95
Features        : swp half thumb fastmult vfp edsp java tls
CPU implementer : 0x41
CPU architecture: 7
CPU variant     : 0x0
CPU part        : 0xb76
CPU revision    : 7

Hardware        : BCM2708
Revision        : 0003
Serial          : 00000000e1a985d1
[root@hobo ~]# █
```

Figure 7-4. *My serial number*

Once you have your serial number, fire up your favorite web browser and go to the Raspberry Pi store at http://www.raspberrypi.com/. Search for the VC-1 license key and MPEG-2 license key.

Select the license you want and enter your serial number as shown in Figure 7-5.

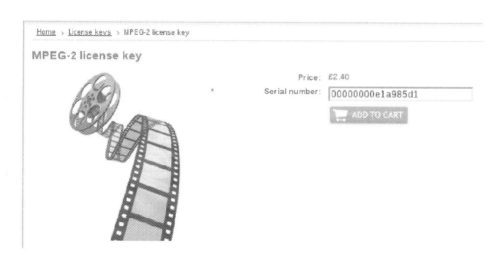

Figure 7-5. *Getting the MPEG-2 license key at the Raspberry Pi store*

Once you are done, go to the checkout and fill in your details. At the moment, the only payment method is PayPal. In the last step you will be redirected to PayPal to provide payment. You're going to need to wait for the good people at the foundation to generate your keys and e-mail them back to you. This process can take up to 72 hours so please be patient.

You should receive at least two e-mails from the foundation.

- The first e-mail will come with a PDF. This PDF will contain instructions for how to use the licenses without license codes.

- Next up you should get an e-mail that will contain the actual license codes. The license codes will have the following format:

decode_MPG2=0x000000

Now that you have your license how do you install it? The license needs to be read by the firmware on boot of the system. With that in mind, there is only one file that meets this need and that is the config.txt on the primary FAT partition of your install. Keep in mind that these keys had needed more recent firmware around August 2012 and the above should be fine. Because you are using the latest version of OpenELEC, this won't be an issue.

The licenses are also applicable to any operating system that can use the underlying hardware. All you are doing is activating a feature of the hardware. There are many ways you can edit the config.txt file. You can edit this file on any machine that has an SD card slot. You could even mount the flash partition from inside a booted operating system on the Raspberry Pi. You will need to edit this file from another PC, because you have not booted up OpenELEC yet.

1. Mount up the boot partition of OpenELEC on your host system.

2. Insert the SD card back into the host system and search your dmesg output as you have done before; this will be the first partition on the SD card you have just created and it will have a label of SYSTEM.

Well, look at that, in Figure 7-6 you will notice there is no config.txt file!

```
$ ls -lah
total 90M
drwxr-xr-x 2 root root  16K Jan  1  1970 .
drwxr-xr-x 8 root root 4.0K Sep 14 10:55 ..
-rwxr-xr-x 1 root root  17K Oct 10 15:42 bootcode.bin
-rwxr-xr-x 1 root root   50 Oct 10 15:42 cmdline.txt
-rwxr-xr-x 1 root root 5.1M Oct 10 15:42 kernel.img
-rwxr-xr-x 1 root root  32K Oct 10 15:42 openelec.ico
-rwxr-xr-x 1 root root 3.7K Oct 10 15:42 README.md
-rwxr-xr-x 1 root root 2.3M Oct 10 15:42 start.elf
-rwxr-xr-x 1 root root  83M Oct 10 15:42 SYSTEM
$ 
```

Figure 7-6. *First partition in OpenELEC*

You're going to need to create this file if it's not already there (and it might be on some builds). Open up your favorite text editor. After you have this file open, add the license keys into the file if you already have a config.txt file that you have created. Then all you need to do is add the two decode lines to the end of your file and then save and reboot the Raspberry Pi. You can see in Figure 7-7 where I have added the two license keys.

```
$
$ cat config.txt
decode_MPG2=0000000000
decode_WVC1=0000000000
$ ▓
```

Figure 7-7. *Decode licenses added*

Once your Raspberry Pi has rebooted, it's worth your time to check that the codecs are working. There are two main ways to check. You could boot into the operating system and check that you could play an MPEG-2 file. Without the codec you won't get any video, just audio. Given that I like to use the command line for everything, I will now show you how to check the codecs via the command line. Log in to the Raspberry Pi and ensure that you can run the following command:

```
# vcgencmd
```

Let's now run this command to check for each codec that has been enabled. First, check for the MPEG-2 decode support. Run the following command to check if the decode is enabled:

```
# vcgencmd codec_enabled MPG2
```

This should return "MPG2=enabled" if your codec is installed and working. Now do the same for the VC-1 codec:

```
# vcgencmd codec_enabled WVC1
```

You can see an example of the MPEG-2 and VC-1 decode support being enabled in Figure 7-8.

```
[root@hobo ~]# /opt/vc/bin/vcgencmd codec_enabled MPG2
MPG2=enabled
[root@hobo ~]# /opt/vc/bin/vcgencmd codec_enabled WVC1
WVC1=enabled
[root@hobo ~]# ▓
```

Figure 7-8. *Enabled codecs fully working*

Now you're all set up and ready to use the media center. Exciting times ahead! Connect your Raspberry Pi to your TV and watch it boot up.

The First Boot

I use HDMI for all connections. I would hope you will do so as well. There is no point trying to watch high-definition content over the composite output. It's time for the first boot: the first thing you will notice is a nice OpenELEC logo and, of course, the Raspberry Pi logo. After a few seconds your screen will go black and then swap to the XBMC dashboard. The first boot may take upward of one minute so be patient and go grab yourself a drink. You can see what this looks like in Figure 7-9: by default OpenELEC will automatically boot and log in to XBMC.

Figure 7-9. The first boot

This is a good thing in this case. After all you don't want to try to log in to the Raspberry Pi with a remote control. Like with most Linux distributions out there, you can also log in via SSH. OpenELEC has a default password for the root account set at "openelec." You can see in Figure 7-10 where I am logging in to the Raspberry Pi.

```
brendan@pcb ~ $ ssh root@192.168.0.55
###########################################
# OpenELEC - The living room PC for everyone #
# ...... visit http://www.openelec.tv ...... #
###########################################

OpenELEC Version: devel-20121008083232-r12055
OpenELEC git: 40cf401c0663aa8a507d1a657576b2a448354f13
root@192.168.0.55's password:
root ~ # 
```

Figure 7-10. SSH login into OpenELEC

You may have noticed that when you first boot up the date and time are wrong. That is because of the missing real-time clock. Unlike Fedora, OpenELEC uses a read-only squashfs filesystem for the root volume. This makes it a little harder to set up network time protocol (NTP), for example. You can no longer enable a service to start or edit a config file in the /etc filesystem so on the next reboot the changes will be gone.

Setting the Date and Time

With this in mind you still want the NTP running, especially if you want to turn your Raspberry Pi into a TV recorder. Recording the wrong TV show because your system clock has drifted an hour would not be a good outcome. Having the correct time is also useful for when you need to check system logs or report faults to XBMC; better timekeeping may help the XBMC team solve your issue quicker. There are two steps to this. The first step is to set your location. This can be done via the GUI. Select System ➤ Settings ➤ Appearances and then select International. Select your time zone and time zone country. You can see my time zone settings in Figure 7-11.

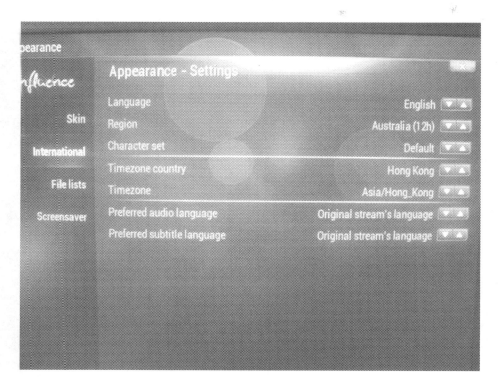

Figure 7-11. *Time zone settings*

Now that you have the correct time zone, you need to keep the NTP daemon running during the OpenELEC install. There is a certain filesystem mount in OpenELEC that is persistent across reboots. This mount is called /storage: anything created under this directory will not get erased on reboot. OpenELEC comes with the NTP daemon: you can find it at /usr/sbin/ntpd. So how can you get NTP to autostart on each reboot? It's not as easy as it sounds if your root filesystem is restored from an image on each boot.

Lucky for you the OpenELEC team allows you to create a script called autostart.sh; this script can be used to run commands when the system starts.

1. Connect to your OpenELEC installation via SSH.

2. You now need to create this file in a certain location for OpenELEC to read it on startup. Change into the /storage/.config directory:

```
# cd /storage/.config
```

3. Now you're going to create two files under the `/storage/.config` directory: an NTP config file and the autostart file. Create a file using vi called `ntp.conf` with the contents of Listing 7-3. Do note I said to use vi, not Vim. Vim is not installed on OpenELEC; the basic commands will be the same as Vim so you're fine.

   Listing 7-3. The ntp.conf File

   ```
   server 0.asia.pool.ntp.org iburst
   driftfile /var/lib/ntp/ntp.drift
   restrict default nomodify nopeer
   restrict 127.0.0.1
   interface ignore all
   interface listen eth0
   ```

4. Change your server to a different NTP server close to your region. Check `http://pool.ntp.org` for this information.

5. Next, in the same directory create a file called `autostart.sh`. Enter the contents of Listing 7-4 into this file. This will start `the NTP daemon` with the config file we created before.

   Listing 7-4. The autostart.sh File

   ```
   #!/bin/sh
   # Autostart for ntp
   /usr/sbin/ntpd -c /storage/.config/ntp.conf
   ```

6. The last step is setting the `autostart` file to have execution permissions. Do that with the following command:

   ```
   # chmod +x  /storage/.config/autostart.sh
   ```

It's now a good time to reboot your Raspberry Pi to make the `NTP` daemon start on boot.

In Figure 7-12 you can see where `NTP` has printed information into the `message` log by running this command:

```
# cat messages | grep ntp
```

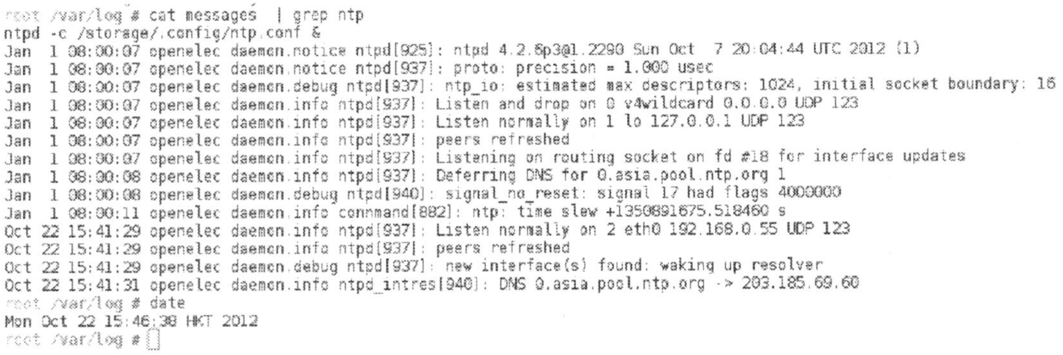

```
root /var/log # cat messages  | grep ntp
ntpd -c /storage/.config/ntp.conf &
Jan  1 08:00:07 openelec daemon.notice ntpd[925]: ntpd 4.2.6p3@1.2290 Sun Oct  7 20:04:44 UTC 2012 (1)
Jan  1 08:00:07 openelec daemon.notice ntpd[937]: proto: precision = 1.000 usec
Jan  1 08:00:07 openelec daemon.debug ntpd[937]: ntp_io: estimated max descriptors: 1024, initial socket boundary: 16
Jan  1 08:00:07 openelec daemon.info ntpd[937]: Listen and drop on 0 v4wildcard 0.0.0.0 UDP 123
Jan  1 08:00:07 openelec daemon.info ntpd[937]: Listen normally on 1 lo 127.0.0.1 UDP 123
Jan  1 08:00:07 openelec daemon.info ntpd[937]: peers refreshed
Jan  1 08:00:07 openelec daemon.info ntpd[937]: Listening on routing socket on fd #18 for interface updates
Jan  1 08:00:08 openelec daemon.info ntpd[937]: Deferring DNS for 0.asia.pool.ntp.org 1
Jan  1 08:00:08 openelec daemon.debug ntpd[940]: signal_no_reset: signal 17 had flags 4000000
Jan  1 08:00:11 openelec daemon.info connmand[882]: ntp: time slew +1350891675.518460 s
Oct 22 15:41:29 openelec daemon.info ntpd[937]: Listen normally on 2 eth0 192.168.0.55 UDP 123
Oct 22 15:41:29 openelec daemon.info ntpd[937]: peers refreshed
Oct 22 15:41:29 openelec daemon.debug ntpd[937]: new interface(s) found: waking up resolver
Oct 22 15:41:31 openelec daemon.info ntpd_intres[940]: DNS 0.asia.pool.ntp.org -> 203.185.69.60
root /var/log # date
Mon Oct 22 15:46:38 HKT 2012
root /var/log #
```

Figure 7-12. *The NTP daemon starting with the correct time*

This command will search the message log for all output from the NTP daemon. You can also see that the date, time, and time zone are now correct. The date changed from January 1 to October 22.

Your XBMC dashboard will also reflect this change. On every boot of OpenELEC, the correct date and time will now be applied.

Memory Allocation

Now that you have OpenELEC working, it may be a good idea to look at memory allocation. By default, OpenELEC uses the 128-MB split. This will give you 128 MB of GPU memory and the rest of the memory will be allocated to the system memory. You should leave this the way it's set. You're going to need a lot more GPU memory for playing back your HD movies. OpenELEC will run fine on 128 MB of memory. To verify that you are running the 128-MB split, check the /proc/meminfo file or take a look inside the GUI of XBMC. Open System ➤ System info and you will see how much memory you have.

Screen Resolution and Display Settings

Depending on your connected screen, you may need to adjust the resolution. To do this go to the settings page and select System. Change the display value to match your screen.

While I am on the topic of displays, it may be a good idea to enable a function called dirty region redraw. By default XBMC will redraw your entire screen whenever something changes in the UI. This could be as simple as a mouse cursor moving or a button becoming highlighted when you select it. No matter what you do the entire screen is redrawn. That sounds rather wasteful, especially on the Raspberry Pi. GPU cycles are very important to you now that you're running a GUI application. This is where dirty region redraw comes into play. With this enabled, XBMC will try its hardest to redraw only parts of the screen that have changed. So now when you highlight that button, only the button, not the whole screen, will be redrawn.

This setting is still a little bit experimental and you may get unexpected side effects.

Dirty region redraw will be disabled the moment you start any form of video playback. To enable this, you are going to need to use SSH to access the system. Once you have connected to the system via SSH, change into the following directory:

```
# cd /storage/.xbmc/userdata
```

This directory holds a lot of the settings for XBMC, including some settings that you configure through the GUI. Next, you're going to need to create a special file called advancedsettings.xml. This file is read on startup of XBMC. Make sure you use vi and not Vim when creating files on OpenELEC. Create the file with the following command:

```
# vi advancedsettings.xml
```

Then fill it with the contents listed in Listing 7-5.

Listing 7-5. Code to Enable Dirty Region Redraw

```
<?xml version="1.0" encoding="UTF-8"?>
<advancedsettings>

  <gui>
    <algorithmdirtyregions>3</algorithmdirtyregions>
    <nofliptimeout>1000</nofliptimeout>
  </gui>

</advancedsettings>
```

Once you have created this file, reboot OpenELEC. Do keep in mind that this setting may cause unexpected side effects and has been known not to work on all builds. If you're having issues, just remove the section from the advancedsettings.xml file and reboot. There are also other small tweaks you could do if you felt that you were seeing issues. You may want to turn off RSS feeds on the main screen; remember, each character is a redraw. To turn off the RSS feeds, go to Settings ➤ Appearance ➤ Skin, and untick the RSS feed option. Also don't use the weather applet if you don't need it: it's a surprisingly hungry part of XBMC.

Next up, you need to do something with your new media center. With XBMC the possibilities are endless: XBMC is capable of so much more than I have room for in this chapter. I know many people who have used XBMC for many different things.

- When I lived in Australia I had a bigger house and a nice audio system. I had it connected to XBMC. I configured XBMC to play back my network share, filled with FLAC music files. XBMC was ideal for this in two ways:

- I could walk around the house and change songs with the remote control, or

- I could sit at my PC and use the web interface.

Now that I live in Hong Kong, closed captions (subtitles) have become a large part of my movie viewing experience. A lot of commercial DVD players are horrible at displaying subtitles or sometimes the movie is just missing them. With XBMC connected to my TV, I now can easily fix the subtitles or add them in if they are missing.

A friend of mine is big into watching TV series but is normally not home at the right times to watch them. He has a few TV tuner cards installed into his XBMC that allows him to record the TV shows to the hard drive and when he's ready to watch it's just a simple matter of turning on XBMC.

The Raspberry Pi is capable of all of the above-mentioned tasks and more. I will list some resources to get you up and running:

- Adding videos to XBMC: http://wiki.xbmc.org/index.php?title=Video_library

- Adding music to XBMC: http://wiki.xbmc.org/index.php?title=Preparing_your_Music

- Recording live TV: http://wiki.xbmc.org/index.php?title=PVR

The best place to start after you have installed XBMC is the XBMC wiki, which details steps for how to configure your media. It's also frequently updated; as with new versions of XBMC, some steps change slightly. Check it out at

http://wiki.xbmc.org/index.php?title=Main_Page

You can also extend XBMC with many add-on applications. Add-on applications can be developed by end users or by the XBMC team. They add functions that are not part of the main build of XBMC. Take a look at the add-on page for more information:

http://wiki.xbmc.org/index.php?title=Add-ons

I hope I have covered most of the setup of XBMC in this chapter for you; you may also want to take a quick look at the Raspberry Pi XBMC page:

http://wiki.xbmc.org/index.php?title=Raspberry_Pi/FAQ

Browser Access

XBMC supports access via HTTP. This allows you to access a few options to control XBMC. You can use your standard web browser of choice to connect to XBMC or you can turn your Android mobile phone into a fancy remote control. To be able to do any of the above cool features, you first need to enable the web server on XBMC. The quickest way to do this is via the command line. You can also enable the web server via the interface but it's a bit of a pain to enter if you don't have a keyboard connected to your OpenELEC install. Also I am sure by now you know that I like my command line a lot. Use SSH to get back into the system and change to the userdata folder:

```
# cd /storage/.xbmc/userdata
```

Open the file named guisettings.xml. Search for the section called <services>: when you have found this section there are two main options you must change. They are webserverpassword and webserver. By default the web server will be set to "false" and the web server password will be blank. You must set a password and set the web server to "true" for the service to activate. See Figure 7-13 for my settings. I recommend you use a better password than what's in Figure 7-13.

```
<webserver>true</webserver>
<webserverpassword>xbmc</webserverpassword>
<webserverport>80</webserverport>
<webserverusername>xbmc</webserverusername>
```

Figure 7-13. *Settings for <services>*

Restart XBMC for the changes to take effect. You will now be able to go to the IP address of your XBMC. If you have not set up any media yet, the web interface will be pretty bland.

In Figure 7-14 you can see the default web site. I've not configured any media.

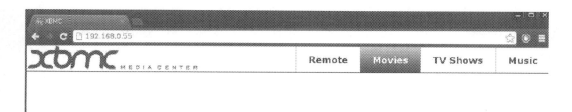

Figure 7-14. *The XBMC default web site*

Remote Control Phone

Now that you have the web server enabled and tested, you can set up your Android phone as a remote. Your phone must be on the local network that the XBMC media center is on for this to work. There are two ways to obtain the official Android XBMC remote.

- The first way is via the web site at http://code.google.com/p/android-xbmcremote/; you can scan the QR code on your mobile and the application will download. The web site also gives you some background on what the application can do. It's well worth your time to take a quick look at the site.

- The second way to get the application is by using the Google Play store. This is the method I will be using.

On your mobile phone, open the Google Play store. Once you have it opened, search for "Official XBMC Remote." There are a few other remote applications for XBMC but you want to make sure you get the official one. You can see in Figure 7-15 the XMBC install screen on the mobile phone.

Figure 7-15. *The Google Play store showing the official XBMC remote app*

Once the app is installed, open it up and you will be greeted with a "no hosts found" message. Click the Settings button. On this screen is where you enter the details of your XBMC installation. The app allows you to have more than one XBMC install configured, so don't worry too much because you won't break anything. Go right ahead and enter the details. The user name and password will be the ones you configured in the XML file earlier on. In Figure 7-16 you can see where I have configured the app to talk to my XBMC installation on 192.168.0.55. If you don't know the IP address of your OpenELEC installation, log in via SSH or check the GUI under "System Information."

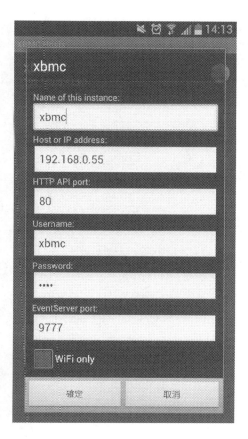

Figure 7-16. *The remote settings page*

There are only a few fields you must fill in on the settings page. They are instance name, IP address, HTTP port, user name, and password: the rest are optional. Once you're done, click OK. As you see in Figure 7-16 the OK button is represented by "確 定,"which means "confirm." The app will now try to connect to your XBMC installation; if there are no issues you will be presented with what you see in Figure 7-17. The app gives you a lot of functionality. You can watch your recorded TV shows or movies, or you can listen to your music and see what's currently playing. The main function you are after is the "Remote Control" feature.

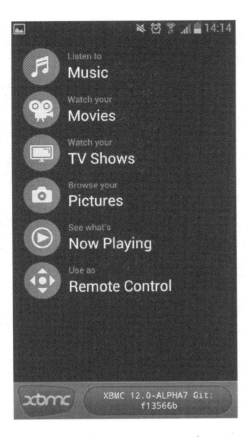

Figure 7-17. *The many options on the remote*

Select the Remote Control option and you will be presented with a very nice-looking remote. You can now control your XBMC via this remote. You can see what the remote looks like in Figure 7-18.

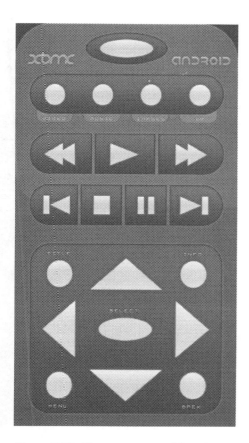

Figure 7-18. *The remote control function*

Summary

In this chapter you got an introduction to XBMC and why I am a big fan of it. XBMC is a very mature project and is supported on a wide range of hardware. I highly recommend you take a look into where else you can take advantage of XBMC in your home. I showed you a Linux distribution that was highly optimized for the Raspberry Pi. This was the first time you moved away from using Fedora, and as you saw OpenELEC is nothing like Fedora! You also found out that just like Fedora sometimes things don't work right away. I showed you how to debug the install script.

Then we looked at a way to get NTP running on OpenELEC; this dealt with the root filesystem and how it gets unpacked on each boot. The choices behind OpenELEC became very clear when I talked about the optimization made to the distribution, especially the GCC compile and link-time settings. Understanding the optimization settings and how the GCC will optimize your code will play a large role in the upcoming chapter on cross compiling for the Raspberry Pi.

Once OpenELEC was up and running, I pointed out a few quick tips for the Raspberry Pi. Do keep in mind that these settings are experimental and may break your installation. If you find you've made it worse, don't panic: just use SSH to enter the OpenELEC install and reverse your change. Luckily you have that root filesystem that you can't change! Lastly I showed you how to set up the web server in XBMC. Please do set a better password than I did!

Now that you have a web server up and running, you could use the amazing remote control for your Android phone. You did not expect me to control an open source media player with an iPhone now, did you? There are many possibilities for the Raspberry Pi, whether it's using it as a streaming music player via the GPIO LCD project or as a small hidden media player for your TV.

In the next chapter I will show you how to build a real-time clock, which would have come in handy with our time issues in this chapter. On to that next!

CHAPTER 8

Adding an RTC

When I first looked at the Raspberry Pi there was one missing piece of hardware that stood out to me. This little piece of hardware has been on pretty much every system you may have used, especially in recent years. What exactly is this missing piece of hardware? It's the real-time clock, or RTC for short. In most modern computer systems you would be hard-pressed not to find the RTC with a quick glance. What you would notice is that little silver coin–shaped battery. Why would the RTC chip need a battery? The main function of the RTC is to keep the current time and date, which has been set into the RTC chip.

This little chip then needs a very small power source in order to keep the RTC counting up. You know by now there is no battery anywhere on the Raspberry Pi. Not all systems have a visible battery though. Take, for example, Figure 8-1: this is an RTC/NVRAM combo chip often seen on early SPARC systems.

Figure 8-1. *A Sun SPARC RTC/NVRAM package*

This RTC/NVRAM package will do more than just keep the date. It would also store system serial numbers and MAC addresses. The battery is built in to this unit, making for fun times when the RTC does go flat. One thing you will soon find out from this chapter is that the overall circuit and parts needed for an RTC have not shrunk much over the years. Sure, you may now have a surface-mount technology (SMT) RTC package but your battery is still quite large when compared to the modern SMT package (I'll cover SMT in this chapter, so don't worry if you're new to it).

There also is one small extra component you must have for the RTC to function. This is a crystal oscillator, and its main task is to provide a timing source for the RTC. Unfortunately, crystals are not the most accurate timing devices. Over time you will notice that your RTC will drift slightly. An RTC is never as accurate as a well-configured NTP daemon. RTCs take up a lot of space, add complexity, and are not as accurate as NTP, so why would you want one? Well, for the most part, you don't need it if your Raspberry Pi will always be connected to a network: NTP will be a better option. What about when your Raspberry Pi never gets used on a network? Let's say, for example, you attach a nice little LCD and use the GPIO pins to do something like read the temperature. Every time you reboot you're going to have issues logging in because your system date and time will have drifted too far back in time. If you had added a hardware RTC to your Raspberry Pi, this would not be a problem. The system would read the time from the RTC on boot and continue on its happy way. If you are going to use your Raspberry Pi as a stand-alone PC or even as part of a non-networked project all hope is not lost if you don't have an RTC. Most common Linux distributions contain a software clock that will record the last shutdown time. This will solve your login issues as your time won't drift back to the 1960s, but it's far from an accurate time source.

The need for an RTC will really depend on your project. Unfortunately it's not some feature you can just enable or plug in. That's what this chapter will cover: how to make an RTC circuit and how to attach it to the Raspberry Pi. This chapter will include some minor SMT, but don't be put off by that work. When I come to the SMT work I will show you some tricks to make it easy for you.

The Beginning of the RTC in PCs

The first PC to use an RTC was the IBM PC/AT, launched on August 15, 1984. As you can see, PCs have used RTCs for a long time. The PC/AT used the MC146818, made by Motorola at the time. The original MC146818 was a 24-pin dual inline package, or DIP package. A DIP package is where you have the chip in the middle of pins that run on each side, and the chip is then placed into a socket or soldered into holes on a PCB. Compare that to the RTC you will be using; it's a rather large chip. I want to talk about how the MC146818 gives out a valid date and time. Once you understand the MC146818, you can move on to using any RTC as they are all loosely based on the MC146818.

The MC146818 had a set of nine registers that you could read and write to.

- Registers 0, 2, and 4 controlled the time: register 0 was the seconds register, 2 was the minutes register, and 4 was the hours register.

- Registers 6, 7, 8, and 9 were responsible for the date functions: register 6 was the day of the week, register 7 was the date of the month, register 8 was the month, and register 9 was the year.

When the RTC is in a fully powered and operational state, you can read any combination of the above registers to get your desired date and time. If you wanted to, you could also write a date and time value back to the registers. This was often done when you first used an RTC to set its time.

At the heart of it, an RTC is just a simple counting device. Every one second it updates the registers to their next value. Exactly how would this chip know what one second is, though? That's where your crystal oscillator comes in. This small device, as the name implies, oscillates at a set frequency. This frequency is printed on the device and you will be using a 32.768-kHz crystal. How can something oscillating at 32.768 kHz give you a one-second timer? Well, it can't. That's where another chip comes into play.

This little chip is part of the main RTC chip. It's called a prescaler and its main job in life is to divide the input frequency into a stable, slow clock rate. This prescaler is what gives us the 1-Hz frequency that in turn gives us the one-second tick value: after all, 1 Hz is equal to one pulse per second. Unfortunately, crystals are affected by the temperature and many other environmental effects. Any of these effects can alter the frequency at which the crystal oscillates. This is where your clock skew comes from. There is nothing that you can do about this and I am sure you have all experienced it: for example, when you turn on an old PC that has been powered down for a while and notice that it's lost a few hours. Of course you're going to need a way to keep this crystal oscillating when your device is turned off. This is where the little coin-shaped battery has its one and only job. Its job is to supply just enough current to keep the RTC chip alive and the crystal oscillating. If your battery goes flat you will instantly lose the stored date and time.

You may have noticed that when I was talking about the registers I skipped a few numbers. There is another function of the RTC and that is an alarm function. The skipped registers provide a way to set an alarm date and time for an event to happen. If you had poked around your PC's BIOS you would have come across a setting that can wake up your PC at a set time. This function directly uses the RTC registers to listen for the set alarm date and time.

Pretty much every RTC you will find today will bear some similarity to the MC146818, so as long as you understand the basic functions of the MC146818 you will be fine to select any RTC for your project. It's time to take a closer look at the RTC you will use for this project.

The DS1338 RTC

The RTC you will use will be a little different from the old MC146818. It's made by Maxim and is called DS1338Z-33 and has fewer pins (only 8, as opposed to 24 on the MC146818). It's also a lot smaller and is no longer a DIP package. What you're looking at is called the SO-8 or SOIC-8. SOIC, or SO for short, is small outline integrated circuit and the 8 simply means how many pads the package comes with. You may notice I said pads and not pins; that's because an SO package is designed to be surface mounted to the PCB. The surface mount components are also quite small and fairly easy to lose if you drop them on the floor.

I will show you how to work with the SO-8 package a little later on. If you have not read the data sheet by now your first question would be how can only eight pads drive all the registers that are needed? Well, I suggest you read the data sheet first.

The DS1338Z-33 is actually an I2C device. All access to the date and time registers will be done with the I2C protocol. If you recall, you used the I2C bus in Chapter 4 and as such I won't be going over how it works. It's now time to show you what each of the pads are used for on this little device. See Table 8-1 for the pad out descriptions, but as always refer back to your data sheet.

Table 8-1. *The pads on the DS1338Z-33*

Pad Number	Name	Function
1	X1	External oscillating crystal connection
2	X2	External oscillating crystal connection
3	Vbat	Battery backup power source
4	GND	Ground
5	SDA	I2C SDA line
6	SDL	I2C SDL line
7	SQW/OUT	Square wave output, if enabled
8	Vcc	Primary voltage source

There are some good reasons for why the DS1338Z-33 is a good fit for the Raspberry Pi:

- It's a 3.3-V logic device.
- It's supported by the Linux kernel.

The downside of the DS1338Z-33 is that it's an SO-8 package with the problems I mentioned above (surface mounting and small size). I will use a small bridge board to allow you to easily plug in the RTC into your breadboards or into jumper cables to get around the surface-mount difficulties. The key issues with surface-mount components are their size. They will be a lot smaller. If you think of the size difference between an SD card and a micro SD card, then you will start to understand the difference. For you this means the pads will be a lot closer together, meaning it will be a little harder to solder. Also because it's smaller they heat up quicker, so you need to solder a bit quicker so you don't damage the chip.

The Crystal

The next important component is the crystal. The most common crystals are made from synthetic quartz. The material that the crystal is made from plays a big part in how the crystal works; there are other materials that could be used but quartz is the least sensitive to outside interference. Quartz by nature is a piezoelectric material. A piezoelectric material is one that will develop a charge when under physical stress. Physical stress can be caused by a small current running across the material in question. When this small current is applied to the quartz, it will resonate at a set frequency. In turn this frequency can be measured by an external circuit.

In Figure 8-2 you can see what the inside of a crystal oscillator looks like. This crystal is from a T6 cylinder package; this will be the same package you use to feed the DS1338Z-33. The quartz crystal needs to be tuned to a set frequency, which is done when the T6 package is made because the shape and size of the crystal are what set its frequency.

Figure 8-2. *The inside of a T6 package quartz crystal*

The T6 package is easy to work with; it can simply be plugged into the breadboard. Crystals do come in many shapes and sizes; the main thing you need to worry about is the frequency. There is one extra critical part you need for this little RTC to function correctly. That is the battery: without this the RTC will still operate normally but every time you power off the device it will lose the date and time, which would seem a little counterproductive for an RTC. I am using a 3.7-V lithium coin battery. There are other sources you could use; for example, you may want to use a double-layer capacitor (EDLC) or supercapacitor. I have picked the coin-shaped battery that everyone has seen on pretty much any recent PC motherboard. This will require you to move away from using just a breadboard but I will cover that later on in the chapter.

You can easily see why the foundation has chosen to leave an RTC off the Raspberry Pi. It would have used up a lot of PCB space. Sure, you can get smaller batteries and smaller RTC chips but they are expensive. When I say expensive, I don't just mean cost, although that is a big one for the Raspberry Pi. Another hidden cost is how you route the circuits. Crystals are a timing device; therefore, they are sensitive to interference. This comes as an expense in terms of how you can place and route the tracks for the RTC and its supporting components. It's now time to take a look at what you will need to build the RTC.

Parts List and Assembly

You're not going to need much for this project because the two main parts are the battery holder and the RTC chip itself. When I chose an RTC for this project I originally wanted to use the DS1307. The DS1307 is well supported by the Linux kernel and is very compatible; it's also a DIP 8 package. Unfortunately it's not 3.3 V. Sure, you could use a level shifter or some other voltage source but I don't like that idea: it's messy and unnecessary. The DS1338 could be powered just from the Raspberry Pi if you wanted to, as it is fully 3.3-V compliant. The same cannot be said about the DS1307. In terms of pin out and function, the DS1307 and DS1338 are very, very close. So now here's the parts list:

- One DS1338Z-33
- One SO-8 adapter
- One 32.768-kHz crystal

- One 3-V CR2032 lithium battery

- One CR2032 battery holder

- A small PCB

I want to bring your attention to the SO-8 adapter. In my haste to get an RTC built for the Raspberry Pi, I just grabbed the first SO-8 adapter plate I saw. Unfortunately for me, no matter what way I placed this into my breadboards, it shorted out some of the pins. This means I had to use jumper wire to connect up my adapter board; it works fine but it's very ugly. Ideally you would want one row of pins on each bank of the breadboard with the RTC chip sitting dead center in between them. This will allow for easy and clean writing. With that in mind I will start by soldering the RTC to the adapter board.

Soldering the Adapter Board

There are two tools I need for SMT soldering jobs:

- A set of handy hands, as seen in Figure 8-3

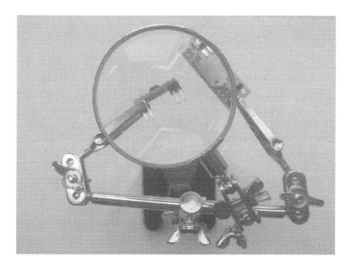

Figure 8-3. *Handy hands: a very handy addition*

- A good thin desoldering wick

My set of handy hands also comes with a small magnifying glass; even if you don't use this to solder with it's a real smart idea to check your work with it after you're done.

Take a look at my completed adapter and the DS1338Z-33 sitting next to it in Figure 8-4. It's quite small. Sometimes these little chips are a real pain to grab. For this I use tweezers: there are special SMT tweezers you can use or you can use the everyday cheap ones as I do.

Figure 8-4. *Adapter and SO-8 chip*

First you need to get some solder onto the pads on the SO-8 adapter board. This method is called sweat soldering. Hold the RTC chip on top of the solder and apply a small amount of heat to the legs of the RTC. If your adapter board has pin numbers, line up pin 1 of the SO-8 chip with pin 1 on the adapter board. Pad 1 is the pad with the little circle next to it on the SO-8 package. I never seem to be this lucky; my board has no pad numbers so just go ahead and solder it on anyway; later on I'll show you how to identify the pads once they are soldered.

It's a wise idea to solder opposite sides first. So solder the top left-hand-side pin first, then solder the last right-hand-side pin. This anchors the component on each corner. By doing this you will prevent the RTC chip from moving when you are trying to solder the rest of the pads. In Figure 8-5 you can see the finished job. Don't be afraid of adding too much solder; I often do (if not, I accidentally join legs together). In fact it happens a lot when I am working with SMT. If this happens get your desoldering wick and apply a small amount of solder to it. Then place it across the pins that have been accidentally joined together and apply heat to the desoldering wick. This will remove the excess solder away and leave the solder between the PCB and chip in place. Do check your solder joints with the magnifying glass. There is nothing worse than missing a connection.

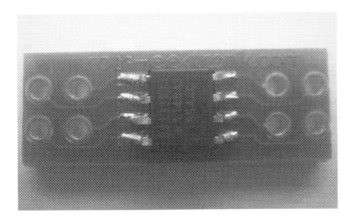

Figure 8-5. *RTC soldered into the adapter board*

Your adapter board now needs some legs. This is pretty similar to soldering the legs for the LCD in Chapter 4. There is only one small tip I have for you. To make sure your pins will fit well into a breadboard when you're done, it's best to do the soldering while the pins are in a breadboard. Place your rows of pins into a spare breadboard, then place the adapter board on to the pins. Once again it's wise to solder opposite corners first and then work inward. You can see in Figure 8-6 where I have placed the pins in the breadboard but have not yet placed the adapter board on top.

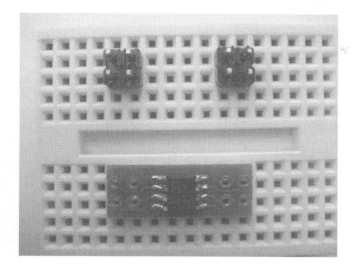

Figure 8-6. *Legs ready to be soldered in*

Try not to heat up the adapter board too much if you can avoid it. You could damage the board itself or you may damage the RTC as well. Once you're done, remove the adapter and RTC from the breadboard. It's always a good idea to remove any excess length from the legs from the top of the adapter board. Use a small set of side cutters for this.

Now the hard part is out of the way and you can make the battery PCB.

Making the Battery PCB

I told you that SMT was not as hard as you thought. Because the battery is so big, I have opted to put it on a separate PCB. You may want to look at smaller holders if you wanted to make this a permanent addition. I don't want to waste an entire PCB on this, nor do I have the need to make a custom PCB.

1. With this in mind, find a small PCB and place your battery holder on it.

2. Once you're happy with the layout, grab a small cutter knife and score the tracks around the sides of the battery holder. Don't do this on the copper side.

3. Remove the battery holder and score the tracks a little more. You don't need to cut all the way though with the cutter: good luck!

4. There a few methods to cutting PCBs. You may want to use a Dremel if you have access to one, but watch out for the dust from cutting the PCB; it's not healthy and in fact is highly toxic. If you don't have access to a Dremel you may want to try a small hacksaw. Failing that, a set of scissors works well, especially if they are the type made to cut up chicken bones or crabs.

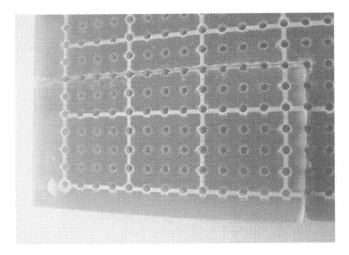

Figure 8-7. *One side cut and one side scored and ready to be cut*

5. Once you're done cutting the PCB, you may have noticed that it's pretty sharp and not very nice to hold. Get out your file and sand down each edge that you cut down. Because you cut through the holes in the board I normally sand down so that the holes and trace are not visible or barely visible.

6. Figure 8-8 shows where I have filed down the cut-down PCB so that it's now ready to use. Give it a good wipe to get any dust off it. That may hamper your soldering.

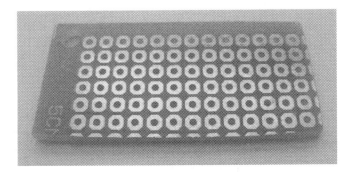

Figure 8-8. *PCB ready to use*

7. The battery holder I bought has the negative terminal at one end of the holder and the positive terminal at the other end. I don't like to have a header at each end of the board; it's just a personal preference for pin placement. However, you can have one if you like: it won't change a thing about this project. I have soldered the two headers at one end of the PCB. To do this, place the legs into the board and flip the board over: this will put pressure on the legs because they are the highest part of the board. You can see in Figure 8-9 where I have run a small trace wire from the negative terminal up to the same side that the positive terminal is connected to.

Figure 8-9. *Top side of the battery holder*

8. On the bottom side, connect the solder pads together to form a track. If you're having issues with this, use a small strip of wire and the solder will stick to the wire and the underlying pad. Figure 8-10 shows how I have done this.

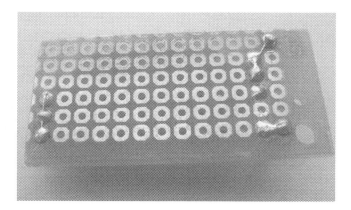

Figure 8-10. *Bottom side of the battery holder*

All the solder work is out of the way now. The rest can be done with hook-up wire and your breadboard.

Building the Circuit

Recall that when you soldered the RTC to the adapter board, I did not talk about which way is the correct way to solder it, unless you were lucky and had pin numbers at hand. There is no correct way. How do you find pin 1 then? You would have noticed that the RTC chip lacked the little crescent shape on one side. SMT components are designed to save space and most of them will not have the crescent that you have been used to seeing in the DIP format. Take a close look at the top of your RTC chip: what you're looking for is a very small circle. Take a look at Figure 8-11 and you can see a close-up of my chip. You will notice the little indented circle.

Figure 8-11. *Pin 1 indicator*

This is the pad 1 indicator. You also may have noticed that the circle is about as wide as pad 1 and pad 2. Pin 1 is always the closest pad to the edge of the chip that's closest to the circle. You need to map this back to the pin leg of your adapter board. This should be pretty easy. You can either follow the tracks on the physical board or use a multimeter to check for continuity between the RTC chip's leg and the adapter board's leg.

It's now a good time to look at the circuit diagrams because you have all your parts assembled and ready to use. There is one small thing you need to keep in mind: you should never place power tracks over the crystal. Nor should you run power tracks under or close by the RTC chip. Both these components can easily be affected by outside interference. So take a few extra moments to work out the best layout. First, let's take a look at Figure 8-12 to see how it should be assembled on the breadboard. Unfortunately, my breadboard in real life doesn't look this neat because of my adapter board.

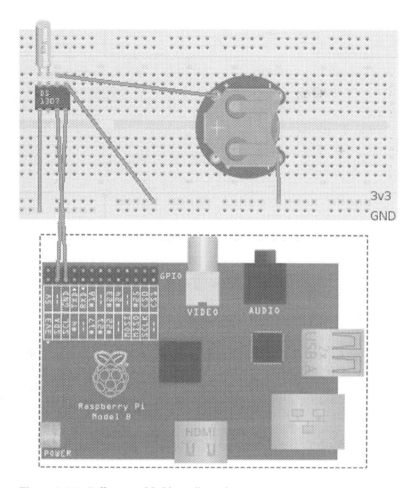

Figure 8-12. *Fully assembled breadboard*

You also will benefit from a schematic drawing and the data sheets for your RTC. Take a look at the circuit schematics in Figure 8-13. As you can see, there is not much to it. If your SO-8 adapter package cannot fit into your breadboard, simply use some jumper cables to connect the legs of the adapter into the breadboard.

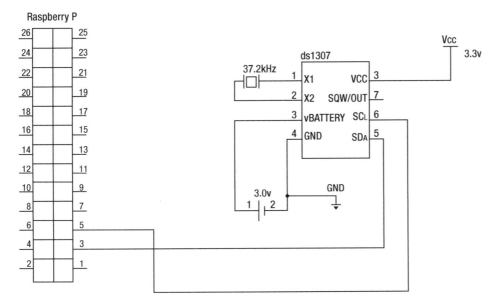

Figure 8-13. *Circuit schematics*

Armed with the above information and your data sheets, you're now ready to do the final assembly. I like to do the power circuits first, although it won't matter what order you do them in.

1. Connect 3.3 V to pin 1.

2. Connect the ground to pin 4.

3. Connect the ground from the battery to the same ground bar.

4. Connect pin 3 to the positive terminal of the battery.

That's it for the power sources: you could do all this from the Raspberry Pi if you wanted to. You can see the completed power circuits in Figure 8-14. I have opted for an external power source but there is nothing stopping you from using the 3.3-V source and ground source of the Raspberry Pi.

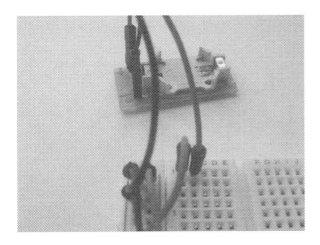

Figure 8-14. *Power circuits installed*

The remaining connections are quite simple.

1. Take pin 1 and pin 2 and connect them to your crystal. The crystal is not polarity-sensitive so feel free to connect it however you want.

2. Next up are the I2C bus lines. Take pin 5 and connect it to the Raspberry Pi's P1-03 GPIO pin, and take pin 6 and connect it to the Raspberry Pi's P1-05 GPIO pin. It's best to do this when the Raspberry Pi is off: you don't want to short out anything.

■ **Note** Because the DS1338Z-33 is a slave device (just like the shift register described in Chapter 4), you could combine it and another I2C device or many I2C devices on the same bus.

---

3. Don't forget to install your lithium battery as well; otherwise, your RTC won't keep any time.

4. Once the connections have been made, turn on your Raspberry Pi.

It's time to put the RTC to use, but where is it? I guess you have never had to think about how to use an RTC before, because it has always just been there.

The Soft Side

Since you expected it to just work, I am guessing the first thing you did was search the dmesg output, only to be disappointed that no RTC was found. Did you really expect it to just work? I sure did not. I am sure you remember working with the i2c-tools in Chapter 4, but if you don't you can find all the details on using i2c-tools there. The first thing I did was load the i2c-dev module manually with this command:

```
# modprobe i2c-dev
```

This will allow you to run an I2C bus scan. If you recall from Chapter 4 you can do that via this command:

```
# i2cdetect 0
```

Keep in mind that you may need to scan bus 1 or bus 0, just like you did in Chapter 4. You can see from Figure 8-15 that I have found a device at address 0x68. Oddly enough I found no way to set an address for this slave device. So it may be wise to plan around this slave device if you want to add more I2C slave devices.

```
[root@hobo ~]# i2cdetect 0
WARNING! This program can confuse your I2C bus, cause data loss and worse!
I will probe file /dev/i2c-0.
I will probe address range 0x03-0x77.
Continue? [Y/n] y
     0  1  2  3  4  5  6  7  8  9  a  b  c  d  e  f
00:          -- -- -- -- -- -- -- -- -- -- -- -- --
10: -- -- -- -- -- -- -- -- -- -- -- -- -- -- -- --
20: -- -- -- -- -- -- -- -- -- -- -- -- -- -- -- --
30: -- -- -- -- -- -- -- -- -- -- -- -- -- -- -- --
40: -- -- -- -- -- -- -- -- -- -- -- -- -- -- -- --
50: -- -- -- -- -- -- -- -- -- -- -- -- -- -- -- --
60: -- -- -- -- -- -- -- -- 68 -- -- -- -- -- -- --
70: -- -- -- -- -- -- -- --
[root@hobo ~]#
```

Figure 8-15. *RTC at 0x68*

Now that you know your RTC is alive on your I2C bus the next challenge is to load a supporting module. Recall how I said the DS1338 was hardware-compatible with the DS1307? If you were to take a look at a module listing for the Raspberry Pi you will notice there is nothing listed for the DS1338.

```
# modprobe -l
```

So how do you know it's compatible? There are two ways to check this. The first method is by using the tool modinfo:

```
# modinfo rtc-ds1307
```

This will give you an alias table and you will find the DS1338 listed there. Another way to find out if the module has support for the DS1338 chip is to use a command called strings. This command will search though compiled code and pull out the text strings:

```
# strings /lib/modules/`uname -r`/kernel/drivers/rtc/rtc-ds1307.ko | grep ds1338
```

You would see the same alias definition. Take a look at Figure 8-16 to see the output on my Raspberry Pi.

```
[root@hobo ~]# modinfo rtc-ds1307
filename:       /lib/modules/3.2.27+/kernel/drivers/rtc/rtc-ds1307.ko
license:        GPL
description:    RTC driver for DS1307 and similar chips
srcversion:     F857655D1929C6AD6033A31
alias:          i2c:rx8025
alias:          i2c:pt7c4338
alias:          i2c:mcp7941x
alias:          i2c:m41t00
alias:          i2c:ds3231
alias:          i2c:ds1340
alias:          i2c:ds1388
alias:          i2c:ds1339
alias:          i2c:ds1338
alias:          i2c:ds1337
alias:          i2c:ds1307
depends:
intree:         Y
vermagic:       3.2.27+ preempt mod_unload modversions ARMv6
[root@hobo ~]# strings /lib/modules/`uname -r`/kernel/drivers/rtc/rtc-ds1307.ko | grep ds1338
ds1338
alias=i2c:ds1338
[root@hobo ~]#
```

Figure 8-16. *Module info and the strings tool*

If you were to run either one of these tools on any of the other RTC modules listed by the modinfo -l command you would soon notice that none of them have DS1338 listed. So this has to be what you need to load. You need to load this module in a very special way, otherwise nothing will happen because the module has no idea what address your RTC can be found at. You're going to need to tell it where to find the RTC. To do that, you're going to use the special file called new_device.

This special file can only be written to and its sole job is to instantiate an I2C slave device at a certain address. This file takes two parameters.

- The first parameter is the name of the kernel module that is needed to support the device expressed just as the device name. It will take care of loading any kernel modules needed. In your case this first parameter will be ds1307.

- The second parameter will be the address of the I2C device in hex. In your case this will be 0x68 as you found out via the i2cdetect tool.

The full command to load the module will look like this; once again your I2C bus may be different, so use the bus that you worked with in the previous steps. In my case, this is bus 0.

```
# echo ds1307 0x68 > /sys/class/i2c-adapter/ i2c-0/new_device
```

You can see in Figure 8-17 the dmesg output and that an RTC was found and that a new device node was created at /dev/rtc0.

```
[root@hobo ~]# echo ds1307 0x68 > /sys/class/i2c-adapter/i2c-0/new_device
[  578.137750] i2c i2c-0: new_device: Instantiated device ds1307 at 0x68
[  578.170597] rtc-ds1307 0-0068: rtc core: registered ds1307 as rtc0
[  578.177690] rtc-ds1307 0-0068: 56 bytes nvram
```

Figure 8-17. *dmesg listing for the new device*

Now that your hardware RTC is installed, it might be a good idea to read from it. Issue the following command:

```
# hwclock -r
```

The date will be a little bit off; after all, the RTC has never been used. Take a look at Figure 8-18; you can see the very wrong date on my RTC.

```
[root@hobo ~]# hwclock -r
Sat Jan  1 00:53:17 2000  -0.161569 seconds
[root@hobo ~]#
```

Figure 8-18. *Invalid date and time on RTC*

It would be a good idea to set the correct date. If you issue the date command, you will notice the date and time have been set back to the date and time in the RTC. Set the correct date and time with the date command:

```
# date MMDDHHMMYYYY
```

This command breaks down as follows: MM is the month, zero padded; DD is the day, also zero padded; HH is the hour in 24-hour format; MM is minutes, also zero padded; and YYYY is the full four-digit year number. After you have done that, set the current system date and time to be the current date and time in the RTC. To do this, use this command:

```
# hwclock -w
```

This will write the system date and time into the hardware clock; it's best to check that the previous command has worked with the hwclock -r command so that you can read the date and time from the RTC. Give your Raspberry Pi a reboot to see your new RTC in action. As expected, nothing happens. The RTC was not even detected. The reason for this is that by default the Linux kernel will not look on the I2C bus for any form of RTC. You are also using a userspace tool to create the device node; the Linux kernel has no way to detect devices on an I2C bus. For the Linux kernel to search the I2C bus for an RTC, you need to have a special command-line option passed to the kernel at boot time. It would look something like the following:

```
rtc.i2c=ds1307,0,0x68
```

This tells the Linux kernel to use the I2C bus to look for an RTC with the device type of DS1307 or an RTC that is compatible on I2C bus 0 with the hex address of 0x68. This command-line option depends on having the i2c-dev and the rtc_ds1307 modules built in as part of the kernel. As you can see on the Raspberry Pi they are not built in; if the module was built into the kernel you would not be able to use a tool like modinfo as it's no longer a kernel module but part of the kernel itself. At this point you have two options.

- First, you could compile your own kernel for the Raspberry Pi with the two above modules built in. If you wanted to do this you could use the fast cross compile environment you configured in Chapter 6.

- If you don't want to recompile the kernel, you're going to need to compromise when your RTC will come online. You've decided you don't want to have it come online early in the boot process but you do not want it coming online too late into the system boot. If the RTC comes on too late in the boot stages, you may find your boot messages are no longer in order or the system logs appear to "jump" in time. It's not the end of the world but it's also not the best outcome.

For this purpose I created an init.d script that will load and unload modules and create and remove the device node. This script is written for Fedora and should work on any RHEL-type operating system. Take a look at Listing 8-1 to see the script. You need to create a file called /etc/init.d/pi-rtc and ensure that it has its execute bit set.

Listing 8-1. The init.d Script for the RTC

```
#!/bin/sh
#
# Author : Brendan Horan
# Description : To load and unload the ds1338 i2c rtc
# you should only need to change the address
#
# chkconfig: 12345 82 82
# description: I2C RTC

# Source function library.
if [ -e /etc/rc.d/init.d/functions ]; then
  . /etc/rc.d/init.d/functions
fi

# set the hex address of the rtc chip
address=0x68

# Change nothing below this line


RETVAL=0

start() {
        echo -n "Starting I2C RTC : "
        modprobe i2c-dev
```

```
        echo ds1307 ${address} > /sys/class/i2c-adapter/i2c-0/new_device
        RETVAL=$?
        touch /var/lock/subsys/pi-rtc
        if [ ${RETVAL} -eq 0 ]
          then
            success
          else
            failure
          fi
        echo
        return $RETVAL
}

stop() {
        echo -n "Stopping I2C RTC : "
        echo ${address} > /sys/class/i2c-adapter/i2c-0/delete_device
        RETVAL=$?
        rmmod rtc_ds1307
        rmmod i2c-dev
        rm -f /var/lock/subsys/pi-rtc
        if [ $RETVAL -eq 0 ]
          then
            success
          else
            failure
          fi
        echo
        return $RETVAL
}

case "$1" in
  start)
        start
        ;;
  stop)
        stop
        ;;
  *)
        echo "Usage: pi-rtc {start|stop}"
        exit 1
esac

exit $RETVAL
```

You can control this script in two ways. You can use the chkconfig tool to set or remove it from system boot or you can use the service tool to start and stop the script when you are logged in. If you wanted to start the RTC when you're logged in, simply run this command as root:

```
# service pi-rtc start
```

I have this script set to start on boot with the following command:

```
# chkconfig  pi-rtc on
```

When you next reboot the Raspberry Pi, your RTC will be loaded and activated.

Now that you have successfully added an RTC to your Raspberry Pi you can use it as either a quick and simple pocket desktop or an offline data logger.

Summary

In this chapter you had the chance to learn about the origins of RTCs and how they can function on a very basic level. You were introduced to the MC146818 and the much-cloned RTC. I gave you information on how you could poke its registers to gain certain date or time values. I then moved on to the DS1338Z-33, which would provide all the RTC functions for this chapter.

You can't have an RTC without a timing source. I talked about how crystal oscillators work and what their functions are. I also talked about why the Raspberry Pi Foundation has left the RTC out. Then we moved on to your first time using SMT components in this book. I showed you some tools to make your life easier and some tricks to make you less nervous when doing small SMT work. It was then time to construct the circuit to hold the battery. This involved cutting a premade PCB and adapting it to your needs. Do remember that the dust from these boards is toxic and you should take caution when working with them.

Lastly you finally got to connect the RTC to the Raspberry Pi via the I2C bus. What a useful bus! Unfortunately, you soon found out that not all was perfect and that your RTC cannot be used at early boot stages without some kernel modifications. Not to worry, because I gave you the second best thing with a fully functional init.d script that takes care of all the hard work for you.

CHAPTER 9

■ ■ ■

Serial Server

By now, many of you may have guessed that I spend a lot of time at the command line. After all, it's my day-to-day work and my pastime at home. Given that I spend a lot of time at the command line, I don't like to open a web browser to access some device's management interface. I am much more at home configuring devices via the command-line tool. Even if this is not your preference, a lot of enterprise-grade equipment must have its initial configuration set up via a serial console, which does not require Ethernet.

Having serial access to the Raspberry Pi may be a good idea for the security sensor in Chapter 5: this way you can access and communicate with the system without the need for an SSH connection over Ethernet that may lead to a security issue. You also may want to use the Raspberry Pi as a temperature display by using the LCD from Chapter 4 and a sensor from Chapter 3; this system would not need to have an Ethernet connection to operate. The serial console would give you a quick and easy way to perform maintenance on the system.

So in this chapter I'll explain what a serial console is, how to configure the Pi's serial ports, and how to access your Pi using this approach.

What Exactly Is a Serial Console Anyway?

When you turn on your home machine the first thing you notice is the boot messages on your monitor. You then sit down and enter text with your keyboard. You then need to access a remote system via SSH, so you open up a command-line console and connect to your remote server. This is all well and good if your remote server is up and running. What would happen if the machine had hung at the grub boot menu? Well, you don't have a screen or a keyboard to look at, so now what? This is where your serial console will come in to play. With a serial console all the boot messages and the grub menu will be redirected to the serial port instead of a physical screen. You can then use an application to connect to the serial port and interact with the serial console in a similar manner as you would with the SSH command console.

It's not just computers that can benefit from a serial console: a lot of enterprise devices extensively rely on serial consoles. Cisco switches come to mind as good examples. Or maybe it's the Raspberry Pi itself you wish to access via a serial line as discussed in the introduction.

In a lot of large organizations you will come across a device that can be known as a serial server, console server, or terminal server. These devices normally have many serial ports that are often accessed via a breakout cable or fan out cable. Their sole purpose in life is to connect you to the serial port of some remote device. Most often this will be a switch or router in the same data center. The logic behind this is that you can fully manage your equipment, no matter its state. For example, if your switches accidentally lose their configuration, you won't be able to access them via the IP address you configured. This is where the serial console in the back of the switch will save the day.

No matter what state the switch is in, you will always be able to find a way to configure or fix the remote device. Given that most data centers have a lot of devices, you need an efficient way to provide access to each one of these serial ports. The best way is to have some form of access over TCP/IP; this will allow you or others to remotely connect to the serial console of a device in a different location. It's quite common to see a Cisco device with an async card or two, providing this function in some organizations. I don't personally have an extra Cisco device at home; also my rack space is limited, just like all space in Hong Kong. Because of this I take a very different approach to building a serial server on my home network.

- First, the extra serial ports are provided by a PCI card with a four-port fan out cable and not via an async port on a router.

- Second, I don't have the ability to use Cisco's software so I have used an open source project called ser2net (http://ser2net.sourceforge.net/). This little open source project is one of my favorites: it's lightweight, easy to build, and functions exactly like its description says.

I have used ser2net for years now so don't be put off by its simple web page; it may be a simple application but it works very well. What ser2net will do is translate a physical serial port address into a TCP port socket and give you a few other nice features that I will talk about later on. This chapter will show you two main concepts. The first concept will be accessing the Raspberry Pi's serial console and the second concept will be using a USB universal asynchronous receiver/transmitter (UART) port to access another device's serial port via TCP/IP. This chapter will also introduce you to a device called a line-level converter because the UART ports on the Raspberry Pi don't work exactly the same as a normal PC's serial port would.

Serial Port, What Serial Port?

Serial ports are becoming harder and harder to find on pretty much any new computer you may come across. After all it's not like you need a serial port to read your e-mail or browse the web. Thankfully the Raspberry Pi comes with two hardware UART ports on board. What exactly is a UART? It is a hardware function that converts between parallel and serial data formats. The UART will take bytes of data and transmit them in sequential manner. On the other side of the connection, the UART will reassemble the bytes in the correct order. Think this sounds like the shift register from Chapter 4? Well, yes, all UARTs include a shift register integrated circuit (IC) to perform the basic function of converting the data. UARTs are used with a communication standard protocol, which is what defines how and when the UART can transmit the data. These standards are known as registered standards. You would have heard of RS-232, RS-485, or RS-422; these are the registered standards for serial communications, hence the RS in the name. How very original!

▓ **Note** I use only RS-232: that's what all of my serial devices use and most likely yours do too. These days you find RS-485 and RS-422 on only serial installations that need to span long distances.

The one thing most people seem to forget when they talk about UARTs is that a UART is never directly receiving or transmitting signals. Its job is only to convert, sort, and store the data in the correct format. You would never plug a serial cable directly into a UART, for example. If you did, you would see a nice puff of magic smoke. After all, an RS-232 connection could have up to a potential of 15 V running across it and a UART normally operates with a maximum voltage range of 5 V. So if the UART is not what you connect to, what are you connecting to when you plug in a serial cable? Directly behind the physical interface you will need an IC called a logic-level shifter. This IC's job is to convert the low-level logic voltage from the UART into the correct voltage levels depending on what RS standard you are using. Most often, it will be RS-232. Take a look at Figure 9-1 to see a high-level overview of a common serial port.

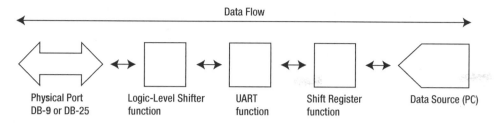

Figure 9-1. *A high-level view of the ICs and steps involved in a serial port*

Of course, there is a lot more to the serial port than what you see in Figure 9-1 but it should give you a general idea. There are two well-known generic UART ICs:

- The National Semiconductor 8250 was a very early UART IC that was in most PCs during the 1980s. This chip was a little slow but was simple to implement.

- One of the main clones of the 8250 was the 16550. The 16550 was originally made by National Semiconductor as well, and it improved on the 8250 but still remained easy to implement. The 16550 gained widespread adoption and can still be found on devices today. Because of this, the 16550 became the main standard for a UART implementation.

Today you will often read about a UART being compliant with the 16550. This means that all the functions that were defined as part of a 16550 IC would still function exactly the same on the computable IC. If you were to look at the data sheets of a 16550 compared to a 16550 compatible, you should notice a lot of similarities.

Serially a Bit of a Letdown

Getting back to the Raspberry Pi, everything but the physical interface and the logic-level shifter functions are already on board. The Raspberry Pi provides you with two UARTs for your use via the GPIO pins. Both UARTs are provided by the Broadcom system on chip (SoC) and are commonly known as the PL011 UART and the mini UART. By default, GPIOs 14 and 15 are set up on boot as the PL011 UART port (also known as UART0). This UART is what I will use throughout this chapter. The second UART (also known as the mini UART or UART1) is not a fully compliant UART port. The mini UART cannot provide the following functionality:

- Break detection

- Framing errors detection

- Parity bit

- Time-out interrupt

- Data Carrier Detect (DCD), Data Set Ready (DSR), Data Terminal Ready (DTR) , or Ring Indicator (RI) signals

In addition to this missing functionality, UART1 is also mapped to the exact same GPIO pin headers as UART0. I cannot see any benefit in using UART1 over UART0. As such, I won't use it at all. Let's move back to UART0; this UART is nearly complete in terms of functionality but the following features are missing:

- Infrared data association (IRDA)

- Serial infrared (SIR) protocol encoder/decoder (ENDEC)

- Direct memory access (DMA)

That should not be too much of an issue unless you're looking at using infrared devices on your UART port.

Finding the Pi's Serial Port

So how can you find your serial port on the Raspberry Pi? Under Linux all serial ports are mapped to a device node known as a teletypewriter (TTY for short). Back in the days of the mainframes you would have many people operating a teletypewriter connected to a TTY terminal on the mainframe. This is where the device node name came from. I would not think there are many physical TTYs around anymore. Today we use the TTY device for serial communications between many devices and of course as a serial console. Take a look at your dmesg output on your Raspberry Pi and use grep for tty. In Figure 9-2 you can see the output from my dmesg.

```
[    0.576414] dev:f1: ttyAMA0 at MMIO 0x20201000 (irq = 83) is a PL011 rev3
[    0.881116] console [ttyAMA0] enabled
```

Figure 9-2. The output of dmesg | grep tty

There are two important things to note from this output. The first part is what type of IC the serial port is. In the case of the Raspberry Pi that is PL011. The PL011 is the UART inside the SoC package. ARM refers to the PL011 as the PrimeCell UART. The PL011 is used on a wide range of ARM devices and not just the Raspberry Pi. The implementation of the PL011 will determine its functionality; after all, it's a pretty generic UART chip that ARM has made. There really is not much interesting about the PL011; it's very close to a generic 16550 IC UART that you would find on most PCs.

The second interesting thing you may have noticed is this ttyAMA0. On most systems you would notice your first serial port is ttyS0. So why is the Raspberry Pi different? To understand why it's different you need to understand what the name ttyS0 means. By now you already know what the tty part of the name stands for but what about the S0? To best explain this, take a look at Table 9-1 to see a full breakdown of the naming syntax.

Table 9-1. The breakdown of the ttyS0 name

Teletypewriter	Bus	Device Number
tty	S	0
tty	AMA	0

It's now very clear that the S is the bus of the device. In a traditional PC with a 16550-compatible IC you would get a serial bus, hence the name ttyS0, which is your first teletypewriter on serial bus zero. In the case of the Raspberry Pi the PL011 is not part of a serial bus. It lives on a special bus called Advanced Microcontroller Bus Architecture (also known as AMBA or AMA). This is why your serial port is called ttyAMA0: it's the first teletypewriter interface on the AMA bus.

The AMBA bus was first introduced in 1996 by ARM. One of the best parts of the AMBA bus is that it is royalty free, high speed, and well documented. You would be surprised to find a lot of devices in the SoC world use AMBA, ranging from network interfaces to flash memory controllers. The serial port is the only device on the AMA bus on the Raspberry Pi that you will have direct access to. Now you know what and where the UARTs on the Raspberry Pi are, and I bet you're keen to access them.

UARTs and Logic Shifters

You probably have caught on by now that I keep using the term "UART" when talking about the Raspberry Pi. There is a good reason for this. From an electronics point of view it is just a UART and it's not going to be useful as a serial port without other components. I want you to understand that a UART is just part of a serial port; it's not a serial port. If you were to connect a serial device to the TX and RX pins on your Raspberry Pi you will be up for a brand-new Raspberry Pi. After all, the Raspberry Pi has no logic-level shifter. So please do not connect a serial device to your Raspberry Pi just yet. I am going to show you how to build a simple logic-level shifter now.

What Does a Logic-Level Shifter Do?

A logic-level shifter solves a very common problem in digital circuits. That problem is how to drive a higher voltage logic circuit from a lower voltage logic circuit. In your case how can you drive a potential 25-V serial port signal from a 3.3-V device? This is where the logic shifter comes in.

The logic-level shifter will take a given signal on the 3.3-V logic side also known as the transistor-transistor logic side, or TTL for short, and convert it up to the correct voltage but still keep the same logic value. Logic-level shifters use a concept called a charge pump to boost the voltage up from the lower input voltage to the higher voltage as needed. A charge pump is a circuit that uses capacitors to store a small charge so that it can boost the voltage when needed. This is why you always see a large number of capacitors near logic-level shifter circuits.

The most widely known logic-level shifter that is known when you are talking about serial ports is the Maxim MAX232 and its clones.

Needed Hardware

The MAX232 has been around for many years and works fine if you have a 5-V supply for it. Because the Raspberry Pi is a 3.3-V logic device I did not want to use the MAX232. You want a logic-level shifter that poses no risk to the Raspberry Pi, one that could be driven from the Pi itself. After all, if you're creating a serial console you don't want to rely on an external power source; otherwise you may miss the start of the boot process. For this task I have selected the MAX3232. This can be powered via 3.3 V and has a very low current draw. It's also in a dual in-line package (DIP) package so it's quite easy for you to work with. Functionality-wise, it is exactly the same as the MAX232. If you have worked with the MAX232 you won't have any issues using the MAX3232.

The MAX3232 is able to convert two pairs of send and transmit signals; now this would have been ideal if we had a second UART on the Raspberry Pi that could be accessed at the same time. You could use one MAX3232 to logic-shift the two UARTs. The MAX3232 converts TTL signals into RS-232-compliant signaling. With the use of the charge pumps, it can supply from -5.5 V to +5.5 V. This will give you a fully RS-232-complaint serial port. The MAX3232 is guaranteed to run at a speed up to 120 kb/s, which makes it easy to support the Raspberry Pi's default UART speed of 14.4 kb/s.

Now that you know what IC you're going to use I will now give you the full list of components for this chapter. You're going to need the following to build the circuit:

- One MAX3232
- Five 0.1-μf capacitors
- One DB9 shell
- Hook-up wire

I like to keep things simple where at all possible. As always, take a look at the electronic schematic in Figure 9-3.

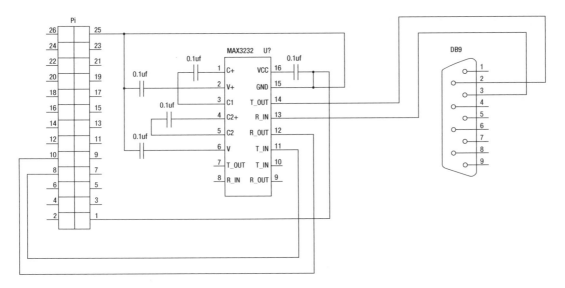

Figure 9-3. *The electronic schematic for the MAX3232*

Building the Circuit

Now let's build the circuit, starting by adding the IC:

1. Insert the MAX3232 into the breadboard. I like to line up pin 1 with a whole number on the board. Check your data sheet to find pin 1.

2. Install two power rails bridging the positive and negative rails on each side of the breadboard. This will make your circuit much neater. You can see my IC and the power rails installed in Figure 9-4.

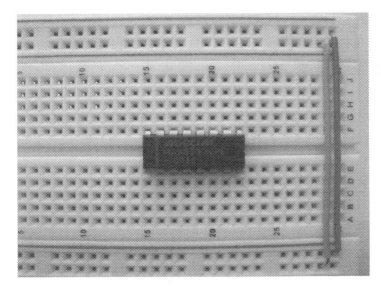

Figure 9-4. *Installed power rails and IC*

Next up, install the five capacitors. It won't matter what sort of capacitor you use as long as it has the correct value of 0.1 µf. Where did I get a value of 0.1 µf? If you are asking this, then I know you have not read the data sheet. Inside the data sheet there is a table of input voltages and their matching capacitors. Because the Raspberry Pi is 3.3 V I should use 0.1-µf capacitors according to the data sheet. Capacitors can be polarized or nonpolarized. I use nonpolarized capacitors but if you use polarized capacitors make sure you install them in the correct orientation.

1. Start off by installing the charge pump capacitors across pin 1 and pin 3 of the IC; then place another capacitor across pin 4 and pin 5.

2. Install the 5.5-V negative and positive charge pumps. Install a capacitor from pin 2 to a spare row. I'll take this to the side of the IC. Do the same for pin 6 as well.

3. Lastly install a capacitor between pins 15 and 16. This will ensure you have a stable voltage input similar to the C6 capacitor on the Raspberry Pi. You can see the installed capacitors in Figure 9-5.

Figure 9-5. *The installed capacitors*

Now you can install the wire links.

1. Connect pin 15 to the ground rail via a jumper cable. Then connect pin 16 to the positive rail.

2. Connect the free leg of the capacitor from pin 2 to the ground rail.

3. Lastly install a jumper cable from the free pin of the capacitor from pin 6 to ground as well. This is why you install the pair of jumper wires between the two sides of the power rails: it makes wiring the MAX3232 a lot easier.

Before you connect the MAX3232 to the Raspberry Pi, I want you to check the potential voltage on this circuit. At this point there should be no connection to the Raspberry Pi.

1. Connect an external 3.3-V source to the board's positive rail and the ground rail to the ground of your external source. There is no need to make this a permanent connection.

2. Power on the circuit.

3. Place your negative probe on the negative power rail and measure the voltage on pins 11 and 12 of the MAX2332. There should be no voltage that is greater than 3.3 V on these pins; if there is, you have an issue with your circuit. Do not connect it to the Raspberry Pi or magic smoke will follow. Less than 3.3 is fine as long as it's not too far off from 3.3; for example, 1.0 V would be bad and may indicate a wiring issue as well.

Now it's time to connect the RX and TX sides of your DB-9 shell to the breadboard and from the Raspberry Pi to the breadboard.

1. Start off by taking P1-08 (TX) to pin 11 on the MAX3232 (T1IN). Then connect P1-10 (RX) to pin 12 (R1OUT) on the MAX3232.

2. Now you want to connect your DB-9 shell. The best way is to solder some wire on to an empty DB-9; cut up hook-up wire for this task but keep the pin header on one side so you can easily work with your breadboard.

3. Connect pin 13 (R1IN) on the MAX3232 to pin 3 (TX) on your DB-9 shell and connect pin 14 (T1OUT) from the MAX3232 to pin 2 (RX) on the DB-9 shell.

4. Lastly connect the hook-up wire from anywhere on the ground rail on the breadboard and connect it to pin 5 (GND) on the DB-9 shell. Take a look at Figure 9-6 if you need help with the pin out from the DB-9 shell.

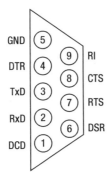

Figure 9-6. *The pin out of a DB-9 shell*

5. For the last two connections, connect your ground rail to P1-25 and your positive rail to P1-01. When you are all done it should look like Figure 9-7.

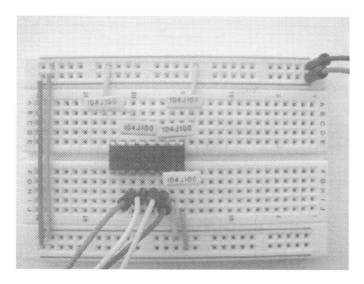

Figure 9-7. *The MAX3232 circuit completed*

The Power On

I hope you did the voltage test before this part. When you power on the Raspberry Pi, you won't see anything different or new. After all, the Raspberry Pi can't talk to the MAX3232; it will only talk to the UART and that's always been there. Now you're going to need a host PC with a serial port and some software to make use of the serial port.

I use a USB to RS-232 adapter with the Prolific PL2303 chip because it is well supported in Linux and does not have any strange behavior. You don't need a null modem cable for the way I have wired the DB-9 shell. If you did want to use a null modem cable, just swap pins 2 and 3 on the DB-9 shell. This would make it a little more like a normal serial port but since I will only be using it for a console I don't mind.

You're also going to need some software to enable your client computer to communicate via the serial port. I like to use Minicom; it's very handy and there is no need for an X-server when you need to configure a lot of serial devices. However, there are many more applications that can talk to a serial port. First, install Minicom with this command:

```
# yum install minicom
```

Start Minicom with the -s flag to get you directly into the setup screen. In Figure 9-8 you can see the setup screen for Minicom.

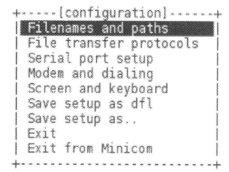

Figure 9-8. *The initial setup screen for Minicom*

Then select "Serial port setup." You need to change three settings for Minicom to be able to talk with the Raspberry Pi.

- Change the "Serial Device" to be whatever your serial port is on your client PC.

- Then set the speed of the port. The Raspberry Pi's UART runs at 115200 like most ARM devices.

- Ensure that you turn off hardware and software flow control.

When you're done, press Enter and then select "Exit."

This will exit the setup and drop you back into Minicom's main screen. Press Enter on the client PC. Nothing happened? No surprise, was it? Reboot your Raspberry Pi. You will now see your boot messages coming in over the serial console if your circuit is working. You will notice that there is no login prompt. If your circuit works, it should look something like Figure 9-9 with no login prompt.

```
ntpdate: Synchronizing with time server: [  OK  ]
Starting ntpd: [  OK  ]
Starting crond: [  OK  ]
vm.min_free_kbytes = 16384

CTRL-A Z for help |115200 8N1 | NOR | Minicom 2.6
```

Figure 9-9. *Working console with no login prompt*

What's going on? It's working but you can't log in. There is a good answer behind this. First log in via SSH and take a look at /boot/cmdline.txt. You will see the following line as part of the file:

```
console=ttyAMA0,115200 kgdboc=ttyAMA0,115200
```

What this means is that Linux should redirect all boot and kernel debug messages to the ttyAMA0 device. This is why you see boot and shutdown messages on your serial console. This has nothing to do with a login prompt also known as a getty process. Fedora manages the gettys; remember in Chapter 2 where I reduced the amount of running tty processes? Well, the serial console is no different; you must start a getty on that device in order to be able to log in via the serial port. Because most people no longer log in to a serial console as their main working environment, Fedora by default won't start a getty process on a serial line. If you are logged in to your Raspberry Pi via SSH you can start a getty with this command:

```
/sbin/agetty 115200 ttyAMA0 vt102 &
```

You will now see a login prompt on your serial console on your client machine. Log in via serial: it's all working. Now log out. What happened to the login prompt? It's gone! It's gone because you spawned a single getty process without initial system management. What happens when you log in is that the getty process will be replaced by your running shell; the getty process no longer exists. This is why when you log off you have no getty process to greet you.

In order to have a getty respawn it must be managed by the system's init process.

In Fedora you need to create a file in /etc/init/ for this to work. I have called this file pitty.conf, which is short for a "pi tty config" file. Take a look at the contents of this file in Listing 9-1.

Listing 9-1. The Contents of pitty.conf

```
# ttyAMA0 - getty
#
# Author : Brendan Horan
# Start and maintain a getty on ttyAMA0
```

```
start on startup
start on stopped rc or RUNLEVEL=[2345]
stop on runlevel [!2345]

respawn
exec /sbin/agetty 115200 ttyAMA0 vt102
```

This file will tell Fedora's init system to start a getty on AMA0 on boot and keep it running. It will also tell init that this process must respawn if it has ended. Ensure that you have saved this in /etc/init/. It's best to check that the init system knows to start this process on the next boot.

Use the following command:

```
# initctl list
```

You should see a line that looks something like Figure 9-10.

```
[root@hobo ~]# initctl list | grep pitty
pitty stop/waiting
```

Figure 9-10. *The pitty ready to start on the next boot*

Give your Raspberry Pi a reboot and now you should see your login prompt; it will look like Figure 9-11 if you have done everything correctly.

```
RaspberryPi Fedora Remix 14 (raspberrypi-fedora-remix)
Kernel 3.2.27+ on an armv6l (ttyAMA0)

hobo login: []
 CTRL-A Z for help |115200 8N1 | NOR | Minicom 2.6
```

Figure 9-11. *Getty process running on boot*

Log in and log back out, and you should see this time the getty process respawns and you can log right back in like magic. If you log in via SSH and leave your serial console logged in, you can see some interesting output from the process list and the who command. You can now see in Figure 9-12 that you have a bash process running on ttyAMA0 and you will see there is no getty process currently running. Remember that it's replaced by the running shell of that user.

```
[root@hobo ~]# ps -ef | grep [A]MA
root       750   745  0 17:34 ttyAMA0   00:00:00 -bash
[root@hobo ~]# who
root     ttyAMA0       Dec  6 17:34
root     pts/0         Dec  6 17:32 (pcb)
```

Figure 9-12. *Running shell and active users*

You can see with the who command that I have logged in as root on ttyAMA0 and a virtual tty called pts/0.

Now log out of your console session and you will see a message from init that getty has respawned. If you check your process listing you will see a getty process and no active shell as there is no user logged in and getty is waiting for you. Take a look at Figure 9-13 to see this in action.

```
[ 1042.843932] init: pitty main process ended, respawning
[root@hobo ~]# ps -ef | grep [A]MA
root       811    1  0 17:46 ttyAMA0   00:00:00 /sbin/agetty 115200 ttyAMA0 vt102
```

Figure 9-13. Getty respawning correctly

Congratulations! You now have a fully functional serial console, which is one of my personal favorite things to have. You can now watch your boot messages scroll across your console or maybe you don't want to have Ethernet connected to your Raspberry Pi.

Serial No Console

What if you want to use the serial port for another function such as a GPS or a modem, for example? The hardware you have just built can support this as well. In fact you don't even need to change anything on the hardware side. You need to make changes to two files. The first file is /etc/init/pitty.conf. You need to use the following two lines:

```
# start on startup
# start on stopped rc or RUNLEVEL=[2345]
```

As you can see I have placed a # in front of them to comment them out. Next you need to edit the /boot/cmdline.txt file. You want to remove the references to ttyAMA0 as the boot console. My cmdline.txt now looks like this:

```
dwc_otg.lpm_enable=0 console=tty1 root=/dev/mmcblk0p2 rootfstype=ext4 rootwait elevator=noop
```

That the console is now on tty1 and there are no references to ttyAMA0. Now reboot your Raspberry Pi. You still may see boot messages but as soon as Fedora takes over you will be free to do whatever you want with the serial port. Now give your Raspberry Pi another reboot. If you check the following command, you will see that the pitty process is stopped/waiting:

```
# initctl list
```

This means the system will not start the process on boot but you could still start it manually. This is why I also left the shutdown line in the pitty.conf file. If you were to check the process listing you would also no longer see a getty process running on ttyAMA0.

Next up I am going to show you one of my favorite software applications for having many serial ports.

Ser2net

For this section, make sure you have no getty process running on ttyAMA0 as it will interfere with the application. You can quickly check for a getty with the following command:

```
# ps aux | grep getty
```

Unfortunately the Raspberry Pi only has one usable UART at a time. This is not the end of the world but it will make things more difficult. Recall in Chapter 1 when I said you have two UARTs? Well, now you can clearly see they are wired to the same pins. By doing this you won't be able to have the serial console and share out the serial port with another device. At this point you're going to need to choose between the serial console and ser2net. You can see how the Raspberry Pi can sometimes be a little limited.

Originally I had planned to use a little chip from Maxim called MAX3100. This little fellow connects via the fast SPI bus and provides a single additional UART. You can easily have two of these on the SPI bus on the Raspberry Pi. There is also a kernel module for the MAX3100. Unfortunately, I could not get this to work and it would have required me to rebuild the Linux kernel to include the MAX3100 kernel module. A kernel rebuild has been something I had been avoiding doing for the entire book. With that in mind I will be using some USB-to-serial adapters. I'd much rather use the MAX3100 if I had a choice.

▓ **Note**   There are also I2C UART chips but sadly many of them are not supported by kernel modules. You're just going to need to make do with the USB and your freshly made serial port.

I need to be able to connect to one of the many serial devices or console ports on devices in my home network. Attaching a console cable would be a very annoying process; in addition to that I would not be able to change a cable remotely. This is where the need came for a serial port as a TCP port. I had looked at many applications to do this and ended up with ser2net.

Ser2net gives you the ability to set the speed, protocol, banner, and a whole host of other neat settings for making your serial ports available over TCP. You can even use ser2net to present a line print terminal (LPT) port out over TCP so ser2net is not just for serial. Just make sure your LPT port won't catch on fire.

ON FIRE?

During the 1950s high-speed printers used a very hot and longish fusing oven. A fusing oven was used to bond the ink to the paper. It was often the case that the printer would jam as they do to this day. Back then there was a large potential for the printer to catch on fire. So the early Unix developers made an error code called "lp0 on fire." While the error did not mean the printer was on fire, it served as a warning that the printer was not in a healthy state and was potentially dangerous.

Connect to your Raspberry Pi and install ser2net with the following command:

```
# yum install -y ser2net
```

You also may want to install Telnet to help you out:

```
# yum install -y telnet
```

As soon as you have ser2net installed I would recommend that you take a look though the man page (I bet you saw that coming). There are two main files you need to be concerned with. The first and most important is the configuration file at /etc/ser2net.conf. I normally make a copy of this file and start afresh. The file has a lot of helpful information and examples but it's far too crowded for me to work in. Make a copy of it now with the following command:

```
# cp /etc/ser2net.conf /etc/ser2net.conf.org
```

The second file is the ser2net binary at /usr/sbin/ser2net. If you run the ser2net binary file with the --help flag as the only option you will be presented with a little bit of information on how you can run the daemon. You're going to need to create a configuration file for ser2net to work. Otherwise it will just exit cleanly.

To create a configuration file, create a file called /etc/ser2net.conf. Use whatever editor you like to create this. Let me explain the configuration file for you. There are three main sections that you can have and only one is mandatory:

- The banner section lets you create a little banner message that will be displayed on that TCP port when you first connect. It is handy to put the remote device name in it and is also an optional setting for ser2net.

- Next you will have the tracefile. The tracefile option allows you to record the Telnet session to a file and it is optional. I personally don't use this.

- Lastly you will see a set of port and device-mapping options. This section is where the real action takes place and it is mandatory. I created Table 9-2 to help you understand its format.

Table 9-2. *The format of the port section in the ser2net configuration file*

Option	Function	Example Value
TCP Port	Sets the TCP port for the given serial device	2001
State	How the port will transmit data	telnet
Timeout	How long before the TCP port times out	600 seconds
Device	The physical serial port device	/dev/ttyAMA0

Now that you can see how the configuration file is set up, it's time to create a simple config file. Each option from Table 9-2 is separated by a colon apart from the last option's section where each suboption is separated by a space. In Listing 9-2 you can see my sample ser2net configuration file.

Listing 9-2. A Working Sample ser2net.conf File

```
# Description : A sample ser2net config file
# Author : Brendan Horan

# Banner Section

BANNER:banner1:Connected to TCP port \p on device \d\r\n\
Remote end:- Brendans Mini210s ARM dev board\r\n

BANNER:banner2:Connected to TCP port \p on device \d\r\n\
Remote end:- Brendans PA-RISC J6750\r\n

# Port config section

2001:telnet:0:/dev/ttyAMA0:115200 banner1
2002:telnet:60:/dev/ttyUSB0:9600 banner2

#EOF
```

As you can see from Listing 9-2, ser2net will listen on port 2001 and 2002 by using the Telnet protocol for both connections. The next sections (0 and 60) are timeout values; if you use 0 as a timeout the timeout function will be disabled. Then I give it the device node name followed by the port speed and lastly I set a banner for each connection. In Listing 9-2 I used some special escape codes in the banner. I will explain them now:

- \p is the TCP port you are connected to
- \d is the physical device you're connecting to
- \r\n is a new line and a carriage return

You can find all supported escape codes in the man page, but you knew that already as you have read the man page, right? Now that your configuration file is complete it is time to connect the remote devices to your serial port and start ser2net. To start ser2net on Fedora, type the following command:

```
# service start ser2net
```

If you want ser2net to start on boot, ensure that you run the following command:

```
# chkconfig ser2net on
```

Give it a try! From another machine on your network, connect to the Raspberry Pi on one of the ports. I will connect to port 2001. Take a look at Figure 9-14 to see this in action.

```
brendangpcb - % telnet hobo 2001
Trying 192.168.0.199...
Connected to hobo.
Escape character is '^]'.
Connected to TCP port 2001 on device /dev/ttyAMA0
Remote end:- Brendans Mini210s ARM dev board
oard type: 2
Running OS 'LINUX'
Loading kernel...
file: /images/Linux/2.6.37.7: 3 MB(3624256 Byte)
Load kernel succeed
Start Linux kernel...
Uncompressing Linux... done, booting the kernel.
[    0.000000] Initializing cgroup subsys cpu
[    0.000000] Linux version 2.6.35.7-FriendlyARM (brendangpcb) (gcc version 4.5.1 (ctng-1.8.1-FA) ) #14 PREEMPT Mon Sep 17 19:27:24 HKT 201
[    0.000000] CPU: ARMv7 Processor [412fc082] revision 2 (ARMv7), cr=10c53c7f
[    0.000000] CPU: VIPT nonaliasing data cache, VIPT nonaliasing instruction cache
[    0.000000] Machine: MINI210
```

Figure 9-14. *A remote ser2net connection working!*

To exit the session, hit Ctrl+] and then just type "quit" to exit the Telnet application. Congratulations! You now have a serial port presented over a TCP connection.

Summary

In this chapter you found out all about how a serial port works and why having a UART will not always mean you can use a serial connection. You then found out the disappointment of UART1 on the Raspberry Pi. This was an unfortunate surprise that you only have one real active UART on the Raspberry Pi. After learning this fact, I talked about the history of a very common logic-level shifter and then showed you how to construct your own logic-level shifter based on the MAX3232. Even with all your hard work, you still could not log in to the Raspberry Pi and then I explained the process of how a getty works and where the name originally came from. Then you set up a getty process to respawn on the console port.

After all that, I showed you how to disable the getty process so that you could set up a favorite application of mine called ser2net. I showed you how to write a basic ser2net config file and then showed you what ser2net looks like in action by connecting to my Mini210S ARM board.

CHAPTER 10

■ ■ ■

Controlling a Mains Device

So far you have been able to do a lot of interesting projects with your Raspberry Pi. There is, however, one topic that always comes up when you talk to anyone about practical uses for a microcontroller or, in your case, for the Raspberry Pi. That question goes something like "how can I turn on some random device in my house?" For example, you may want to turn on a lamp at night or your air conditioner before you get home. Nothing like a cron job to turn on your air conditioner! Now if you think about this quickly, getting the Raspberry Pi to turn on a random device is an easy task. In theory, turning a mains-powered device on or off is no different. It's just interrupting the flow of electricity to that device; after all, this is what your common wall switch does. Unfortunately, here are two big issues that you will face and they both have the same source. That source is alternating current, or AC.

- The first issue is that the Raspberry Pi is obviously not tolerant of 110/240 V AC; putting that sort of voltage anywhere near your GPIO pins will let the magic smoke out.

- The second issue is that this voltage can kill you. The fact that it can kill you won't be much of an issue to your Raspberry Pi but it will greatly impact your ability to finish this book.

So you and the Raspberry Pi are not tolerant of the mains voltage. What now?

There are a few device options you can take to safely interface with the mains voltage. All of these devices provide some form of isolation to the mains current but some offer more than others.

- The device that offers the most isolation is opto-isolation and this would be my preference but it's not often seen on less expensive devices.

- Another common device you may see being used to switch AC is a power metal oxide semiconductor field-effect transistor (MOSFET). You will know if you encounter a power MOSFET by the size of the heatsink it uses. A power MOSFET will generate a large amount of heat so it is not often used in small circuits or anything encased in plastic for that matter.

- Lastly and most commonly you will find a relay. You will come across two types of relays: the standard mechanical relay and the solid-state relay. A mechanical relay is easy to spot, because it will be a little bigger than the solid-state version and, more obvious, has a distinctive click that the device makes when activated. Both the solid-state and mechanical relays work in a similar manner and offer the lowest level of isolation. If something bad were to happen, there is a good chance it will fry more than just your relay.

The last thing you need to be concerned about aside from your safety is what your local laws allow you to do. Some countries may not allow you to change any part of a mains circuit unless you have the appropriate qualifications.

So let's take a look at how the AC mains works and how it's different from direct current (DC); after that I will show you the different ways to switch AC mains power. At the end of the chapter I will introduce you to the method I use to switch the power. This method is easy and risk-free. Read on to find out what it is.

Alternating Current

Let's take a look at what AC is. Why exactly is it called alternating current? If you recall, in the book's introduction I talked about DC. DC is when the flow of the electric charge flows in only one direction. So your flow of current will always remain the same. For example, your current will flow from negative to positive only. With alternating current, the flow of the current will change direction according to a frequency. You can see an example of this in Figure 10-1. The voltage will go from +240 to -240 V.

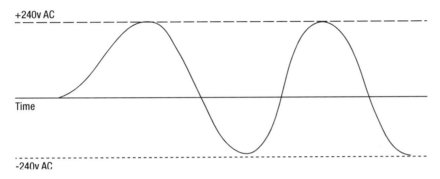

Figure 10-1. *An example of an AC voltage graph*

This frequency is measured in hertz (Hz for short). An AC usually runs at a frequency of 50 or 60 Hz. For example, a 50-Hz 240-V circuit will have its direction of current flow changed 50 times a second. There are a few very good reasons why AC was eventually selected as the method of distribution across the world.

- First, converting AC power to different voltage levels is very easy and requires no complex circuits, and a simple transformer can take care of this. On the other hand, converting DC power to different voltage levels is not an easy task. In recent years this has become easier but at the time when AC and DC were fighting it out for dominance it was a very hard task that required large machinery. In your home or at your place of work you will have many different devices that use a wide range of voltage. Under the original DC power network, you would have needed a separate feed for each different voltage device. As you can see, that would not be very convenient or a good use of resources.

- AC also has another big advantage. The fact that AC could easily have its voltage converted up or down made it ideal for a large distribution range. The distribution network could run at a very high voltage with less current, then be easily stepped down to your household voltage. The advantage of using less current is that the potential voltage drop over longer runs of cable is smaller. You can then use smaller wire, thus giving you less resistance, unlike DC, which needs thicker wires for a higher current flow, resulting in more lost energy.

Your mains voltage will be somewhere from 100 to 240 V at 50 or 60 Hz. This won't matter for this project, so don't worry that I will be using 240-V devices. With that in mind, all high voltage should be treated with a lot of respect, whether it's AC or DC. Each has the potential to kill you and most certainly will kill your Raspberry Pi. Now that you have some background on AC, it's time to take a look at the devices that will do the hard work for us.

Isolation Devices

First up, and my personal favorite, is full opto-isolation (devices that use this approach are also referred to as opto-couplers).

Opto-Isolation

What exactly is opto-isolation? Opto-isolation stands for optical isolation, where the isolation part of this refers to each side of the circuit, with one side being high voltage and the other side being low voltage. An opto-isolator works by separating each side of the circuits by an optical connection. Take a look at Figure 10-2 to see what the inside of an opto-isolator would like.

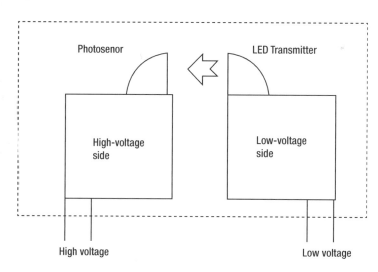

Photosenor

LED Transmitter

High-voltage
side

Low-voltage
side

High voltage

Low voltage

Figure 10-2. *A high-level design of an opto-isolator*

As you can see, there is not much to an opto-isolator. The most common opto-isolator you will encounter will use an infrared LED and a photosensor. You are most likely to have walked though many infrared photosensors as they are often found on doorway entry systems.

In your common opto-isolator, when a current is passed through the low-voltage side the LED will emit an infrared light. This light is detected by the photosensor on the high-voltage side. When the photosensor detects this light, it will break or connect the high-voltage circuit depending on its current state. With your common infrared opto-isolators there is a small delay of up to a few nanoseconds. That may sound very small; indeed, for your needs to switch a mains device it's more than fine. It's not so fine if you wanted to use an opto-isolator to transmit sound though. The best thing about opto-isolators is that there is no way at all the high-voltage side can get onto the low-voltage side. An opto-isolator is a very safe way to isolate your projects and is not all that expensive.

MOSFET

Another common way to isolate the mains voltage is via a power MOSFET. MOSFETs are simply transistors used to amplify or switch electronic signals. Power MOSFETs are a little different than normal MOSFETs: the gates inside a power MOSFET are created vertically rather than horizontally. This allows the power MOSFET to sustain a large blocking voltage, say, for example, a 240-V AC mains source. You will often encounter power MOSFETs in audio amplifiers that are attached to massive heatsinks, because they tend to put out a large amount of heat. The reason you find them in audio equipment is they have a very fast switching time, unlike an opto-isolator. Let's take a quick look at Figure 10-3 to see how a MOSFET works at a high level.

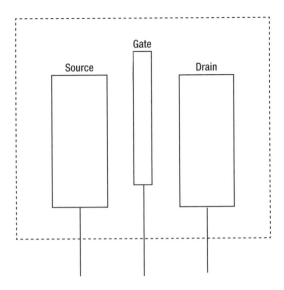

Figure 10-3. *A basic overview of a simple MOSFET*

There are three main elements: a gate, drain, and source. When a current is applied across the gate, a connection can be made from the source to the drain. When the current is removed from the gate, the circuit is broken. Unlike the opto-isolator the gate in a MOSFET will start to conduct with a lower amount of voltage and will rise in a linear value until the saturation point has been reached. The saturation point is when the MOSFET is in a fully open mode and there will be a linear change in voltage at the drain side. Power MOSFETs, unlike normal MOSFETs, have much more stable behavior at the saturation point. This won't matter to you if you are switching only a mains device but would matter a lot if you were amplifying an audio signal. The last thing you need is unpredictable behavior at a certain voltage. It's uncommon to find a power MOSFET in such a simple circuit to switch mains power.

Relays

Relays are quite common these days (they never used to be). In the pre-transistor-era, relays were state-of-the-art technology along with valves. All computers during this time used relays and valves to do their calculations. This made computers of that era very noisy, very large, and supplied with very high voltages. Nowadays I would be surprised if you found many relays in your home computer (if you found any at all). The two main, common types of relays are mechanical and solid-state, although there are many more types.

Mechanical relays are, as the name suggests, mechanical; they work by a magnetic force that pulls or lets go of an armature. It's simply a magnetic field being switched on or off. This magnetic pull is what gives you that distinctive click that you hear. Take a look at Figure 10-4; in this figure you can see how a basic relay would operate. In practice there is a lot more to it.

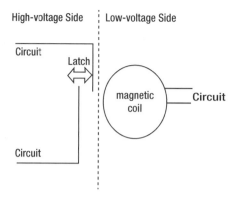

Figure 10-4. *A high-level overview of a mechanical relay*

In this very high-level diagram you can see that if we applied a current flow to the circuit attached to the magnetic coil the latch would move to the left to complete the circuit on the left-hand side. When the current is removed, the latch moves back to the right and the circuit is broken.

The other type of relay you may come across will be a solid-state relay. Solid-state relays use MOSFETs inside to achieve the same outcome as a mechanical relay. They have the benefit of being quicker and less prone to failure. Unfortunately they also generate more heat and when they do fail they have a habit of failing and short-circuiting. You are not likely to come across a solid-state relay in a mains AC switching circuit unless one of the selling points is low noise. After all, they do cost more than their mechanical counterparts. Now that you know the most common ways to switch the AC mains, what method will this chapter use?

The AC Mains Remote Control

All through this chapter I have said you won't need to touch the AC mains and even after all this talk of how to switch the AC mains you won't be getting anywhere near it. You're going to be using a remote-controlled AC mains switch (I'll show you which of the above techniques it uses in a little bit). Make sure it has a separate remote control; I don't want you busting open the main unit that connects to the mains socket. Let me warn you about AC mains again. **Don't ever work on live AC mains circuits.** Don't even think about opening an AC mains device unless you know what you're doing. Remember that capacitors may hold lethal voltage for upward of 30 minutes after you have unplugged the device. You can see in Figure 10-5 the device I have picked up. This device operates over a radio frequency, which I feel is better than an infrared device.

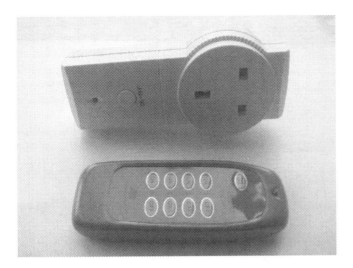

Figure 10-5. *The remote control unit and the socket unit*

As you can see from the remote it can control more than one power socket device too. By using a remote control you gain a few advantages.

- The first one is that you won't get electrocuted by the AC mains voltage.

- The second part is that it gives you the best form of isolation for the Raspberry Pi.

I have opened my unit to show you that it's using a relay device to do the AC mains switching (take a look at Figure 10-6) but I could easily tell it was a relay from the click sound. You don't need to open your unit and I would recommend against it; the image is for demonstration purposes only and is not required to complete the project.

Figure 10-6. *Inside the AC mains unit*

Once again there is no need for you to open your unit; I'm doing it so you don't have to. After all it's the remote control unit you care about, not the technology used to switch the AC mains. Moving on from the wall-socket side of the unit, let's look at the circuit and open the remote.

Putting the Circuit Together

Let's put all this knowledge to use and build the circuit to control a mains appliance. For this you will need the following parts:

- A mains remote-controlled plug

- Two 3-V relays (RY3W-K or equivalent)

- Two 1N4007 diodes (or equivalent)

- Some wire

First up, as always I want to show you an electronic schematic. There really is not much to this circuit (see Figure 10-7). Most of the work will be in software land again.

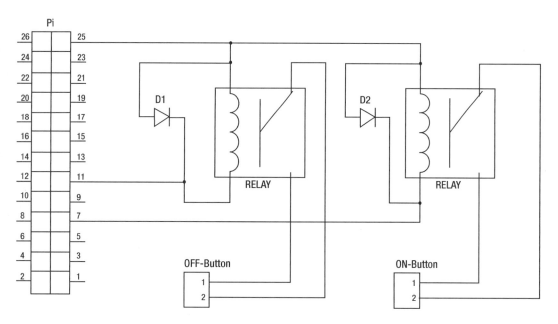

Figure 10-7. *The electronic schematic for the circuit*

Dissecting the Remote Control

The first thing you're going to need to figure out is exactly how your remote control works. With that in mind, open up the remote control. In Figure 10-8 you can see the back side of the remote from my device. I did say I like to open electronic devices up!

Figure 10-8. *The inside of the remote control unit*

Most of the little tactile buttons you will find on remote controls will have four pins on the back side of the remote: you don't need four pins to make a simple switch, because two are all that is needed. Four pin switches are often used as they add stability to the mount of the switch. You may have noticed that all four pins are soldered into the board. If you take an even closer look you will notice a few patterns between each set of switches. The first and most obvious thing you may have noticed is that two pins between a switch set are simply joined together by a track on the printed circuit board (PCB). This usually indicated the ground pin of the switch as it's easier to join the two ground pins together than to route two separate tracks on the board itself. This will become one side of your circuit on the breadboard. This now leaves three pins left.

You now need to find out what pin closes the circuit when the switch is pressed. There are two ways to do this:

- The first way and the way I have used it is to set your multimeter to the ohms setting: connect one probe to the ground pins you found before and then connect the other probe to any of the remaining three pins. You will have two possible outcomes at this point. The multimeter will either read a very high resistance (indicating no connection) or a very low resistance (indicating a closed circuit, which means the switch connects the two pins). If you have found a pin with low resistance then this will be the other side of your circuit on the breadboard. If this pin was not the right one, move on to the next pin until you find a pin that has a closed circuit when you press the switch in. It should not take long: there are only three choices after all.

- The second way is to take a look at the PCB; in most of the cheaper remotes the PCB is a single layer, which means you can visually trace each connection on the board. You want to trace the pin that goes back to an integrated circuit (IC). Given that there should be only one IC, this is a simple task. The other two pins will either be connected to nothing or connected to another switch. What the other pins connect to is not important. You're only interested in the pin that leads you back to the IC.

Now that you have worked that out, let's build the remote control part of the circuit:

1. Take a look at Figure 10-9 to see how I have wired my remote. I have fully connected only one switch to better display the pins of the switch. You will need to connect one ground wire and one positive wire to each switch.

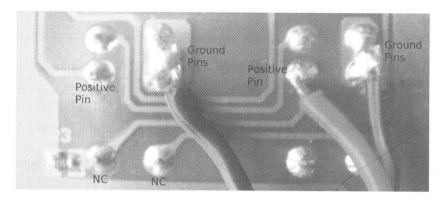

Figure 10-9. *The wiring of the remote control*

2. It won't really matter what side is ground or positive. After all, you are just closing a circuit. I have used these terms to make it easier to understand. I like to solder breadboard pins on each of the wire ends to make it easy to connect to the breadboard. You can see my finished job in Figure 10-10.

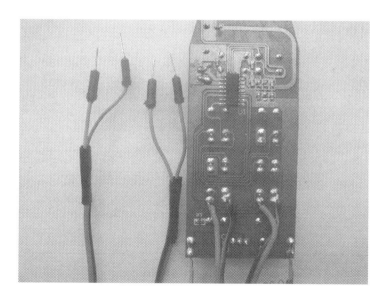

Figure 10-10. *The completed wiring for the remote*

That's now the hardest part done. Next up, get your breadboard and the relays.

Adding the Relays

Pick up a relay. If you are lucky you will have two things: a model number so you can read the data sheet, and a little squiggly-looking drawing. If you're unlucky you will get neither of the two. You know what to do with the data sheet by now but what is that little squiggly drawing on the side of the relay? That's the connection diagram and it should look something like Figure 10-11.

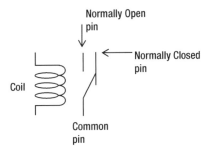

Figure 10-11. *A single pole-relay diagram*

In Figure 10-11 you can see the pin connections for the relay. You want to use the normally open side of the relay. When you apply a current to the coil, the circuit on the other side of the relay between the common pin and the normally open pin will become closed. This is simulating pressing the button on the remote control. You don't want to connect anything to the normal closed side of the relay. If you are really unlucky and your relay has no part number and no circuit diagram, you're just going to need to figure it out manually. This is not difficult:

1. The easiest connection to identify is the normally open and common pins, as they will have no connection without power applied to the relay coil.

2. The second easiest connection to identify is the normally closed side. When measured with your multimeter it should read very close to zero resistance.

3. The last pins should obviously be the relay coil but it's wise to check them, especially if your relay has more than one pole inside the relay. The resistance between the coil terminals can vary between makers of relays but it should not be an open circuit or a closed one, so the multimeter should read some resistance.

Once you understand how the relays work, you can begin to connect them:

1. Place two relays into the center of your breadboard so that the relay has one side of its legs on one side of the breadboard and the other legs on the other side. Take a look at Figure 10-12 to see how I have placed my relays.

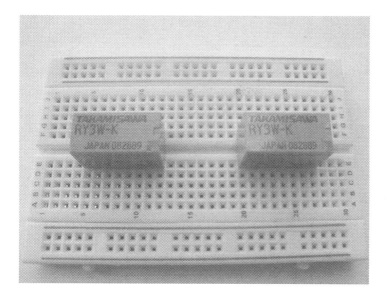

Figure 10-12. *Relay placement on the breadboard*

2. Install the diode across the terminals of the relay coil. This diode is used to prevent a potential voltage spike from the relay coil traveling back down into the Raspberry Pi. Remember that when you install a diode it is polarity-sensitive. The side with the stripe around it will be the cathode. Install a diode next to the coil and across the two halves of the breadboard in the exact same manner that you did for the relays.

3. Install jumper wire between each side of the relay's coil and the diode.

4. Install a jumper wire between the ground and one side of each of the relay coils. The ground side of the relay coil must be the same side that the anode of the diode is connected to. Take a look at Figure 10-13 to see my jumpers and diodes installed.

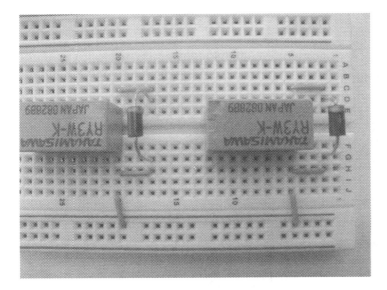

Figure 10-13. *The installed diodes and jumper wire*

5. Connect the two wires from one switch on the remote to one of the relays. Ensure that you connect it to the normally open side of the relay. Do the same for the second switch. The connections from the remote switches are not polarity-sensitive so don't worry about connecting them backward.

6. You're now ready to connect the circuit to the Raspberry Pi. Connect your ground rail first. I have selected P1-25 for my ground connection.

7. Now connect P1-07 (GPIO-4) to the front of the diode on the coil side of the relay connected to the on button on the remote. Then connect P1-11 (GPIO-17) to the relay that is connected to the off button. Once again, ensure that it's in the front of the diode. Don't worry too much if the on/off buttons are the wrong way around; you can swap them at any time.

The finished breadboard should look like Figure 10-14.

Figure 10-14. *A finished breadboard connected to the Raspberry Pi*

That's all the hardware work! The last thing you may want to do is ensure that the remote button you have wired to the breadboard is mated with the mains plug. For my unit I had to hold the on button for a few seconds until the mains unit stopped flashing. You are still able to use the remote control buttons as you normally would at this point in time. It may be a wise idea to make sure that your remote control and mains unit work before moving on to the next section. Now that you know the unit works, it's time to make it work from the Raspberry Pi.

The Soft Side

Log in to the Raspberry Pi. Just like in Chapter 5, you're going to need to export the GPIO pins and configure them first.

Using the GPIO Pins as Output

First, export the two pins with the following command:

```
# echo 4 > /sys/class/gpio/export && echo 17 > /sys/class/gpio/export
```

Once that is done you need to set the GPIO pins as an output this time. Unlike in Chapter 5 where you detected the high or low state of the external circuit, this time you want to set the external circuit high or low. To do that, run the following command:

```
# echo out > /sys/class/gpio/gpio4/direction && echo out > /sys/class/gpio/gpio17/direction
```

Now it's time to see if you got your hardware corrected right. Run this command to turn on your mains device:

```
echo 1 > /sys/class/gpio/gpio4/value
```

This command sets the logic level of the GPIO pin to high. If you were to now place a multimeter on P1-04 and P1-25 you would see that it is running at 3.3 V. This is known as setting the pin high. If you were to set it low by echoing 0 into the value file your voltage would drop back to 0.0 V, thus setting the pin low. If everything has gone according to plan your mains device should be on. If you are lucky your remote will have an LED on it that lights up when you press a button. If your unit has this, take a look at it: you will notice it's constantly lit. That's not really simulating a button press! That's because you have just set the GPIO pin high, which is the same as holding down your finger on the button. You now need to run the following command to pull the GPIO pin back down to low:

```
# echo 0 > /sys/class/gpio/gpio4/value
```

This will simulate a button press. However, coding this is a little trickier than simply reading a value from the GPIO pins.

Coding a Simulated Button Press

There are many ways to solve this issue. I use a bash script, as seen in the code in Listing 10-1.

Listing 10-1. A Simple Bash Script to Simulate a Button Press

```bash
#!/bin/bash
# Description : command line tool to turn on/off a device
#  You must have the GPIO pins set up first. Use gpio-setup.sh
# Use : ./cmd-ctl.sh on|off
# Author : Brendan Horan

# Turn on
  function on {
    /bin/echo 1 > /sys/class/gpio/gpio4/value
    sleep 1
    /bin/echo 0 > /sys/class/gpio/gpio4/value
    # Create a file to indicate current outlet state
    /bin/echo power-on > outlet-status

  }

# Turn off
  function off {
    /bin/echo 1 > /sys/class/gpio/gpio17/value
    sleep 1
    /bin/echo 0 > /sys/class/gpio/gpio17/value
    # Create a file to indicate current outlet state
    /bin/echo power-off > outlet-status

  }

# What shall I do ?
  $1
```

This script won't give you any feedback, and you cannot query the GPIO pin to get an indication of the current outlet status. This is where a handy flag file comes in hand. This little file gets written to the filesystem and echoes the status of the physical outlet. You can see the flag file in this line:

```
/bin/echo power-on > outlet-status
```

This will write a file to the current directory called outlet-status, with the value of power-on. When you turn off the outlet the file contents will get overwritten with the value of power-off. This will also persist across a reboot so you will always know the status of the outlet.

Save this script into /usr/local/bin and call it power-ctl.sh. Make sure you set the execution bit on the script. This script only accepts the command-line arguments on and off. I am sure you can guess what they do. Take a look at Figure 10-15 to see the script in action.

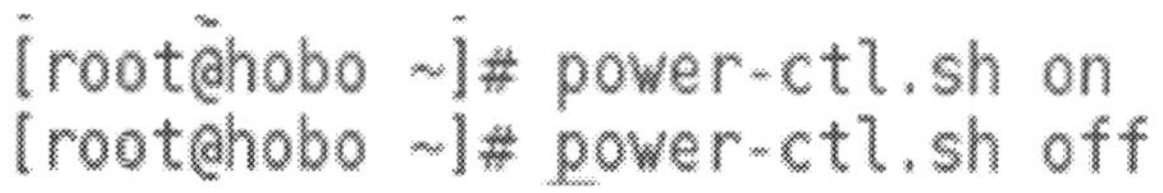

```
[root@hobo ~]# power-ctl.sh on
[root@hobo ~]# power-ctl.sh off
```

Figure 10-15. *The power-ctl.sh script in action*

You're going to need to take my word when I say that my mains device did turn on and off. After all it's a little hard to embed video into a book. This script uses two functions to replicate what you did on the command line. The reason that you see "sleep 1" in between each value toggle is that the remote control takes a few milliseconds to register the button press. Without this you may toggle the GPIO pins too quickly for the remote to notice. If you read all the lines of code you would have also noticed I referenced another script called gpio-setup.sh. This little script is part of a bigger project. After all I am sure you don't want to use SSH to get into the Raspberry Pi every time you want to turn this mains device on. What happens if you have many mains devices?

Back to the WEBrick

I will be giving you another nice little web page to provide convenient management. I will be using Ruby's WEBrick again for a lightweight web server. Just like in Chapter 5 this web server needs to be run as root for this example.

To get started, create a folder called power-ctl; however, the name of this folder or its location do not matter. After all I have set up WEBrick to work from its running directory. In your newly created directory, place the following files into the directory:

- gpio-setup.sh
- index.html
- off.cgi
- on.cgi
- server-power-control.rb

Take a look at Figure 10-16 to see my directory listing.

```
[root@hobo power-ctl]# ls -la /root/power-ctl
total 28
drwxr-xr-x    2 root root 4096 Dec 10 13:39 .
dr-xr-x---.  15 root root 4096 Dec 10 13:39 ..
-rwxr-xr-x    1 root root  680 Dec  8 13:30 gpio-setup.sh
-rw-r--r--    1 root root  336 Dec 10 13:39 index.html
-rwxr-xr-x    1 root root  462 Dec  8 13:12 off.cgi
-rwxr-xr-x    1 root root  458 Dec 10 13:37 on.cgi
-rwxr-xr-x    1 root root  888 Dec  8 13:03 server-power-control.rb
[root@hobo power-ctl]# []
```

Figure 10-16. *The power control application directory and scripts*

The first script I want to show you is the gpio-setup.sh script. Because I wanted the WEBrick server to be able to be run from boot, I needed to create a script that would configure the GPIO pins the way I needed them to be. Take a look at Listing 10-2 to see the contents of the script.

Listing 10-2. The gpio-setup.sh Script

```bash
#!/bin/bash
# Description : Set up GPIO pins, exit if they are already one
#  GPIO 4 is the ON switch
#  GPIO 17 is the OFF switch
# Author : Brendan Horan


function check {
  if [ -e "/sys/class/gpio/gpio4" ]
  then
  exit
  fi
}


function export {
# Export the GPIO pins
  echo 4 > /sys/class/gpio/export
  echo 17 > /sys/class/gpio/export
}


function direction {
# Set the GPIO pins to be outputs
  echo out > /sys/class/gpio/gpio4/direction
  echo out > /sys/class/gpio/gpio17/direction
}
```

```
        # set the pins to low to start with
          function setlow {
            echo 0 > /sys/class/gpio/gpio4/value
            echo 0 > /sys/class/gpio/gpio17/value
          }
```

```
check
export
direction
setlow
```

This script is separated into four functions.

- The first function checks to see if the script has already run by checking for the presence of the exported gpio4 directory.

- The second function exports the GPIO pins, exactly like you did on the command line.

- After that, the next function sets the direction of the pins: once again, this is nothing you have not done before.

- The last section is not really necessary but I like to set the GPIO pins to a known state.

You can now use this script to set up the GPIO pins automatically. The gpio-setup.sh script takes no command-line arguments and will exit quietly upon failure or success.

Next up, take a look at Listing 10-3.

Listing 10-3. The Simple HTML Page to Control the GPIOs

```
<!--
Description : Simple HTML page to activate the cgi scripts
Author : Brendan Horan
  -->


<html>
    <head>Pi Power Control</head>
    <body>
      <form action="on.cgi">
         <p>Turn On: <button>ON</button>
      </form>
      <form action="off.cgi">
         <p>Turn Off: <button>OFF</button>
      </form>
    </body>
</html>
```

As you can see, there is not much to this index page at all. You have two buttons that run either the on.cgi or the off.cgi scripts.

Next up will be the two common gateway interface (CGI) scripts because I have just referred to them. Ruby's WEBrick HTTP server by default supports CGI scripts. The CGI is a method for a web server to access and run a script on itself. I will be using a bash script to form my CGI scripts. Take a look at Listing 10-4 to see the on.cgi script.

Listing 10-4. The on.cgi Script

```
#!/bin/bash
# Description : cgi script to toggle gpio 4 high -> low
# Author : Brendan Horan

# Required by cgi to set content type
  echo "content-type: text/plain"
  echo ""


# Pull the pin high
 /bin/echo 1 > /sys/class/gpio/gpio4/value


# Sleep for 1 second to allow the remote to receive
  sleep 1
# Pull the pin low
  /bin/echo 0 > /sys/class/gpio/gpio4/value
# Create a file to indicate current outlet state
/bin/echo power-on > outlet-status


# Give the user a nice message
  echo "Power is ON"
  echo "Click your browsers back button to return"
```

This script is very similar to the on function in the `power-ctl.sh` script. There are two differences. The first is that you need to tell the server what type of data your CGI script will return. In your case this line sets that:

```
echo "content-type: text/plain"
```

This line tells the WEBrick CGI server that this script should return plain text. As you can see, right at the bottom of Listing 10-4 the CGI script returns plain text.

The second difference is that the script will echo some text back to the web server. In the last two lines you can see the text that would appear inside your web browser after you click the button.

In Listing 10-5 you can see the `off.cgi` script.

Listing 10-5. The off.cgi Script

```
#!/bin/bash
# Description : cgi script to toggle gpio 17 high -> low
# Author : Brendan Horan

# Required by cgi to set content type
echo "content-type: text/plain"
echo ""


# Pull the pin high
/bin/echo 1 > /sys/class/gpio/gpio17/value
```

```
# Sleep for 1 second to allow the remote to receive
 sleep 1

# Pull the pin low
/bin/echo 0 > /sys/class/gpio/gpio17/value

# Create a file to indicate current outlet state
/bin/echo power-off > outlet-status

# Give the user a nice message
echo "Power is OFF"
echo "Click your browsers back button to return"
```

There really is no difference between these scripts except that you are toggling different GPIO pins.

Last up is the server-power-control.rb Ruby script. This Ruby script is where all the above scripts come together. Take a look at the script in Listing 10-6.

Listing 10-6. The WEBrick HTTP Server Used to Pull Everything Together

```ruby
#!/usr/bin/ruby
# Description : Ruby webrick html server and gpio setup
#  this app will run out of one directory self contained
#  ensure on.cgi, off.cgi and index.html are in the same dir
# Author : Brendan Horan

# Include
require 'webrick'
include WEBrick


# Set up the webrick
 dir = Dir::pwd
 port = "80"
 access_log_stream = File.open('access.log', 'w')
 access_log = [ [ access_log_stream, AccessLog::COMBINED_LOG_FORMAT ] ]


puts "Access at :-"
puts "URL: http://#{Socket.gethostname}:#{port}"

# run a script to configure gpio
 puts "Setting up GPIO on pid:"
pipe = IO.popen("./gpio-setup.sh")
puts pipe.pid


server = HTTPServer.new(
  :Port            => port,
  :DocumentRoot    => dir,
  :AccessLog       => access_log
 )
```

```
# trap exit safely and start the webrick
 trap("INT"){ server.shutdown }
  puts "Running.. Hit Ctrl+c to stop."
  server.start
```

You may have noticed that this script looks pretty close to the one from Chapter 5. You are correct. Only this time I am running the gpio-setup.sh script when starting up the WEBrick HTTP server. Start up the WEBrick HTTP server with the following command:

```
# ./server-power-control.rb
```

Open your favorite web browser and navigate to the Raspberry Pi's IP address. You should be greeted with a screen that looks like Figure 10-17.

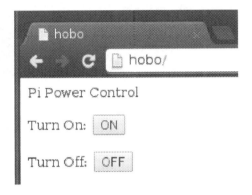

Figure 10-17. *The web page of the GPIO control*

By using the two buttons on this page you can now control your mains device. If you click the on button you will see your mains device turn on. You will also see the output from Figure 10-18; now just hit the back button on your web browser.

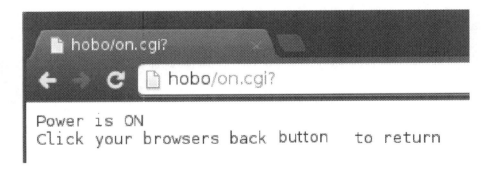

Figure 10-18. *The on button pressed*

If you wanted to have the WEBrick HTTP server start on boot of the Raspberry Pi, you could simply add the two lines listed in Listing 10-7 to your /etc/rc.local file.

Listing 10-7. A Simple Command to Start the WEBrick HTTP Server on Boot

```
# start the webrick server for GPIO
cd /root/power-ctl/ && ./server-power-control.rb &
```

Summary

Congratulations! You can now turn a mains device on and off safely. Your Raspberry Pi is protected by two layers of electrical separation. This chapter has talked a lot about the AC mains and how it works. I also stressed how dangerous it can be to you and, of course, to your Raspberry Pi. I then talked about the main ways that low-voltage circuits are isolated from high-voltage circuits. This is where you found out all about relays and the big part they play in this chapter. Then I stripped down my mains unit and remote control so you could see what they look like and what parts they use. Then I guided you though hacking the remote control unit so that you could connect it to your breadboard. I then described how to use a relay and talked about the funny patterns on the sides of them and lastly we returned to WEBrick to build another web site to control the GPIO pins. In the process you gained an understanding of simple CGI scripts. In the next chapter I leap away from the hardware and the GPIO pins in order to focus solely on alternative operating systems. Yes, that includes Android and, more important, some operating systems you may have never heard of.

CHAPTER 11

■ ■ ■

Other Operating Systems

I am a huge fan of trying just about any operating system I can get my hands on. At this point in time I could use anything from Plan 9 to OpenVMS as a workstation (although I don't think I would want to). I very much like my Gentoo Linux desktop but the thing I would like you to think about is why you like your desktop operating system. You're going to have a very hard time to justify your reasons unless you have tried another OS. I don't just mean install it and then decide it's all too hard and different and give up. You need to give yourself a few days or weeks to use it and work with it. Only then will you see each operating system's strong points and weak points. Far too many people just stick with Windows or OSX. There is nothing wrong with any of the mentioned operating systems but they just don't fit my needs. I know they don't fit my needs because I have used them for a decent amount of time. If you take a look back, many years ago you would have found a vast range of operating systems to use, each with their strong points and each with their loyal supporters. Unfortunately just as much as available architectures have shrunk so have available operating systems. I find it a little sad that our choices are so limited nowadays.

Now given that the Raspberry Pi may be your first non-x86 architecture machine, it's a good choice to also try out a different operating system as well. After all you don't want to just go and replace your main desktop with an alternative operating system. The Raspberry Pi will give you the opportunity to install many different operating systems without risk. In fact this book covers at least two different Linux distributions. While it's still Linux they act very differently. There is a growing list of officially supported operating systems for the Raspberry Pi and there is also a large amount of work done by individuals to get alternative operating systems onto the Raspberry Pi.

In this chapter you're going to be introduced to four different operating systems.

- First will be everyone's favorite, Android. How could you not put Android on an ARM device at least once?

- Next up you will take a look at RISC OS and get an understanding of its deep history with the ARM architecture.

- Then to really throw something odd into the mix you will learn about Bell Labs' Plan 9.

- Lastly I will give you a quick guide on how to install Gentoo Linux onto the Raspberry Pi. Gentoo is my favorite Linux distribution so there is no way I could leave it out. After all, every machine I have runs Gentoo.

Whatever operating system you end up leaving on your Raspberry Pi, you can feel content with the fact you have explored other options and not just blindly accepted what everyone else is doing. The operating systems discussed in this chapter may not be suited for you but please do give them a go and see what's different and what you find interesting about them. When you do go back to your preferred operating system, I can guarantee you will appreciate it more.

Android

First I want to show you an operating system that I am sure you all have come across at some point in time. This operating system is still a distribution of Linux although its main purpose is very different from any of the other distributions I have covered in this book. Of course I am talking of the one and only Android.

The first thing a lot of people ask when they learn that the Raspberry Pi has the same architecture as most mobile phones is if they can install Android onto the Raspberry Pi. Well, you will be happy to hear that the Raspberry Pi can support Android. While I have wanted to see the inside of the Android distribution for some time now it has been quite low on my list of operating systems to install. The Raspberry Pi raised this quite a lot: after all, I no longer needed some strange development board or an expensive ARM board. I now have a cheap board that supports a range of operating systems; it sounds like a perfect time to install Android.

A History of Android

It might be a good idea to know where Android came from. Android, Inc., was first established in 2003 and its main product was supplying an operating system for phones called Android. Not a lot of development on the Android operating system was seen by the public eye until 2005 when it was bought by Google. Then in 2007 the Open Handset Alliance and the first Android project were revealed. The world had to wait until 2008 before it got its first glimpse of a real Android-powered phone.

At this point in time Android was seen as an impressive project but with little power to ever end up as a mainstream mobile-phone system. After all, at this time there were many smartphone vendors with a well-established commercial product; with the likes of Apple and RIM's BlackBerry, Android was in for a challenge. Google did something that paid off and that was creating the Open Handset Alliance alongside the Android project. Google could now bring chip-set makers like Texas Instruments and Qualcomm alongside wholesale carriers like Sprint and T-Mobile and of course the hardware giant Samsung. Now all these different vendors could openly talk about a hardware and software platform to meet their needs. No longer were the wholesale carriers just selling a service: they were influencing the devices for their service. The hardware vendors knew exactly what end consumers wanted. This was Android's big advantage. Android needed all the help it could get: if any of you had the misfortune of using an Android phone with the 1.6 (donut) version of Android, you know that it was a very immature platform.

Another big advantage Android had was that not only could you make a super top-of-the-line smartphone but you could also take the exact same code base and apply it to a cheap handset and easily remove some features. You now had a constant end-user experience and your developers could write applications for a wide range of devices with ease.

Android, unfortunately, has not always played nice with the open source community. During the 2.6 kernel era it split off its development because of issues merging back into the mainline tree. In addition to this a lot of the main handset makers lock down their smartphones to prevent end users from modifying the system. So now you have an Open Alliance using mostly open source technology on a closed hardware platform. This is where the Raspberry Pi comes in. You can now easily get a small taste of the Android operating system from the initial installation and, yes, you will have root.

▓ **Note**   There are other ways you can experience Android like hacking your smartphone or buying a more expensive development board. Some of the more expensive development boards will give you a better all-around experience especially when it comes with a touch screen. None of them will be close to the Raspberry Pi's price point!

Android Considerations

There a few things you must be aware of before you decide to use Android on your Raspberry Pi. The first and biggest one is that there is no support from the Raspberry Pi Foundation. There is no supported image of Android for the Raspberry Pi and there never has been. The foundation was working on a port of Android 4 with Broadcom, but that never got released for reasons unknown. If you think Fedora was in a bad state, then Android on the Raspberry Pi is in an even worse state.

The second point to keep in mind is that since there is no official support from the foundation there are no official Broadcom modules for Android. This means your GPU won't be able to help accelerate the graphics and all rendering will be done in software and that is going to be slow. This means no Android 4 at all. You're going to be going back to a 2.3 version to be even somewhat usable, but without GPU acceleration it's still going to be slow.

Installing Android

No matter how harsh I sound about Android, it's still a good exercise to install it. After all, it's a good idea to know how Android works behind the scenes especially if you use an Android phone. If you still want to go ahead and try out Android you're going to need to download an image. You can get an image from `http://rosefire.us/~razdroid/aaa801/Gingerbread+EthernetManager.7z`.

Once you have this image downloaded, extract the 7zip image to your host machine. You're also going to need an SD card that is bigger than 2 GB to write the image to.

1. Find your SD card on your host machine and use dd to write the image; this will take some time to write. I used the following command to write the image to my SD card:

   ```
   # dd bs=4M if=Gingerbread+EthernetManager.img of=/dev/sde
   ```

2. If you need to edit the `config.txt` file to support your output device, insert your SD card into the host machine and select the 80-MB-sized partition. This is the boot filesystem and contains the firmware and configuration files. This is optional as HDMI just works for my system.

3. Now place the SD card into the Raspberry Pi and turn on the device. At first you will see your normal dmesg boot output scroll past your screen very fast. Then you will notice it stops after activating the network card. At this point I want to warn you that the boot process will stall for quite some time and then again while the Android interface loads. Soon after you will see the Android logo on your screen: you're close now. If all has gone to plan you will see the lock screen of the Android operating system. Take a look at Figure 11-1 to see the lock screen just after the boot process is finished.

Figure 11-1. *The Android lock screen*

Using Android

You can now use Android. Take a look at the version information within the Settings section. In Figure 11-2 you can see that I have Android 2.3.7 running on the Raspberry Pi.

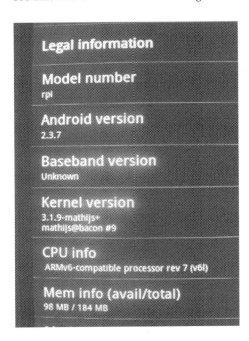

Figure 11-2. *The Android information screen*

You would have noticed by now how slow this version of Android is. Recall that all graphics rendering is now done in software. This means more CPU cycles used on a very limited machine. There is not much more you can really do with the Android operating system on the Raspberry Pi. Without an officially supported image with full GPU support, Android is not usable. It is unfortunate that the operating system that first pops into everyone's head when you say ARM is the one that works the least. Not to worry: this chapter will be filled with other very interesting operating systems that do work better.

RISC OS

You could not have a chapter on other operating systems for an ARM system without talking about RISC OS. What has RISC OS got to do with ARM? Read on to find out.

A History of RISC OS

RISC OS was originally created by Acorn Computers back in 1987 and takes its name from the type of architecture that the operating system was designed to run on. That architecture was RISC (Reduced Instruction Set Computing) and that is exactly what the ARM is. RISC OS was developed to run on the very first ARM CPUs developed for the Acorn line of computers. Over many years RISC OS has become somewhat less important and as such it has suffered in the amount of machines you can run it on, emulators excluded. It's now nice to know that RISC OS has been ported to run on your Raspberry Pi and is provided at no extra cost. It would seem only fitting after all for a computer that makes reference to the BBC Micro to be running RISC OS at least once.

RISC OS Considerations

It's a good idea to talk about the key features or differences of RISC OS before you jump into installing it. The first thing you may want to know is that RISC OS, unlike Linux, is a single-user operating system. A single-user operating system is an operating system that only one user can use at any one point, unlike Linux where you can have more than one user logged into the system, say, via SSH or even via a physical terminal. This makes RISC OS less than ideal for a headless terminal.

One of the most interesting parts of RISC OS is the way it achieves its multitasking. Most operating systems that you will have come in contact with (including Linux) multitask very differently from RISC OS. They use a system called preemptive multitasking, or PMT for short. Under PMT the operating system calculates a time slice for each running process. This time slice may be calculated from a hardware timer or another timing source. When a process enters the running state the operating system starts counting how long it has been running. At this point two things can happen: either the process will finish executing by itself or the operating system pauses the process after a fixed period and lets another process run for its allocated slice. This ensures that all processes get an equal chance to be in a running state on an active CPU. The downside is that no one process can sit in a running state until it's finished. For most users this would not be an issue but for anyone with a latency-sensitive application this can be a problem. So, for example, a place where PMT falls down is aircraft controls. Sometimes you must have a certain process run regardless of current running processes: after all you don't want the autopilot being interrupted by a nonimportant running service.

RISC OS uses a very different system called cooperative multitasking, or CMT. Unlike PMT, CMT is controlled by the processes themselves. In a CMT environment each process should regularly talk to the operating system. When it talks to the operating system a process will indicate if it needs to gain more time on the active CPU or if it can yield time on the active CPU to another process. The reason why it's called cooperative is that each process should inform the operating system as soon as it can about its state and all processes cooperate to ensure that no one process hogs time on the active CPU. Unfortunately this aspect of CMT is also its downfall. If you have one process that spends too much time on the active CPU, every other process will fail to respond in a timely manner, effectively locking up your entire system. Now if you can't control that process your operating system will eventually crash. On the other hand if you are in total control of that application you may want it to have full access on the CPU and run until completed, no matter what else is trying to run. Some flight-control systems still use a CMT-based operating environment. Another defining characteristic of RISC OS is that it relies heavily on the WIMP concept; if you have spent any time on Apple's OSX you're not going to feel too far from home on RISC OS. WIMP is short for windows, icons, menu, and pointer, which is a graphical user interface design that relies heavily on the use of a mouse and the drag-and-drop principle. The WIMP style of interaction was first developed at Xerox in 1973, although the operating system that popularized this style was of course Apple's Mac OS. Designers of WIMP interfaces pride themselves on the interfaces' abstraction and ease of use. For example, to install new applications you simply drag the binary file into the filesystem. To run the exact same application you just launch it from the filesystem where you copied it.

On the topic of filesystems, RISC OS uses a filesystem called Advance Disk Filing System, or ADFS for short. ADFS is by far the most limited filesystem in this chapter. For example, you won't be able to put a few hundred files into a directory or make use of that new 1-TB hard disk you have, nor will you be able to rip a DVD to the filesystem in one single file. These points aside, there are a few small things you need to know about ADFS in order for you to be able to use it efficiently. The first and most confusing part of ADFS is how a filesystem path first looks. Take, for example, this path:

ADFS::HardDisk4.$.Mystuff.Pi

This looks a little confusing at first so Table 11-1 breaks down the layout for you.

Table 11-1. *An example of a filesystem path broken down*

Path Element	Definition	Filesystem Delimiter
ADFS	Filesystem type	::
HardDisk4	Device name and number	.
$	Root of the HardDisk4 device	.
Mystuff	A directory under the top level of the filesystem	.
Pi	A file	None

The first thing you may have noticed is that parts of the path use different delimiters, unlike in Unix or Linux where all paths are delimited by a forward slash /. The filesystem type and the physical device are delimited by ::. Thankfully you won't need to worry too much about this delimiter unless you are changing between physical devices or network devices. The rest of the directory structure is delimited by a single dot.

The next thing you may have noticed is that my example file called Pi has no extension! How do you know this is a text file, I hear you ask? Recall that RISC OS is based around a WIMP user interface and this interface uses something inside every file called metadata. Metadata are information about a file that is saved with the file. The metadata are set on a per-file basis and the WIMP interface reads the attributes. Once it has read the metadata for file type it will change the icon of the file. This is how you know it's a text file; the icon will be of a text file and a zip file has a little zipper on it and so forth. It's all part of the way a WIMP interface works. Take a look at Figure 11-3 where you can see how I have set the file type metadata on an application file.

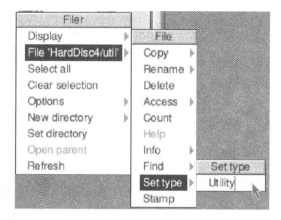

Figure 11-3. *Setting the metadata in the WIMP interface*

One very nice thing about ADFS that some other operating systems have made use of recently is a loop-style device to mount archived filesystems. For example, when you double-click a zip file in a recent version of Windows it will open up the contents of the archive. RISC OS and the ADFS have been able to do this for many years. This all comes back to the WIMP interface: the end user should not need to go into a command line and extract the files from the archive and then view them. The WIMP approach is to make all of that seamless, and the archive just opens up for the user and provides access to exactly what is needed. This is the loop filesystem working in the background to mount the zip file as a working filesystem for you.

Now what would happen if you were to copy your Nginx `error.log` file into your RISC OS system? RISC OS already knows it's a little different from other operating systems and will change the extension on the file automatically to help you out. If you were to copy your `error.log` into the `Mystuff` directory from Table 11-1, your RISC OS system would save the file as `ADFS::HardDisc4.$.Mystuff.error/log`. You may need to set the metadata on the file if RISC OS cannot automatically recognize the file type (this only needs to be done once).

The ADFS implementation is also very modular. The entire filesystem stack consists of three modules each with a very special task.

- The module ADFS is responsible for block access and user interface interaction.

- The FileCore module is responsible for the actual filesystem on disk behind the ADFS module.

- The Fileswitch module gives out access to the application programming interface (API).

This all makes for a very stable filesystem stack. Because of the modular system it makes it very simple for other developers to port their filesystems to RISC OS. Sadly not many people have ported filesystems, given RISC OS's limited popularity.

All of this is starting to sound quite interesting. It's time to get the image and create your SD card.

Installing RISC OS

Point your browser to `http://raspberrypi.org/downloads` and select the RISC OS download image. At the time I wrote this, the image was called `RiscOS-2012-11-01-RC6.zip`.

Once you have this file downloaded, extract it from the zip archive to a temporary directory on your host machine. Once it is extracted, you will notice there is no installer, just the image file and a text file. You are going to need to write this image file to your SD card by using the `dd` command.

Find your SD card's whole block device entry and write the whole image to it; in my case the device is /dev/sde and the command would be as follows:

```
# dd if=ro519-rc6-1876M.img of=/dev/sde
```

While that image is writing, take a look at Figure 11-4 to see the contents of the SD card.

Figure 11-4. *The contents of the RISC OS SD card*

There is not much on the SD card. You will have the firmware, the RISC OS image, and a config file that will allow you to set the GPU memory. There is a small difference between the Raspberry Pi and a traditional RISC OS machine. The RISC OS operating system is normally sorted on a ROM filesystem or inside flash memory on the machine and not on the first hard disk. This traditionally made RISC OS has an amazingly fast boot-up time and very little operating system corruption. Given that the Raspberry Pi only has the SD card slot you won't be able to boot it like a traditional RISC OS machine. Not to worry: you will still get very fast speeds from the SD card.

By now your RISC OS image should be written to your SD card. Insert the SD card into the Raspberry Pi and power on. If all is good you will see a boot screen like in Figure 11-5.

Figure 11-5. *The RISC OS boot screen*

This should pass fairly quickly and you will be dropped onto the wonderful RISC OS desktop. On the first boot the operating system will set up a few things and you should be greeted by a few tasks running as you can see in Figure 11-6.

Figure 11-6. *The first boot and the WIMP interface*

Once the setup tasks are all done, you will be presented with a warning from an application called NetSurf. This warning will look like Figure 11-7.

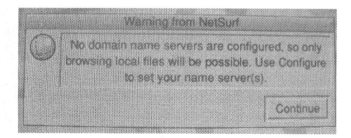

Figure 11-7. *The NetSurf warning*

This warning is pretty harmless if your Raspberry Pi is not connected to a network. My Raspberry Pi is connected to a network and I would like to have Internet access from RISC OS as well. The warning is telling you that the NetSurf application cannot resolve any Domain Name System (DNS) names. I will show you how to configure your network now. On your desktop, click on the icon called !Configure. This will open up a configuration folder as you can see in Figure 11-8.

Figure 11-8. *The Configuration folder*

This is where you configure the settings for RISC OS. There are no files to edit or obscure configuration files: it's all WIMP.

1. Click the Network icon. You will then have another window pop up with three options: AUN, Access, and Internet. I want to show you what each network technology is before you go and fix your network access.

   - The first network type is Acorn Universal Networking, or AUN for short. When the BBC Micro was released it had the ability to be networked via a network system called Econet. Econet was originally used to share small files between the machines and to share floppy and hard disk devices across the network. As time went by and Ethernet and TCP/IP became more of the industry standard, this meant Econet was losing a lot of ground. Acorn Computers ported Econet to run over TCP/IP and AUN was born. If you have more than one RISC OS machine on your network, you may want to enable AUN. Access allows you to share system resources over a network. This network may be AUN or a TCP/IP network. The Access option is enabled by default. You can see it's enabled as it has a green dot under the icon whereas the other two networking options have gray dots.

   - The last icon is Internet and this allows you to configure TCP/IP settings.

2. Click the Internet icon and you should see the Internet configuration window like in Figure 11-9.

Figure 11-9. *The Internet configuration options*

3. Click Enable TCP/IP Protocol Suite.

4. Click the Interfaces icon. You should see that USB Ethernet over USB is selected.

5. Click the Configure button next to this and you can now configure your IP settings. In Figure 11-10 you can see I am using DHCP for the network settings.

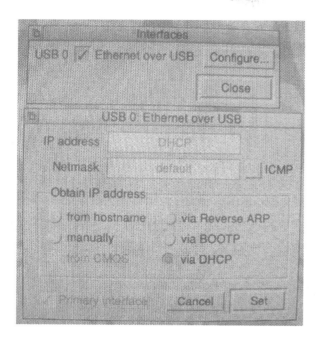

Figure 11-10. *The IP configuration window and the Interfaces window*

6. Once you have configured your network settings, click the Set button and close each of the windows.

7. Once they are all closed the RISC OS system will ask you if it can reboot to enable the changes. It's best to restart the system now.

Once your system has restarted you can test out the Internet access. Click the !NetSurf icon on the desktop. Hang on: where is your browser? Why did nothing appear onscreen? In RISC OS when you first open an application it will be placed into the application tray on the bottom right-hand corner of the screen. From there you can do something with the application. See Figure 11-11 to see the NetSurf application loaded into the application tray.

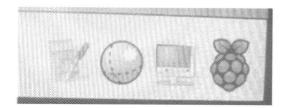

Figure 11-11. *The application tray with NetSurf loaded*

Left-click the icon and NetSurf will launch a new browser window. If your network is configured correctly you should be able to browse to a web site. In Figure 11-12 you can see that I opened the Google web site.

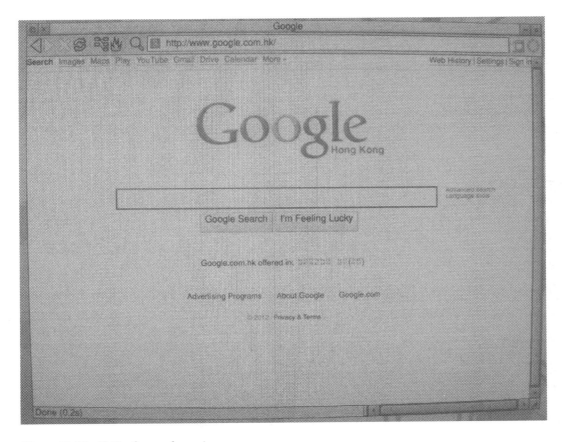

Figure 11-12. NetSurf up and running

Having a working web browser is your first step and a very useful one as you are going to be searching a lot on how to use RISC OS.

Using RISC OS

Let's take a quick look around RISC OS. You have already seen the Configuration Settings screen but how can you launch an application? There is no menu. Take a look at the lower left-hand corner of your screen; you can see mine in Figure 11-13.

Figure 11-13. *The applications and filesystems sections*

In this part of the screen you can see a few icons. The first two, Discs and :0, are your filesystems. There will not be much under the Discs icon as you have no hard disks attached to the system yet. You only have an SD card filesystem, or SDFS for short; this is represented by the :0 that you see. If you click this icon you will see the contents of your SD card. The next icon is the Apps folder. This is a shortcut to the applications directory on the RISC OS operating system. This is where you install new applications and access existing applications. Mac OSX users will be most familiar with this kind of application folder. You can see the applications folder in Figure 11-14.

Figure 11-14. *The Apps folder*

There are not a lot of applications installed by default. That's not a problem; the Raspberry Pi version of the RISC OS provides two ways to get more software. The first one is called PackMan. PackMan not only will allow you to install new applications but also will keep the RISC OS operating system updated. Always check PackMan first to see if your application is available for download. Take a look at Figure 11-15 to see PackMan in action.

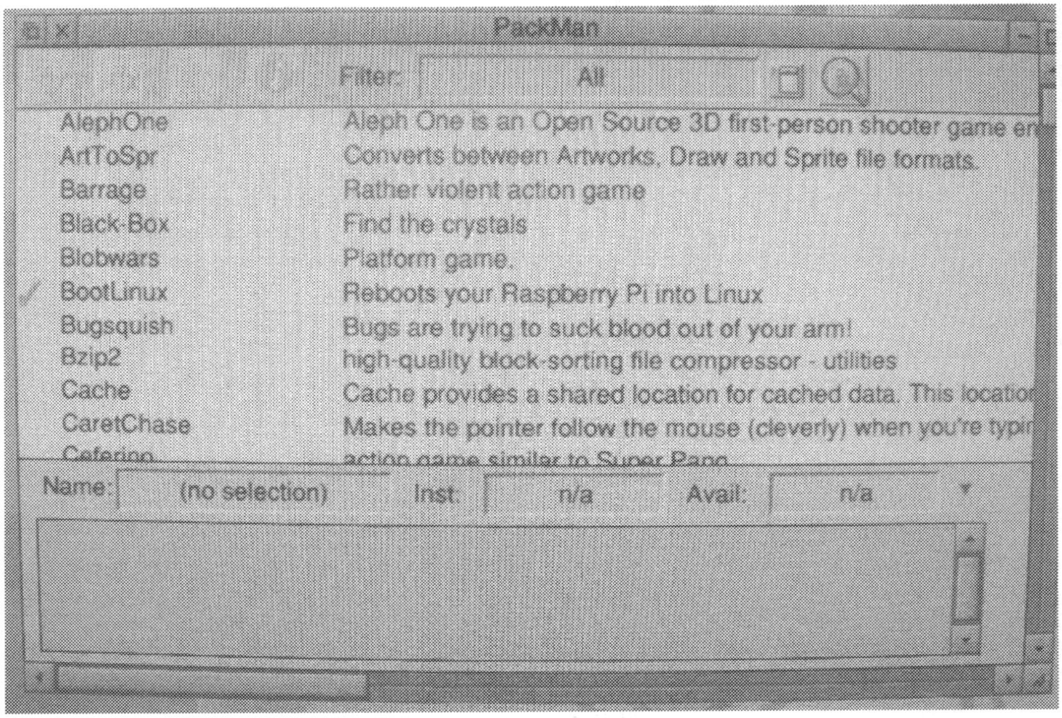

Figure 11-15. *PackMan in action*

Those are not all the applications RISC OS can provide. If you take a look on your desktop, you will see an icon called PlingStore. This is another application you can use to find free and paid software for a Raspberry Pi that is running RISC OS. There is a large amount of software you can gain access to in PlingStore so do take a look around. You can see the two main screens of PlingStore in Figure 11-16.

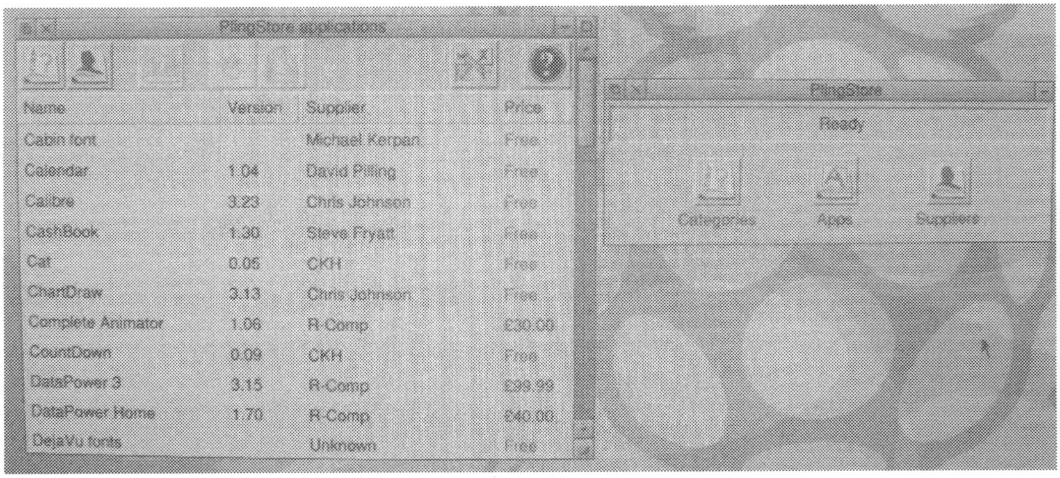

Figure 11-16. *PlingStore application running*

As you can see, RISC OS is a fully functional lightweight desktop. You may also now appreciate where some of our modern graphical user interfaces came from. Take some time to use RISC OS; I am sure you will find some things you like about it.

Plan 9

Plan 9 was developed at Bell Labs. Bell Labs is a division of Alcatel-Lucent, and it has developed and pioneered a large range of technologies over the years. One such project is Plan 9.

A History of Plan 9

Plan 9 was an operating system designed to evolve Unix's concepts. It was extensively worked on inside Bell during the 1980s and even managed to replace Unix on some of Bell's internal research systems. It was only in 1992 that the first edition of Plan 9 was released to universities. Soon after that a commercial version of Plan 9 became available. Around the same time Bell Labs opened up Plan 9 for distribution under a noncommercial license, which allowed any one with supported hardware to install Plan 9. The license was not the GNU General Public License (GPL) but was an in-house Bell Labs license model, which added a lot of confusion for the end users of Plan 9 because the license was less than clear about what you can and cannot do with Plan 9. With the fourth release of Plan 9 in 2002 Lucent moved Plan 9 to a much clearer license model.

Sadly by 2002 a lot of people had lost interest in Plan 9, but lucky for you there is now a port of Plan 9 to the Raspberry Pi. Let me talk about why you may want to take a look into Plan 9 and what makes it so very different from any of the operating systems listed in this book. You need to understand that Plan 9 was originally designed to meet Unix's shortcomings. Unix during the 1980s was a fantastic multiuser operating system that gave end users a lot more freedom than the batch job-oriented alternatives at the time. Unix was not perfect and it fell short in distributed computing. This is where the people originally behind Plan 9 saw the chance to improve, and Plan 9 was born.

Plan 9 Considerations

Plan 9 is a distributed grid computing platform; it's designed for the network and is part of the network at a very low level. What exactly is a distributed grid computing platform? A grid style of computing is where each node is part of a larger grid of systems that is spread across any location. Applications running on one node may pull resources and even CPU time for any members of the grid. The grid can be made up of one node or many nodes across any form of commutation and across any administrative boundaries. There would be no technical reason why your Plan 9 system could not be a member of the same grid that my Plan 9 system is in. This gives Plan 9 a huge benefit from the ground up as Plan 9 is fully distributed, including in CPU time.

In a Plan 9 grid there are normally three types of systems:

- A system called a terminal is what the end user would sit in front of and operate with a keyboard and mouse.

- A system called a CPU has one job: to process commands from terminals on the grid. A system called file stores files, although the file server is a little more advanced than that.

Terminals don't necessarily need a local disk and it's not the best way to get Plan 9 up and running as well. Plan 9 terminals can be run right off the network with all their storage hosted on a file server. This is seamless to the end user as Plan 9 makes all requests for any resources over the network to start with. Even if you're sitting at a local terminal with a local disk, Plan 9 will not treat this any differently than if you were connected to a remote file and CPU server.

Plan 9 achieves this via a protocol called 9P, or more recently 9P2000. This protocol is what ties all of Plan 9 together. The 9P2000 protocol has one strange aspect that can take some time to get used to. There is no API. There is no API for anyone; it's not hidden or reserved for special people at Bell Labs, there just is no API (you'll see why this is the case later in this section).

Now the absence of an API is not always a good or bad thing. If you used Plan 9 every day and wrote programs and tools just for Plan 9 it would not matter in the slightest that it did not have an API. After all, you would be so used to the 9P2000 protocol. Now you will notice there are very few programs from other operating systems ported to Plan 9. This is where not having an API comes at a huge cost. Most modern operating systems such as Linux, Mac OS, and Windows all have APIs. So if you wanted to port the LibreOffice package to Plan 9 you would need to change every single API to fit with Plan 9's 9P2000 protocol. That's not an easy task for anyone!

Plan 9 makes heavy use of the concept that all objects are files on a filesystem. In Plan 9 you manipulate a file to get something to happen in much the same way you can in Linux or Unix for that matter, but Plan 9 uses this concept for everything. The logic behind this is simple: if everything is a file it's very easy to distribute something across the network as part of the grid. Let me give you an example. In Plan 9 your keyboard and mouse of your local terminal can be represented as /dev/kbd and /dev/mouse and they are just simple stream devices. On a remote terminal node I can mount up your /dev/ filesystem and write to your /dev/mouse stream device file. I would then be moving your mouse on your terminal. This concept can be applied to any device connected to the Plan 9 systems. After all, everything from your mouse to your local storage is just a file on a filesystem somewhere.

Given the fact you can mount (or *bind* as it's referred to in Plan 9) any remote filesystem how do you manage paths? Under Plan 9 you can bind many directories to one top-level directory. Say, for example, you have the following list of directories:

- /usr/local/bin

- /usr/contrib/bin

- /home/brendan/bin

In Unix and Linux you would fiddle with your system's path variable to ensure your applications can be executed. In Plan 9 you would bind the directories to the main /bin directory. This would make any files under /usr/local/bin appear as if they were part of the /bin directory. This concept is similar to hard links in Unix and Linux but works on a directory level and is not destructive.

There are two other filesystems in Plan 9 that have a lot of functionality: they are the /proc and /net filesystems. The /proc filesystem is similar to what's found in Unix and Linux but has many more features. With Plan 9's version of /proc you can control applications with basic system tools to get the same functionality as an API call to an application in Unix and Linux. This is why Plan 9 has no API: you manipulate files on the filesystem instead.

Then you have /net: this is how you set up your network and gain information about your network. Each configuration is read or written into files inside /net. There are even files to represent TCP and UDP data streams.

This all sounds pretty interesting, but before you jump into Plan 9 there are a few small things you must understand. First, Plan 9 is built around a three-button mouse. In Plan 9 the left mouse button is solely used to select text on the screen. The middle mouse button is for menu and context choices and the right mouse button is for high-level options like moving a window around. You can simulate the middle mouse button with the Shift key and the right mouse button, or your mouse's scroll wheel can sometimes act like a third button. Using this method gets annoying quite quickly so see if you can find a three-button mouse.

Another odd thing is that when you're using an application that gives out scrolling text, Plan 9 will not scroll the output of any window by default. This means that if your text file is three pages long, unless you scroll the window yourself you will be stuck on page 1. You can use the arrow keys or the scroll wheel on your mouse to move the output.

■ **Note**   Unlike in Linux and Unix, the Delete key, not Crtl+C, in Plan 9 will terminate a running job.

Plan 9 also has some funny jargon. Take a look at Table 11-2 to see some of the more common ones.

Table 11-2. *Plan 9 jargon*

Jargon Term	Meaning
Chord	Press more than one mouse button at the same time
Put	Save something to the filesystem
Snarf	Copy text to the clipboard
Sweep	Move the mouse across the screen while holding down a button
Zerox	Duplicate a window and its contents

Now that you have a brief idea what Plan 9 is and why it's good, it's time to install Plan 9.

Installing Plan 9

You're going to need to download the Plan 9 image for Raspberry Pi first. Do note that this image is not supported by the foundation or by Bell Labs. Download the image from here:

`http://plan9.bell-labs.com/sources/contrib/miller/9pi.img.gz`.

Once you have this downloaded on your host machine, you need to extract the image and write it to the SD card. You won't need to compile Plan 9 as it's a premade ready-to-go image. All you need to do is write the image to your SD with the following command on a Unix-like system:

`# dd if=9pi.img of=/dev/sdX`

Replace sdX with the name of your actual SD card device. This should not take too long. When that is done take a look at the contents of the SD card; in Figure 11-17 you can see my SD card contents.

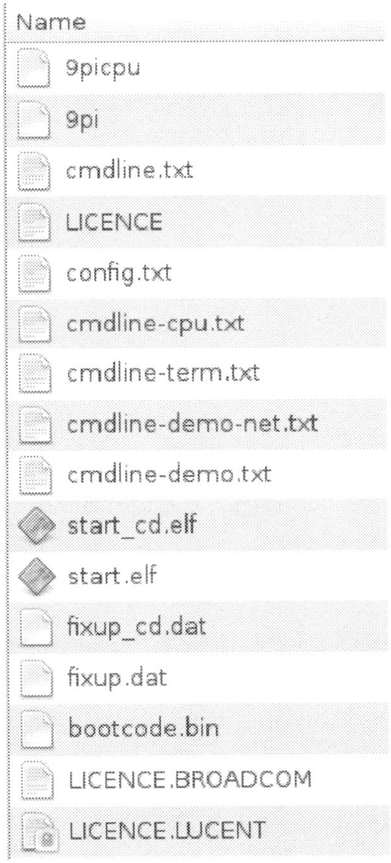

Name
9picpu
9pi
cmdline.txt
LICENCE
config.txt
cmdline-cpu.txt
cmdline-term.txt
cmdline-demo-net.txt
cmdline-demo.txt
start_cd.elf
start.elf
fixup_cd.dat
fixup.dat
bootcode.bin
LICENCE.BROADCOM
LICENCE.LUCENT

Figure 11-17. *The contents of the Plan 9 SD card image*

A few files may interest you. The first one is config.txt; unlike in Fedora this file is well commented and easy to use. The first line of this file will set which kernel is booted when you power on the Raspberry Pi. By default, that will be the 9pi terminal image. You could change this to 9picpu just to get a CPU server rather than a terminal (useful for you if you have a cluster of Raspberry Pis in your possession). It's wise to leave the kernel set to 9pi for the first time.

Looking back at the main directory again, you will see the 9picpu file and the 9pi file that I just talked about. These are the two systems you can boot. The default cmdline.txt file will ensure that Plan 9 boots all the way into the rio window manager without your intervention.

The rest of the files can be left alone or are similar files as you would find on any other boot partition for the Raspberry Pi. For your first boot of Plan 9 you should not need to edit any files on the SD card. Insert the SD card into the Raspberry Pi and connect an HDMI cable, mouse, and keyboard. When you turn on your Raspberry Pi and your image is good, you will be greeted with a boot message like you see in Figure 11-18.

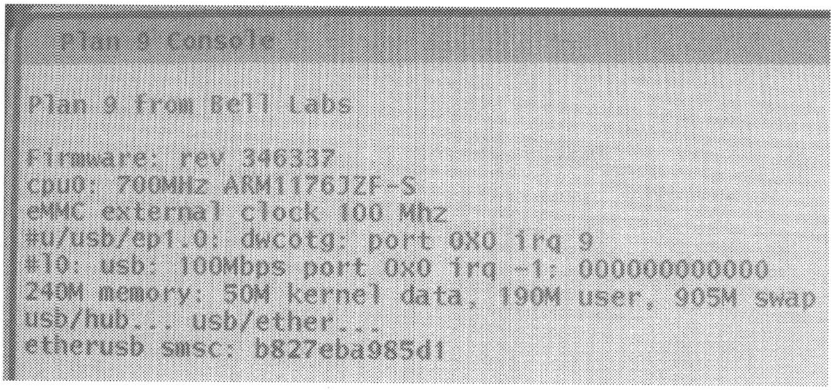

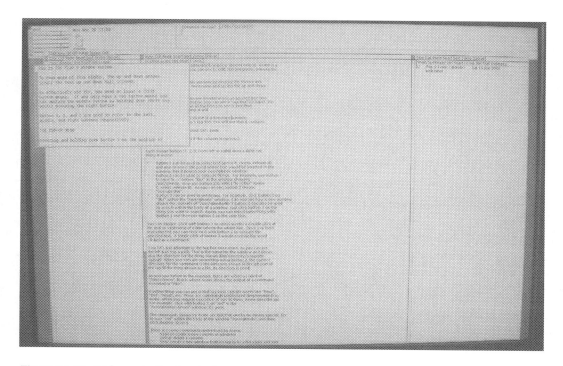

Figure 11-18. *The boot message of Plan 9 on the Raspberry Pi*

The boot process is fairly quick. Once it's done you should be greeted by the rio window manager. The image will also launch a lot of Acme windows with useful help information for first-time Plan 9 users. Acme is Plan 9's visual text editor. You can see the rio window manager in Figure 11-19.

Figure 11-19. *Welcome to the rio window manager*

As you can see, the rio window manager is very different from any of the operating systems in this chapter and most likely any operating system you have used before. Take a look though the help screens that have been displayed for you as part of the first boot sequence. You will also notice that all the windows have no close or resize buttons. To close a window you need to use the right mouse button and select the kill option, then hover the cursor over the window you want to kill and left-click on it. It is a little strange at first, but you will soon get used to it.

After reading though the help screens you may want to enable networking via DHCP in Plan 9. To do this, draw a new window in rio and use the ip/ipconfig command; to do this type the following command:

```
term % ip/ipconfig
```

This should return with no error. Since this returns with no information how can you find your IP address? Remember the special /net filesystem and that everything in Plan 9 is a file? With this in mind, just cat the /net/ndb file; the command would be as follows:

```
# term% cat /net/ndb
```

This should print back your IP configuration. Take a look at Figure 11-20 to see the output of these two commands.

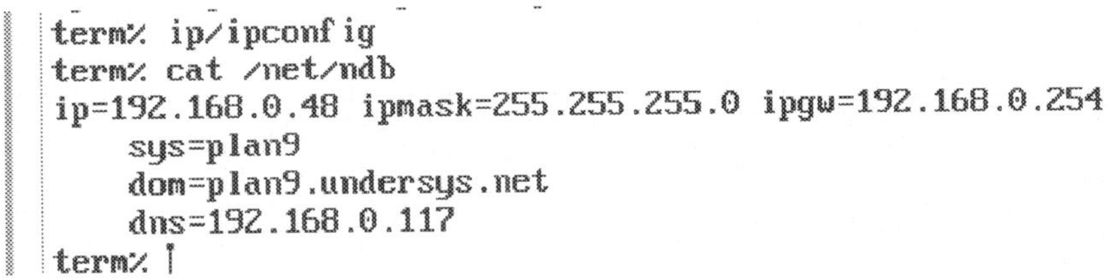

```
term% ip/ipconfig
term% cat /net/ndb
ip=192.168.0.48 ipmask=255.255.255.0 ipgw=192.168.0.254
    sys=plan9
    dom=plan9.undersys.net
    dns=192.168.0.117
term%
```

Figure 11-20. *The output of the ip/ipconfig and the cat /net/ndb commands*

Using Plan 9

Now that you have your network connection you're going to want to access a web browser. Under Plan 9 your choices are very limited; on the Raspberry Pi you must use the browser called Abaco. It's very basic but it will get you up and running.

1. Draw a new window in rio and type abaco at the term% prompt. Oh that did not work, did it? You got a nice error about the webfs not being initialized. You really need to keep in mind that everything in Plan 9 is a file on a filesystem, including any web page you are browsing. The webfs filesystem is another special filesystem that handles HTML requests. You are going to need to enable the cookies subsystem as well because the webfs system depends on cookies.

2. In your current window, run the following commands to enable the webcookies filesystem and the webfs filesystem. Take a look at Figure 11-21 where I have done this. There should be no output or error.

   ```
   term% webcookies
   term% webfs
   ```

```
term% webcookies
term% webfs
term% ls /mnt
/mnt/exportfs
/mnt/factotum
/mnt/plumb
/mnt/temp
/mnt/web
/mnt/webcookies
/mnt/wsys
term% |
```

Figure 11-21. *The commands to enable the webcookies and webfs filesystems*

3. You can also see in Figure 11-21 where I have listed the contents of the /mnt directory; you can see that the web and webcookies directories are mounted and ready for use. Now try to run Abaco again. If all has gone well you should have a window running Abaco.

4. Open a new window inside of Abaco to browse a web page. To do this, press Shift and right-click on the word New or use your middle mouse button if you have one.

5. In the lowest empty green box, enter the web site URL. In Figure 11-22 you can see I have browsed to the Plan 9 home page.

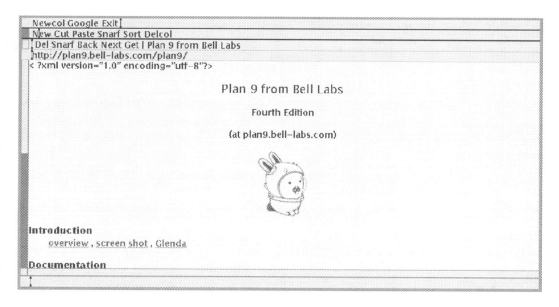

Figure 11-22. *The Abaco web browser*

Abaco is quite basic as you can see, and you would have also noticed how much Plan 9 relies on a three-button mouse. Plan 9 contains no real usable end-user applications that are suitable for everyday use. If you want to see what applications are installed in Plan 9, just list the /bin directory and you will see applications that you can run. This is a good example of the directory binding in action. Unlike RISC OS, the sole purpose of Plan 9 is to demonstrate an alternative operating system to you and introduce new concepts of how an operating system can work. After all Plan 9 is classed as a research operating system. What you should take away from Plan 9 is not how featureless Abaco is, for example, but how Plan 9 considers everything as a file and grid computing concepts.

Gentoo

Lastly I will show you how to get Gentoo up and running on the Raspberry Pi. Gentoo is my personal favorite distribution of Linux.

A History of Gentoo

Gentoo Linux (originally known as Enoch Linux) was created by Daniel Robbins and a small group of developers around 1999. His goal was simple: to create a Linux distribution with no precompiled binaries and tuned to the hardware that it's running on. This goal struck a huge roadblock when developers behind Enoch found out that the GNU Compiler Collection (GCC) has issues building itself from the source correctly. The Enoch development team found solutions to resolve the issues. Not only did this allow the GCC to build correctly, but those contributions optimized the GCC's ability to compile binary files.

At this point Enoch was renamed as Gentoo. The name Gentoo was selected because a gentoo is the fastest swimming penguin. Gentoo at this point lacked a crucial item. It had no package management system. For a period of time Daniel Robbins halted Gentoo and switched to FreeBSD as his operating system. It was during this time that he was inspired by FreeBSD's package management system. From this Gentoo gained its own package management system called portage.

The fact that Gentoo is free of binary components and has a package tree that consists of just source code makes it an ideal operating system to port to other architectures. There are very few machine types that are not supported by Gentoo; if the Linux kernel has support, then there will be a Gentoo installation possible as long as you have a lot of spare time. Gentoo has its shortcomings: for a start the installation process is long and involved compared to other main Linux distributions.

Gentoo Considerations

Gentoo is a little different from most of the more popular Linux distributions. There is no installer for Gentoo although there is a live CD. If you wanted to, you could even install Gentoo from your currently running Linux operating system. When you install Gentoo, everything is done by hand and via the command line. There are no wizards and there are no GUI tools. I did tell you that I was quite fond of the command line. Don't be too put off by that; Gentoo has a very useful install time guide that they call the handbook to help you out. The handbook will be your new friend during a Gentoo install.

The next difference about Gentoo, compared to Fedora, is that there is no distribution version. Gentoo is a meta-distribution. A meta-distribution is a distribution that continues to update forever. You install new kernels and new versions of LibreOffice as they come down from the upstream providers, whereas Fedora takes a known working set of packages from the upstream provider and assigns them to a distribution version number. You would have a hard time installing the latest LibreOffice on Fedora Core 11 via yum if you tried to today. In contrast, with a meta-distribution you can do this no matter the age of the original install, although you may need to update a lot of packages to get there. The benefit of a meta-distribution is that you can always update to the latest version and bring any age of the original install up to date. The downside is that you end up with a very mixed package version that has not been as thoroughly tested as a Fedora release package at a set version.

Gentoo also has another difference in the way it handles its packages. Most of the popular distributions of Linux use a binary package format to distribute packages. You may have come across this with packages ending in .rpm or .deb. Gentoo's system of distributing packages is called portage. Gentoo's developers were inspired by the FreeBSD ports collection where only the source code and a small file on how to build that source code is distributed to the end user. This is known as source distribution, unlike Fedora, which is a binary distribution. Gentoo's portage system is made of a set of files called ebuilds and the necessary patches are created by the Gentoo community. Ebuild files are read by a tool called emerge. This tool has a similar function as yum or apt-get. Take a look at Listing 11-1 to see a sample ebuild file.

Listing 11-1. A Sample ebuild File (Copyright 1999–2012 Gentoo Foundation)

```
# Distributed under the terms of the GNU General Public License v2
# $Header: $

EAPI=4

DESCRIPTION="A useful Description of the package"
HOMEPAGE="http://the home page of the package"
SRC_URI="mirror://the full path to the exact source archive"

LICENSE="What license the source is under"
SLOT="Which slot to install into"
KEYWORDS="Any keyboards if needed"

        # Configure the source
src_configure() {
    econf --Place your configure options hear

}

        # Install the source
src_install() {
    emake DESTDIR="${D}" install

            # Create documentation for the source.
    dodoc FAQ NEWS README
    dohtml EXTENDING.html ctags.html

}
```

As you can see, this file just runs your standard ./configure, make, and make install tools. This means that every application you want on your Gentoo system from the ping utility all the way up to your window manager must be compiled from source code. Gentoo compiles everything from source and because of this the distribution was responsible for a large number of bug fixes to the GCC tool chain that resulted in a lot of performance improvements for the GCC. So everyone in the Linux community has benefited from Gentoo's slightly odd way of building an entire operating system from source.

Aside from this benefit to the Linux community as a whole, the source distribution provides a very big advantage for the end user as well. When you go to install a package in Gentoo you will be given the option to specify something called *use flags*. Use flags interact with the configure stage of the build and set what parts of the application you would like compiled in with the application binary. For example, you may want to install nmap but you don't like using the GUI (after all, the command line is better). Under Gentoo's use flag system you simply instruct the emerge tool not to build nmap with the GUI. This gives you a faster and cleaner lightweight system. It also may give you a lot of headaches when you notice that some applications depend on some feature that you had removed and you now require two hours of recompiling to enable a very small feature.

In the binary world of package management like in Fedora you do not get this choice: the package builder has already selected what will be part of the package for you. This makes for better compatibility between packages and stability between packages but it comes at the lack of choice for the end user. Gentoo is all about end-user choice. If you wanted to, there would be nothing stopping you building a system with no X and just installing Minicom or having an eye-candy display of KDE 4. You can also have a mix of both: the choice is yours and its Gentoo's strength and its weakness.

Getting support for your Gentoo system is not as easy as you would hope; after all, everyone has a slightly different install configuration and different use flags. In this respect, community support for a packaged version distribution will be much better. Gentoo teaches you to understand your system and then you can better support it yourself when you know where every little application and setting have been configured.

Gentoo's sourced based system makes it an ideal distribution to port to other architectures because there no longer is a need to cross compile: you already have a working tool chain in your initial build environment. Gentoo also sets up the GCC right at the start of the configuration of your build so that you have an optimized GCC binary for your target architecture. Gentoo takes full advantage of this with the Raspberry Pi by enabling hard-float and link-time optimization.

Installing Gentoo

The installation of Gentoo is not as simple as extracting an image and writing it to the SD card. If you wanted to make an image of your finished Gentoo install, that method would work though. Nor will this install of Gentoo be like a traditional install. You will do most of the installation from your host machine and the cross compile environment you configured in Chapter 6.

I use a 16-GB SD card for my Gentoo install; you could easily get away with a 4-GB card but given that SD cards are cheap in Hong Kong I've gone for bigger ones. The first task you're going to need to do is to create the partitions for the Gentoo installation. At a bare minimum you're going to need two partitions:

- The boot partition, which is fat32

- A root partition that can be EXT4 or another Linux filesystem of your choosing

I will be using fdisk under Linux to create my partitions but nothing stops you from using any tool you want. Figure 11-23 shows my partition layout.

```
Disk /dev/sde: 16.0 GB, 16009658368 bytes
64 heads, 32 sectors/track, 15268 cylinders, total 31268864 sectors
Units = sectors of 1 * 512 = 512 bytes
Sector size (logical/physical): 512 bytes / 512 bytes
I/O size (minimum/optimal): 512 bytes / 512 bytes
Disk identifier: 0x000ef81f

   Device Boot      Start         End      Blocks   Id  System
/dev/sde1            2048      206847      102400    c  W95 FAT32 (LBA)
/dev/sde2          206848    31268863    15531008   83  Linux

Command (m for help): []
```

Figure 11-23. *Gentoo partition layout*

Next, format the partitions in their respective filesystem formats. For the boot volume (sde1), I used the following command:

```
# mkfs.vfat -F 32 /dev/sde1
```

I then used the following command to make the EXT4 filesystem on the second volume (sde2):

```
# mkfs.ext4 /dev/sde2
```

Now you will have two filesystems that are ready to use. You'll need to mount the boot and root partitions onto the host machine. I like to mount them under /mnt but you can mount them wherever you want. I used the following two commands to mount my filesystems:

```
# mount /dev/sde1 /mnt/rpi-boot/
# mount /dev/sde2 /mnt/rpi-root/
```

In Figure 11-24 you can see my mounted partitions.

```
pcb / # df -h | grep rpi
/dev/sde1               99M   13M   87M  13% /mnt/rpi-boot
/dev/sde2               15G  1.5G   13G  11% /mnt/rpi-root
```

Figure 11-24. *The mounted partitions on the host machine*

The boot partition is like any other Raspberry Pi boot partition. It contains the firmware from the foundation, the command-line arguments and configuration files, and lastly the kernel itself. The first step in building the boot filesystem is to obtain the firmware files from the foundation's GitHub site:

```
https://github.com/raspberrypi/firmware/tree/master/boot
```

Here are the files you will need:

- bootcode.bin

- start.elf

- fixup.dat

Use wget to copy them from the GitHub site onto the mounted boot partition. Once you have the three files, your mounted boot partition should look like Figure 11-25.

```
pcb rpi-boot # ls -lrth
total 2.3M
drwx------ 2 root  root   16K Dec 17 16:40 lost+found
-rw-r--r-- 1 root  root   18K Dec 18 14:30 bootcode.bin
-rw-r--r-- 1 root  root  5.2K Dec 18 14:31 fixup.dat
-rw-r--r-- 1 root  root  2.3M Dec 18 14:31 start.elf
pcb rpi-boot # █
```

Figure 11-25. *The boot partition with the firmware files*

Next, you're going to need to create the cmdline.txt file and the config.txt file. In Listing 11-2 you can see the contents of the cmdline.txt file. Create the cmdline.txt in the boot partition.

Listing 11-2. The cmdline.txt File

```
root=/dev/mmcblk0p2 rootdelay=2
```

Next create the config.txt file. In Listing 11-3 you can see the contents of my file. You may need different options if you're using HDMI or composite video outputs. Once again, save this file in the boot partition.

Listing 11-3. The config.txt File

gpu_mem=32

Once you are all done your boot partition should look like Figure 11-26. All that is left is the Linux kernel to go on the boot filesystem.

```
pcb rpi-boot # ls -lrth
total 2.3M
drwx------ 2 root root  16K Dec 17 16:40 lost+found
-rw-r--r-- 1 root root  18K Dec 18 14:30 bootcode.bin
-rw-r--r-- 1 root root 5.2K Dec 18 14:31 fixup.dat
-rw-r--r-- 1 root root 2.3M Dec 18 14:31 start.elf
-rw-r--r-- 1 root root   32 Dec 18 14:41 cmdline.txt
-rw-r--r-- 1 root root   11 Dec 18 14:42 config.txt
```

Figure 11-26. *The boot filesystem with firmware and configuration files*

Now it's time to unpack the stage 3 tarball. What's stage 3? This is a pretty valid question if you have not used Gentoo before. Stage 3 refers to a very minimum environment compiled for your given architecture. This environment includes all the tools you need to bootstrap the system and chroot into the new install. It's just enough of a Linux system to be able to build a new system.

CHROOT?

What is this chroot thing? chroot is short for change root. This command allows you to change the root directory of all future running processes. You cannot chroot between different architectures; hence you cannot do this on the Gentoo install for the Raspberry Pi unless you are building Gentoo from another ARM system.

There are also stage 1 and stage 2 tarballs but I do not recommend you use them on the Raspberry Pi. They will not gain you any advantage.

HANG ON, WHAT'S THIS STAGE 1 OR 2 BUSINESS?

A Gentoo install is broken down into stages. Each stage will gain you some functionality. Stage 1 will just give you enough tools to bootstrap the system; you will need to compile the rest of the tools by hand. Stage 2 builds on that functionality and gives you more tools and more of a complete filesystem. Stage 3 gives you all filesystem entries and all base tools with your build tools compiled for your architecture. Gentoo no longer supports an install from stage 1 or 2; because they are unsupported I do not recommend you do it.

On the other hand if you were porting Gentoo to a brand-new architecture you would most definitely need a stage 1 install.

To unpack this baseline system, change into the mounted root partition for the Raspberry Pi. Then open your browser to the following web page:

http://distfiles.gentoo.org/releases/arm/autobuilds/current-stage3-armv6j_hardfp/

In this directory you will find a file that has the format of stage3-armv6j_hardfp-YYYYMMDD.tar.bz2. wget the latest file to your hosts filesystem. This was the command that I used at the time of writing:

```
# wget http://distfiles.gentoo.org/releases/arm/autobuilds/current-stage3-armv6j_hardfp/
stage3-armv6j_hardfp-20121213.tar.bz2
```

Once this is downloaded into the root partition, you need to extract the stage into the root partition. Use the following command to extract the archive:

```
# tar xfj /tmp/stage3-armv6j_hardfp-20121213.tar.bz2 -C /mnt/rpi-root
```

You can see that I have saved the stage 3 tarball under /tmp on my host machine. Replace this location with where you saved your stage 3 tarball. This may take a little time but once it's done it will look like Figure 11-27. This should look familiar to any Linux user.

```
pcb tmp # ls -la /mnt/rpi-root/
total 92
drwxr-xr-x 20 root root  4096 Dec 18 15:38 .
drwxr-xr-x 10 root root  4096 Dec 17 16:45 ..
drwxr-xr-x  2 root root  4096 Dec 13 19:48 bin
drwxr-xr-x  2 root root  4096 Dec 13 12:03 boot
drwxr-xr-x  3 root root  4096 Dec 13 12:03 dev
drwxr-xr-x 29 root root  4096 Dec 13 19:52 etc
drwxr-xr-x  2 root root  4096 Dec 13 12:03 home
drwxr-xr-x  5 root root  4096 Dec 13 19:43 lib
drwx------  2 root root 16384 Dec 17 16:40 lost+found
drwxr-xr-x  2 root root  4096 Dec 13 12:03 media
drwxr-xr-x  2 root root  4096 Dec 13 12:03 mnt
drwxr-xr-x  2 root root  4096 Dec 13 12:03 opt
drwxr-xr-x  2 root root  4096 Dec 13 09:15 proc
drwx------  2 root root  4096 Dec 13 12:03 root
drwxr-xr-x  4 root root  4096 Dec 13 19:43 run
drwxr-xr-x  2 root root  4096 Dec 13 19:52 sbin
drwxr-xr-x  2 root root  4096 Dec 13 12:03 sys
drwxrwxrwt  2 root root  4096 Dec 13 19:52 tmp
drwxr-xr-x 11 root root  4096 Dec 13 19:52 usr
drwxr-xr-x  9 root root  4096 Dec 13 12:03 var
```

Figure 11-27. *The stage 3 tarball unpacked*

Now that you have a base filesystem and its tools, it's time to configure the system. I won't be using any nondefault make flags for the GCC but if you wanted to use some you can edit the /etc/make.conf file.

The next step is to configure the fstab file, otherwise you may have an issue trying to boot anything. Listing 11-4 shows the contents of my /etc/fstab file.

Listing 11-4. The Contents of the /etc/fstab File

```
# /etc/fstab: static file system information.
# <fs>                  <mountpoint>    <type>      <opts>            <dump/pass>
/dev/mmcblk0p1          /boot           vfat        noauto,noatime    1 2
/dev/mmcblk0p2          /               ext4        noatime           0 1
```

Don't try and use /dev/sdX device references from your host build machine. You will end up with a nonbootable system as the SD card is seen as /dev/mmcblk0 on the Raspberry Pi. Because you cannot chroot into the new build environment you need to set up a few things by hand.

The first thing you need to do is generate a new root password for your Gentoo install. Use the openssl toolkit for this with the following command:

```
# openssl passwd -1
```

In Figure 11-28 you can see the output of this command.

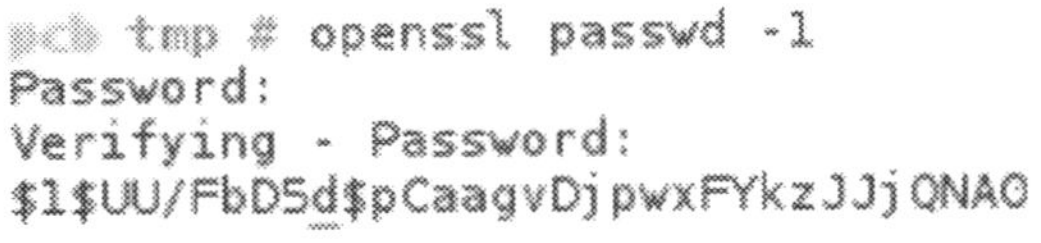

```
▓▓ tmp # openssl passwd -1
Password:
Verifying - Password:
$1$UU/FbD5d$pCaagvDjpwxFYkzJJjQNA0
```

Figure 11-28. *Generating the new root password*

The last line in Figure 11-28 is your encrypted password that needs to be placed into the /etc/shadow file. Open the /etc/shadow file from the mounted root filesystem and replace the * with the new root password that you generated with the openssl command. Once you are done it will look like the text below.

```
root:$1$UU/FbD5d$pCaagvDjpwxFYkzJJjQNA0:10770:0:::::
```

That's all the system configuration that needs to be done at the moment. Remember that Gentoo's initial install should be just enough to get the system booting; it's not your final system state. Now you must extract the current portage collection so that you can build applications once your Raspberry Pi can boot. Download the following file to your host machine:

```
http://distfiles.gentoo.org/releases/snapshots/current/portage-latest.tar.bz2
```

This will always give you the latest snapshot of the portage tree. Portage is the collection of ebuild files I talked about before. Once this file has finished downloading, extract it to the mounted root partition with the following command:

```
# tar xjvpf /tmp/portage-latest.tar.bz2 -C /mnt/rpi-root/usr
```

This will take quite some time as there are a lot of small files to extract. After this step, you need to build a kernel for your new Gentoo Raspberry Pi system. For this you will use the cross compile environment that was configured in Chapter 6. You're going to need a copy of the Linux source: I recommend you use the kernel source from the foundation as it will have all the Raspberry Pi patches already applied. You can download a zip file of the kernel source or use GitHub to clone the repository. I will show you the zip file method.

Open your web browser to this site:

```
https://github.com/raspberrypi/linux
```

Click the "download as a zip" button to get a copy of the kernel source. This was the command I used at the time of writing:

```
# wget https://github.com/raspberrypi/linux/archive/rpi-3.2.27.zip
```

Extract this on your host machine where you installed the cross compile environment. In the next few steps I will show you how to configure the kernel and how to cross compile it. Remember that the cross compile is installed at /home/`whoami`/x-tools/arm-unknown-linux-gnueabi/bin/. Also remember that the cross compile tool chain was built with Fedora and is soft float and not hard float. You have two choices to fix this:

- Redo your cross compile environment.

- Rebuild the kernel on the Raspberry Pi itself.

The install will boot with a soft-float or hard-float kernel. You will use the original cross compile environment to first build the kernel to boot the Raspberry Pi. Once Gentoo is up and running, rebuild the kernel as hard float to ensure Gentoo can rebuild itself. That is optional and you can leave the kernel as soft float if you want.

I will use the preconfigured cut-down kernel configuration for the initial boot that is supplied with the kernel source. To do this, change into the kernel source directory that you have just extracted and run the following command to generate the .config file:

```
# ARCH=arm make bcmrpi_cutdown_defconfig
```

This will write out a .config file that you can use to build the kernel. After you have generated the .config file you need to ensure that the generated .config file has all the options found in your downloaded kernel source. To do this, run the following command and ensure that you replace my username with yours:

```
# ARCH=arm CROSS_COMPILE=/home/brendan/x-tools/arm-unknown-linux-gnueabi/bin/arm-unknown-linux-
gnueabi- make oldconfig
```

This may prompt you for missing options if there are any. If there are no missing options it will exit cleanly. Now you need to build the kernel itself.

I have used -j8 to ensure I am using all eight cores of my host machine but you should adjust this to suit the number of cores in your host machine. This is the command you need:

```
# ARCH=arm CROSS_COMPILE=/home/brendan/x-tools/arm-unknown-linux-gnueabi/bin/arm-unknown-linux-
gnueabi- make -j8
```

Once the kernel is compiled you need to make the kernel modules and install them onto the mounted root of the Raspberry Pi. To achieve this I used the following command:

```
# ARCH=arm CROSS_COMPILE=/home/brendan/x-tools/arm-unknown-linux-gnueabi/bin/arm-unknown-linux-
gnueabi- make modules_install INSTALL_MOD_PATH=/mnt/rpi-root/
```

The install_mod_path is the path to the mounted root filesystem on my host machine. Don't forget to change the CROSS_COMPILE path to suit your system. Once the kernel has been built and the modules installed into the mounted root filesystem the last step is to copy over the uncompressed kernel image to the mounted boot partition. You must not use the compressed kernel source because the firmware loader has no support for reading the compressed image.

With this in mind, copy over the uncompressed kernel image to the mounted root filesystem. You can find the uncompressed kernel source from the following directory inside the kernel source directory named arch/arm/boot/Image. Copy the image file to the root filesystem with this command:

```
# cp arch/arm/boot/Image  /mnt/rpi-boot
```

Congratulations! It's time to eject your SD card from the host machine and see if your system boots. One thing to keep in mind is that this install of Gentoo will be lacking pretty much any useful tools and all configuration will be missing.

If your installation has gone well you should be greeted by a login prompt. Don't worry so much about any errors on the first boot: a few fixes need to happen before you will get a clean boot. Log in as root; you're now going to fix a few things to enable an SSH login and some other issues that just affect the Raspberry Pi.

The first thing you need to fix is the initial time and the hardware clock errors on boot. To turn off the hardware clock, run the following command:

```
# rc-update del hwclock boot
```

You're going to need to add the software clock to the boot level now:

```
# rc-update add swclock boot
```

For the software clock to work, you need to set the initial date on the system. Set the date and time with the date command:

```
# date MmddHHmmCCyy
```

This is my command as an example:

```
# date 122013402012
```

You also need to copy your time zone file to overwrite /etc/localtime; this sets your machine's time zone. Take a look in the /usr/share/zoneinfo/ directory for your time zone file. I used the following command to set my time zone to Hong Kong:

```
# cp /usr/share/zoneinfo/Asia/Hong_Kong /etc/localtime
```

Now that the time is close to being correct, reboot your machine. This will allow the swclock script to write the current shutdown time to a file that it can reference on the next boot.

Log back in to your Raspberry Pi; it's time to get the network up and running. Change into the /etc/init.d directory and run the following command:

```
# cp net.lo  net.eth0
```

You can now set the network card to start on boot with this command:

```
# rc-update add net.eth0 boot
```

Also add sshd to start on next boot with this command:

```
# rc-update add sshd default
```

The last thing you must do before you are able to log in via SSH is to configure an IP address. You do this in the file /etc/conf.d/net or you use a DHCP client. If you select DHCP, nothing needs to be added to /etc/conf.d/net. If you're going to use a DHCP client, you must install a client. To install a simple DHCP client run this command:

```
# emerge net-misc/dhcp
```

Now go and have dinner or a few drinks: this is going to take a while. Once the DHCP client is installed or you have configured a static IP address you can reboot your system and log in via SSH.

The last step I am going to do is copy the kernel build root from the host machine across to the Gentoo installation. Some packages need a valid kernel source tree to build. On the host machine change into the directory with the kernel source and copy it across. I have used scp with the following command:

```
# scp -r linux-rpi-3.2.27/ root@192.168.0.46:/usr/src/
```

This will take a while as there are a lot of files to copy. Once that's done, log back in to the Raspberry Pi and create a symlink to point the current kernel source to /usr/src/linux:

```
# ln -s /usr/src/linux-rpi-3.2.27/ /usr/src/linux
```

Using Gentoo

Now that the Raspberry Pi–specific parts of the installation are done, I would recommend you read though the Gentoo handbook and finish off the install so that it suits your needs; after all, it's your custom system and only you know how you want to use it. Gentoo offers a lot of customization in the install process. You can find the handbook at this site:

```
http://gentoo.org/doc/en/handbook/
```

Summary

This chapter has been wide-ranging and I hope you got something out of it. First up we looked into the current state of Android on the Raspberry Pi. This was a sad start because we found out that the official Broadcom version of Android is unlikely to ever be released. This means Android will never get any optimization or support for the GPU. Right now you're stuck with an unusable version of Android 2.3 with no support. This is far from ideal. At least you can say that you have at least installed Android once rather than just buying a device with it already installed.

Next up was a nice surprise with RISC OS. The RISC OS distribution hails all the way back to the original ARM platform and is still very usable as a lightweight desktop. In this section you found out about CMT-based systems and the benefits that CMT may bring you and your applications. You also found out where a lot of the ideas for some of the modern desktop user interfaces came from. In addition to this the RISC OS comes with a large online repository of applications.

After spending some time inside RISC OS I then showed you one of my favorite experiential operating systems called Plan 9. Plan 9 is where Unix may have ended up; after all Plan 9 set out to fix what were seen as the shortcomings of Unix. Plan 9 is a very good example of a grid computing platform system and it has been executed very well in this regard. Plan 9 takes the concept of everything as a file and acts on it with vigor. You really need to get your head around this concept to get into Plan 9. Plan 9 won't be your replacement desktop anytime soon or most likely it will not even remain on your Raspberry Pi but it's an excellent learning tool (or at least an excellent demonstration of what could have been the future of Unix).

Last was Gentoo, my personal favorite Linux distribution. Gentoo is built from the ground up to be exactly what you want it to be. This is an amazing feature in that you get a lean, clean, and fast distribution. This exact advantage also has its downsides in that you are going to need to do a lot of your own support work and be able to fix the system when it crashes. Gentoo is a good teacher of Linux (if a little unpractical for all purposes). I hope this chapter has whetted your knowledge of other operating systems and why there is no one best operating system. Every operating system has its good points and its weaknesses.

Index

▓ T

▓ U, V, W, X, Y, Z